Jump into the Story

Jump into the Story

The Art of Creative Preaching

RAY R. FRIESEN

WIPF & STOCK · Eugene, Oregon

JUMP INTO THE STORY
The Art of Creative Preaching

Copyright © 2019 Ray R. Friesen. All rights reserved. Except for brief quotations in critical publications or reviews, no part of this book may be reproduced in any manner without prior written permission from the publisher. Write: Permissions, Wipf and Stock Publishers, 199 W. 8th Ave., Suite 3, Eugene, OR 97401.

Wipf & Stock
An Imprint of Wipf and Stock Publishers
199 W. 8th Ave., Suite 3
Eugene, OR 97401

www.wipfandstock.com

PAPERBACK ISBN: 978-1-5326-7040-4
HARDCOVER ISBN: 978-1-5326-7041-1
EBOOK ISBN: 978-1-5326-7042-8

Manufactured in the U.S.A.   FEBRUARY 27, 2019

Scripture texts quoted in this collection are from one of five possible sources:

New Revised Standard Version Bible, copyright ©1989, Division of Christian Education of the National Council of the Churches of Christ in the United States of America. Used by permission. All rights reserved. These will be identified as NRSV in the book.

The Holy Bible, New Living Translation, copyright ©1996, 2004, 2007, 2013, 2015 by Tyndale House Foundation. Used by permission of Tyndale House Publishers, Inc., Carol Stream, Illinois 60188. All rights reserved. These will be identified as NLT in the book.

THE MESSAGE. Copyright © by Eugene H. Peterson 1993, 1994, 1995, 1996, 2000, 2001, 2002. Used by permission of NavPress. All rights reserved. Represented by Tyndale House Publishers, Inc. These will be identified as *The Message* in the book.

King James Version. Public Domain. These will be identified as KJV.

My own paraphrases. In writing my paraphrases, I always start with the NRSV and am indebted to the NLT and *The Message* for inspiration.

*This book is dedicated to my father,
Diedrich (Dick) Friesen,
whose passion and commitment
to have the Ancient Texts
become the Living Word of God for all who knew him
and even those who only met him once or twice,
served his congregation well,
touched the lives of many with God's Love & Good News,
and was an example to all
who experienced his preaching and conversation.*

Contents

	Acknowledgements	ix
	Introduction	1
Chapter 1	Jump into the Story	25
Chapter 2	Jesus's Autobiography	36
Chapter 3	Same Text, Different Sermon	44
Chapter 4	The Twelve Little Guys	60
Chapter 5	Story Sermons	74
Chapter 6	Ancient Writings and Twenty-First-Century Gurus	83
Chapter 7	Sing Me a Song About Jesus	92
Chapter 8	Movies and the Word	106
Chapter 9	Advent	120
Chapter 10	Christmas #1	124
Chapter 11	Christmas #2	134
Chapter 12	Christmas in the Community	146
Chapter 13	Community Preaching	159
Chapter 14	Easter and the Community	166
Chapter 15	Funerals	173
Chapter 16	Children's Stories	183
Chapter 17	Scripture Reading	194
Chapter 18	Lent	208

| Chapter 19 | Songs | 211 |
| Chapter 20 | Thanksgiving | 218 |

Appendix A: For Further Reading | 233
Appendix B: The Bible and the Word of God | 235
Bibliography | 245

Acknowledgements

THERE ARE MANY PEOPLE who deserve thanks for what follows in this book. Just because you helped me and supported me and are not mentioned, does not lessen my sense of gratitude. However, a few groups/individuals deserve special mention.

Thank you to the people of Aberdeen Church in Winnipeg, MB. They had to "endure" my earliest development as a preacher, and did so patiently and with encouragement. Special thanks to John Schlamp who would give me his running commentary in note form after every sermon.

Thank you to the people of Zion Mennonite Church in Swift Current, SK who welcomed us when we arrived in SC in 1991 and then called Sylvia and me as pastors in 1997. They were there for me as I continued to develop as a preacher and as I, as one friend—a senior in the church—said, had a tendency to "skate near open water." It was here at Zion that I started developing the creative side of my preaching.

Thank you to the folks at Emmaus Mennonite Church in Wymark, SK. For thirteen and a half years they gave me pretty much a blank cheque to preach what I thought needed preaching. They joined me in my own spiritual journey. They affirmed my attempts at creative preaching. They held me accountable, like the Bereans did Paul when they "examin[ed] the Scriptures to see if they supported what he said."[1] Without you, this book could not have happened.

Thank you to the people at Wipf & Stock for being willing to take a chance on this book. A special thanks to George Callihan, a very patient typesetter who worked with me, a rookie author, as I learned the trade and made change after change.

Thank you to Lisa Goudy for her competent assistance as a copy editor.

1. Acts 17:11. *The Message*.

Thank you to my parents, Dick & Dora Friesen. Dad shared my passion for education and study and made my college and grad school studies financially possible. Mom was a great cheer-leader for my preaching and money from the inheritance I received from her made the publication of this work possible.

Thank you to our daughters, Larissa and Rachelle. As teenagers they had to sit through Dad's preaching every Sunday, knowing he could well ask them on the way home or over Sunday lunch what had been taught in the sermon. They endured (mostly) patiently. Thank you to them for how they, each in their own way, carry on Dad's passion to partner with God to make this world a better place, and do it so much better than he did.

Thank you to Sylvia, my life's partner and companion. Throughout our 40+ years of marriage she has supported me when I needed support and challenged me when I needed challenging (whether or not I thought I needed it). In 2015 when I went through cancer surgery and chemotherapy, I could not have asked for a better wife, companion, and helper, even as the drugs weakened me physically and sent me into the darkness of depression. For twenty years, most weekends, she read my sermon on Saturday (always a gentle and helpful critic) and listened (at least she was in the pews) on Sunday. Thank you, Sylvia!!

Introduction

I think preaching is part of my DNA and is woven into the very fabric of my being. After son, husband, and father, nothing says who I am as much as "preacher." My father was a preacher, four of my uncles in Dad's family were preachers, and at least twelve of my cousins in the Friesen family are or were preachers. My brothers both do a lot of public speaking, one calling himself an "evangelist for agriculture." My wife Sylvia, for as long as I can remember and to this day, insists that she is not a preacher. And yet when I was on leave due to chemotherapy, she wrote and preached several sermons between June and October and then wrote and preached, following the assigned texts of the Lectionary, all four Advent sermons. Our older daughter used to be a youth pastor and preacher until the church asked her to leave because she was divorced. This was their loss and the school system's gain as she now works as a youth pastor—known as a social worker in the secular world—in a school system. Our younger daughter is an old-fashioned street corner preacher, preaching justice, freedom, peace, and equality at protests.

As a pre-teen, I loved playing "program." I would plan a program that included singing, poetry, Scripture reading, and a sermon. I always assigned the preaching to myself. Our family photo collection includes pictures of me standing on a chair, proclaiming boldly whatever I thought the needed message was. As a teenager, I was hungry for good preaching and went looking for it where I could find it.

It wasn't always present in the churches I attended as a child and joined as a teen. My childhood and youth were spent in a tradition where preachers were unpaid and were called from within the congregation by election. Men and boys who were members of the congregation voted,[1]

---

1. In a misguided reading of the New Testament, my tradition was convinced that the text in 1 Corinthians about women keeping silent in church meant they were not

guided by the Holy Spirit. The rules were strict. To make sure it was the Holy Spirit and not personal preference or "campaigning" that determined the outcome, there was no discussion in the weeks ahead of the election as to who might be a good preacher or whom God might be calling. There were times the Holy Spirit seemed to pay more attention to family connections than preaching ability. This made for some truly boring sermons.

I still longed to hear good preaching—good meaning interesting to listen to. So I went looking. Each year in early July, our denomination had what they called "Conference." Saturday of the weekend was filled with denominational business. However, Friday night, Saturday night, Sunday morning, and Sunday afternoon were worship times. Worship meant preaching. We had come to hear God speak through a preacher. We were not about to waste time on too much frivolous stuff.

If an evangelist came through town, Barry Moore, for example, I would go to the meetings several nights of the week, not to be born again each time, but to hear interesting preaching. One of my first dates with the woman who is now my wife was to a Barry Moore Crusade. On Sunday afternoons, before I left to play softball or football with my friends, I could be found next to the radio, listening to *Hour of Decision* and Billy Graham. The program fed, not my need for salvation, but my hunger for good preaching.

My father was elected to the ministry of preaching in 1964 or 1965. In 1966, he became the lead minister (unsalaried) in our small rural congregation and that meant, among other things, that he generally preached twice a month. Dad had an innate ability and did the best he could. However, his education and training were limited. He did not finish high school. He did not have seminary training, though he did have a couple

---

allowed to have any input into a congregation's decision making, except by telling their husbands at home and hoping the husband would agree and speak for both. That meant when I was baptized at the age of fourteen, I was deemed better able to help a congregation decide things than my mother, simply because of my gender. Female preachers were forbidden and still are in 2018 in the denomination of my youth (as they are in many Evangelical churches). The exception was when the denomination needed people to train pastors in the mission field. White women, who dare not teach a white man, were sent to Mexico to teach Mexican men of color who then taught Mexican women of color. Such is the pecking order in this tradition's understanding of the Church where "There is no longer Jew or Greek, there is no longer slave or free, there is no longer male and female; for all of you are one in Christ Jesus." Gal 3:28. NRSV.

of years of Bible school. His library was basically *Halley's Bible Handbook*[2] and the *Tyndale* commentary series.[3] I recall, on a fall Saturday, Dad in his study, praying, studying, and making notes while my brother and I were harvesting the wheat and oats. God's call on his life came first.

I have been a preacher for forty years or so—most of my adult life. I started as a student pastor at Aberdeen Church (part of the Evangelical Mennonite Conference) in Winnipeg. I was a co-pastor in that congregation from 1978 to 1980. Given our commitment to lay preacher involvement and because we had two co-pastors, I preached once or twice a month. When Karl, the other co-pastor, was called to be the full-time pastor, I stayed in the congregation while attending grad school in the same city. With the change in pastoral leadership, we strengthened the teaching team we had created earlier. I was chair of that team and we as a team were responsible for the preaching and the adult Sunday school. Our pastor was better known for his counseling and visitation skills than his preaching and so he preached twice in six weeks, three of us preached once in six weeks, and once in those six weeks we asked someone else, often a visitor, to preach. The team planned the preaching, usually three series a year—OT, Gospel, and Epistle. The text was assigned to each Sunday, the preaching schedule was created, and the two were merged. You preached on your assigned text. It was a good developmental experience, for you had to preach what you were assigned, no matter how difficult or easy the text.

From 1987 to 1991, my wife and I were co-pastors of that same congregation. Though I still worked with the teaching team, given what was seen as my gift for preaching, my preaching load increased dramatically.

In 1991, I began as interim principal at Swift Current Bible Institute. The position changed to president and lasted until 1996 when the school closed. During that time I would speak in chapel regularly, preach in various congregations as I visited them on behalf of the school, and, for a period of time, took a regular turn in our local congregation while we were without a pastor.

In 1997, Sylvia and I began as co-pastors at Zion Mennonite Church. Her primary responsibility (as a 20 percent assignment) was pastoral care, with a particular focus on the women in the congregation who, for

---

2. By Henry Haley. The book was first published in 1924 and has gone through numerous editions and printings since.

3. Originally published by The Tyndale Press. My dad's editions would have been published by Eerdmans. Currently they are available from InterVarsity Press.

too many years, had been pastored through their husbands.[4] I preached about forty Sundays a year. In 2004 we added Emmaus Mennonite Church to our circle of responsibility. For a year I preached twice every Sunday, first at Emmaus at the 9:00 a.m. service and then at Zion at the 10:50 a.m. service. A year later, we left Zion but continued at Emmaus, sharing a half-time position. However, since we had originally been hired to make sure Sunday mornings got done, I continued to preach about forty times a year.

During my time in these two congregations, there are a few things that have guided my preaching. Generally I have used the Lectionary every Advent and every other Lent. I decided in the fall of 1997 that I would preach through a Gospel every other winter, starting after Epiphany and going until Easter or later. Often this meant June 30. I started with Mark, a Good News Story Collection that I, at that time, saw as basically a simple Jesus story.[5] Two years later it was Luke, whose focus on the social justice aspect of the Kingdom of God is often missed. I never much cared for John's Collection and was often puzzled by Evangelicalism's almost obsessive focus on it. I have since come to appreciate it as the Gospel of the Inner Life. Finally, in 2004 it was Matthew's turn with his message of the end of religion and the Gospel's universal message. I continued that cycle every eight years and so in winter and spring of 2018, I made my third journey through John.

At the same time, I tried to keep in mind the balance we worked at back in Winnipeg so that I would preach about equal number of series from the Old Testament, the Gospels, and the Epistles. There are some Epistles I have never preached (who wants to tackle Hebrews?) and some I've journeyed through at least twice. In 2017 I traveled my third journey through Colossians. When I preach a book I have preached earlier,

---

4. This continues to be a problem in many congregations where church and pastoral leadership is restricted to men. There is a real need in many congregations to place pastoral care in the hands of deacons, men and women, who can care for people. Whether or not that gets done, it is time we stop overriding the gifting of the Spirit by barring women, strictly based on gender, from the leadership and preaching ministries God has called them to. Men, get out of God's way or who knows what will happen! What is happening now is that congregations and the church at large are deprived of much that God wants to give us through female preachers. I can't see God taking kindly to that.

5. With the help of N.T. Wright's *How God Became King*, I have since realized that Mark's Collection is a teaching that leads to the crucifixion as Jesus's coronation. This has profound implications for our understanding of the cross and the Kingdom of God.

I rarely look at the old sermons. I have changed. People have changed. The times have changed. I want to preach a sermon for that time in that place. As you will note as you read the sermons that follow in this book, I have preached other series as well, many of them represented in this collection.

Looking back, I have done a lot of preaching. From spring 1997 to spring 2018, it's been twenty-one years. I took a break of about nine months in 2015 as I dealt with cancer and chemo. Allowing for that, nineteen and one-third years at forty sermons a year, that's in the neighborhood of seven hundred seventy sermons. In addition, I would preach at weddings and funerals.

I am deeply grateful to the people at Aberdeen, Zion, and Emmaus for walking with me as I developed and grew as a preacher. I highly commend their long suffering patience, especially the folks at Aberdeen where I started. My development and growth continues. Sylvia says she noticed a significant change to "more interesting" in my preaching when I returned after chemo. I also thank her for my development as a preacher. Most of the weekends I preached, she read the sermon on Friday or Saturday and then listened to it on Sunday. She has had to put up with having a preacher husband who feels a lot more comfortable than she does with sharing personal stories publically. I confess that when we first started on this joint-journey, I could be supersensitive and found her suggestions very threatening. However, with time I realized that if something in my manuscript was confusing, hard to understand, or said with a sentence that was waaaay too long, I needed to make changes to better communicate the intended message to the congregation that would be listening Sunday morning.

I have been a fierce critic of preaching, including my own, for most of the years that I've been a preacher. I firmly believe that as preachers we have been called by God, are being paid by our congregations (by and large), and people sit and listen to us when there are lots of other things they could be doing. Therefore, it is imperative that we make sure of at least three things.

1. *We must do our homework.* It is absolutely crucial that we pump time and energy into prayer and study. Prayer and study is important in general and a necessary discipline each week as we start on yet one more sermon. Eugene Peterson, in one of his books on pastoral ministry, says that the words "busy" and "pastor" go together in the same way that

the words "adultery" and "husband" go together.[6] We must have time for prayer and study.

Here are some of the practices I use to fulfill my commitment to "doing my homework." I have no illusions that I am the perfect pastor nor the perfect preacher. However, I share my practices as a way to hopefully help you think about yours. I try to read between forty and fifty books a year. This includes novels (see below). When preparing a sermon, if at all possible, I consult four different commentaries: *The New Interpreter's Bible, Interpretation* series, *Westminster Bible Companion,* and *The NIV Application Bible Commentary.*[7] This gives me not only the perspectives of at least three different interpreters, it also gives me variety across a fairly wide theological spectrum. Sometimes I consult the *Believers Church Bible Commentary.* However I find its format restricts its usefulness, being more backward looking than forward looking. Two authors that seem to have been able to transcend these limits are Tom Yoder Neufeld (*Ephesians*) and John E. Toews (*Romans*). I have not had the opportunity to use some of the more recent ones. There are also occasionally other books I may consult or other commentaries I read. Any time I can get help from Walter Brueggemann, Eugene Peterson, or N.T. Wright, I jump at the chance. In addition, I have been significantly influenced by Brian McLaren.

The other thing I do in terms of research is consistently consult three different translations: *New Revised Standard Version, New Living Translation,* and *The Message.* With the help of the website, Bible Gateway,[8] I print the three versions side by side and then read each one carefully, noting things that seem important and/or catch my interest and imagination. Depending on the text, I may spend a fair bit of time comparing and contrasting and then following up certain words in Greek to see how else they are used in other parts of the NT. I find this often helps me get to stuff I would miss otherwise. It also helps me see the text pointing me

---

6. Having read many of Peterson's books, I have no idea in which one he taught me this lesson.

7. I have found Gary M. Burge's volumes on the Gospel of John and on the Epistles of John in to be particularly insightful and helpful in this series. I also appreciate the series' focus on three parts: Original Meaning, Bridging Contexts, and Contemporary Significance.

8. Bible Gateway, "BibleGateway.com."

INTRODUCTION 7

in new directions both my tradition and context[9] have not necessarily identified.

2. *We must be relevant*, connecting the Ancient Writings with life in the twenty-first century. This will, of necessity, take significant imagination. In preaching, we are attempting to make connections between Ancient Writings and twenty-first-century situations that are separated by time (two thousand to three thousand years), geography (ten thousand kilometers), and culture. Nothing translates directly. Nothing can be taken from the Ancient Writings and simply plopped into a twenty-first-century context. Everything requires interpretation, most of it with huge leaps that can only be made if our imaginations are in high gear.

On a weekday afternoon in 1986, browsing in a Bible college library in Winnipeg, I encountered a small book that piqued my curiosity. It turned out that this small book would open my mind in a big way. The book was *The Bible in Human Transformation* by Walter Wink. It started with the line "Historical biblical criticism is bankrupt."[10] According to Wink, the way to read and study the Bible taught by most seminaries and practiced by most preachers was no longer able to build the bridges necessary between Ancient Writings and the contemporary world to engage the imaginations, and therefore the faith, of the people in the pews.

Either Wink or one of my grad school professors, Dr. Larry Hurtado, made the point that our preachers attended seminaries where they were learning languages, historical criticism, and everything about the context in which the Ancient Writings were produced and collated. They graduated with a great education, but then, come the first Saturday night in their first posting as they faced their first sermon, they were in trouble. They realized they had nothing to offer their congregation the next morning. Then came a sinking feeling. We must not let that happen to us.

Later that fall, I studied an article by Paul Ricoeur that formed the basis for a paper I wrote.[11] In the article, Ricoeur argued that once a piece

---

9. This includes my fundamentalist Evangelical tradition, my Anabaptist/Mennonite tradition, and the twenty-first-century context I am in, culturally, sociologically, theologically, and ecclesiologically.

10. Wink, *The Bible*, 1.

11. I don't remember the name of the article nor where it was published and I no longer have the paper. However, a few years ago, in reading Walter Brueggemann's book, *The Word Militant*, I encountered references by Brueggemann to Ricoeur and his ideas. Brueggemann's endnotes pointed to "From the Hermeneutics of Texts to the Hermeneutics of Action," in *From Text to Action* (Northwestern University Press, 1991), 105–222. This may have been a reprint of an earlier periodical article that I used.

has been written, it is "no longer in the control of the 'author' but makes its own testimony and insists on interpretation."[12] This creates a kind of freedom for the interpreter as s/he seeks the relevance of the text for her or his setting and life. It struck me as possibly being the solution to the problem raised by Wink.

As Chiam Potok has one of his characters say in *Davita's Harp*: "Did he believe that God wrote stories with only one kind of meaning? It seemed to me that a story that had only one kind of meaning was not very interesting or worth remembering for too long."[13]

In the early nineties, I bought and began reading the book, *The Book of God: The Bible as Novel* by Walter Wangerin, Jr. On the flyleaf the publishers declare that "*The Book of God* reads like a fine novel, bringing a wise and beautiful rendering of the Bible . . . Wangerin recreates the high drama, low comedy, gentle humor, and awesome holiness of the Bible story."[14] This helped feed my interest in reading the Bible in a new way, as story best interpreted with imagination. I have found the focus on story and the use of imagination has made the Ancient Writings more meaningful and relevant to my life and in my preaching.

The two people who have been most influential in how I now read Scripture and interpret it for myself and our congregation are Eugene Peterson and Walter Brueggemann. Each in his own way has helped me understand that what we call the Bible is essentially a collection of stories, poems, and writings that tell a story, the story of people trying to make sense of God, life, and history. I make regular use of Peterson's translation of the Ancient Writings known as *The Message*.

Of particular help in reading the Bible and developing my spirituality have been Peterson's five-volume series on spiritual theology;[15] his book, *Five Smooth Stones for Pastoral Work*,[16] his commentary on 1 and 2 Samuel; his book on the Psalms;[17] and the book, *Leap Over a Wall: Earthy Spirituality for Everyday Christians*. In this work on the life and

---

12. Brueggemann, *The Word Militant*, 23.

13. As quoted in Rachel Held Evans, *Inspired*, vii.

14. Wangerin, *The Book of God*, flyleaf.

15. *Christ Plays in Ten Thousand Place, Eat This Book, The Jesus Way: A Conversation, Tell It Slant,* and *Practice Resurrection*.

16. In this book, he interprets the Old Testament books of Song of Songs, Ruth, Lamentations, Ecclesiastes, and Esther in ways never before encountered by me, making full use of their setting in Jewish literature, Bible, and interpretation.

17. *Answering God*.

spirituality of David, he says, speaking of his mother who had a profound influence on how he came to read the Bible: "She held the entire Story, from Genesis to Revelation, in her believing *imagination*, with Jesus as the central and controlling presence throughout."[18]

He continues by saying that the Ancient Stories have been and can be used for "training the believing *imagination* to think *narratively*, immersing the praying *imagination* in *earthiness*."[19] I was hooked on both the idea of Bible as story and the use of imagination in interpreting the Story and its stories for the twenty-first century.

It seems to me that using the imagination is precisely the approach used by Walter Brueggemann in opening up the Ancient Writings, especially those of the Old Testament, to many, including myself. His commentaries, no matter what book of the Old Testament, grab my imagination. It's like what was ancient and has been read through the centuries and was taught in a particular way to me in my Christian tradition is opened up in a whole new way, pointing to truths and understandings both profound and powerful.

In addition, I have been particularly helped to read the Ancient Writings as Story and to use a Spirit-guided, trained imagination to interpret them by reading his books, *The Practice of the Prophetic Imagination*, *The Word Militant: Preaching a Decentering Word*, and *The Bible Makes Sense*. In reading and interpreting Ancient Poetry I have been helped by his books, *Spirituality of the Psalms*, *Praying the Psalms*, and *The Message of the Psalms*.

Here is an example from personal experience that may make the point about relevance better than any detailed explanation. In 2014, at my mother's request, I preached the funeral sermon when our family and Mom's friends said good-bye to her. There were a minimum of two things I wanted my sermon to do. One, I wanted it to be a fitting farewell and reflection on Mom's life and spirituality.

Secondly, I was keenly aware that eight of Mom's eleven grandchildren would be present. None of them were involved in church in any way, shape or form. Three of my nephews camp in atheism's neighborhood. The other grandchildren were at various places in their spiritual journeys. I wanted to preach a sermon that would create the possibility of engaging their imagination and remind all of us, children and grandchildren alike,

---

18. Peterson, *Leap Over a Wall*, 2. Emphasis mine.
19. Peterson, *Leap Over a Wall*, 2. Emphasis mine.

that Oma's faith and spirituality, reworked for our time and situation, was relevant and could be nurtured in our lives in a meaningful way. (See the sermon in chapter 14.)

A year or so later, I attended a friend's father's funeral. Most of his grandchildren were in attendance, many of whom were not connected to the church. This was another opportunity to affirm a grandfather's faith and spirituality to his children and grandchildren. The family had decided to ask one of his former pastors to officiate and preach the sermon. Unfortunately he went off on some historical, critical[20] tangent about Israel and Babylon that was simply boring for everyone there, including this preacher, and had nothing to do with the wonderful man we were there to remember and honor. The message to all of us seemed clear: "Grandpa's faith was boring and has absolutely nothing to offer you." What a wasted and botched opportunity!

Sunday morning we face a crowd that equally deserves to be respected and therefore what we preach must be relevant to them, their situations in life, and the history and society in which they live. I recall chatting with a young adult and new Christian back in the eighties. She had been introduced to a church by her then-boyfriend. They had since separated. The two had originally come to me because they were looking for a Bible. At that initial visit, they indicated they were interested in classes on the basics of Christian faith and spirituality. In a later chat, the young woman confessed that she became a Christian as the result of our classes. Now, she wanted to change churches (she was attending a very Fundamentalist church, not ours). All she heard in the fundamentalist worship she was attending was the need to be born again and that Jesus was coming back any time. She needed more in her journey. This is true of all our people.

In 1997, John Toews, then of MB Biblical Seminary[21] in Fresno, California, spoke to a group of pastors in Winnipeg. He was bold to declare that in a post-modern era, we had to rewrite the Gospel. He gave one example. Until the late twentieth-century, people were dealing with guilt and needed to be told about God's forgiveness. Post-moderns, however, were not dealing with guilt. They were dealing with shame. It is not forgiveness, but love and acceptance that they were looking for.

---

20. Even as his fundamentalist faith would have him disavow historical criticism.
21. Now Fresno Pacific Biblical Seminary.

Those are the kind of changes we as preachers need to make, sensitive to where the people in our congregation are at. Penal substitutionary atonement may have spoken forgiveness to people—in an unfortunate, to say the least, misreading of the Gospel and a horrible image of God[22]—but it does nothing for those dealing with shame and looking for love and acceptance. An angry God who needs to be pacified and who insists on punishment before he[23] will forgive is a God who is neither needed by nor attractive to twenty-first-century people.[24] Such a view of God also has done and continues to shape a way of thinking that does a lot of harm. This kind of rewriting is needed in a variety of other ways and the responsibility is ours as preachers to do that for our people.

I think making changes to be relevant is not just about concepts, but also about language. For example, I rarely refer to the Bible as the Bible. The word "Bible" immediately brings up what are often old, tired, and probably erroneous concepts of what the Bible is.[25] I tend to refer to the compilation that the church has chosen to be a collection that speaks God's Word to us as the Ancient Writings. I refer to Ancient Poets, Ancient Folk Singers, and Ancient Storytellers. I am hoping that this, along with the teaching I have done and am doing, will help people see, read, and hear the Bible differently.

Use of language is even more important when we speak about and refer to God. It is time to throw aside—permanently —any use of the male pronoun when we refer to God. Yes, I know, the Ancient Writings use male pronouns for God and refer to God, among other things, as Father. However, the original writings never use "Father." In the Old Testament they use the Hebrew word for "Father" and in the New Testament they say "*Patros.*" If we translate from Hebrew and Greek into English, we not only can, but must translate from culture to culture and from historical time period to historical time period. There are many female, mothering images of God used in the Ancient Writings. Even when there

---

22. For more on this see Zahn, *Sinners*, especially chapter 1.

23. I use the male pronoun deliberately in this case for the male warrior God is part of the foundation of the patriarchy that has done and continues to do so much damage in our churches and our society.

24. A good alternative vision of God and salvation can be found in Brian Zahnd's *Sinners in the Hands of a Loving God.*

25. On the question of what the Bible is, I invite you to read Peter Enns's *The Bible Tells Me So* and Rob Bell's *What is the Bible?* On making a distinction between "Bible" and "Word of God," see Appendix B.

are not, it is time to make it clear God is no more father than mother, and our preaching needs to reflect that.

I would say the same thing about how we refer to people. Yes, in the first century, *anthropos* could refer to both men as in male and humanity as a whole. *Adelphoi* could include brothers and sisters. Their English counterparts did the same for a good bit of history on into the mid—and late mid-twentieth century. But now we are in the twenty-first century and it is time we spoke in twenty-first-century English. Never mind that there are still many who scoff at "political correctness," we are tasked with the responsibility of speaking God's Word to our people in our time and we need to do that as best we can in twenty-first-century English. No longer should women have to imagine that they belong in God's Kingdom and in our congregations.

3. *We dare not be boring.* Given the money most of us as preachers get paid and given that people listening to us Sunday morning could be golfing, at the lake, or out for brunch, we are compelled to be interesting and creative in our preaching. I think my earlier preaching at Aberdeen must have been boring at times, and long, often going thirty-five to forty minutes. I find that at this stage in my preaching life, with the tools I have available to me, finding out what the text means and what it might mean to people today is relatively easy. What faces me each week, however, is how I will start, the hook I will use for the sermon, and how I will preach it so it has a hope of connecting with people's imaginations.

When I was president of a small Bible school and we, as faculty members, were helping out a local congregation that did not have a pastor, a colleague told me that he'd give me five minutes to convince him that listening to my sermon would be worth it. If after those five minutes I had not grabbed his attention, he was gone. His butt would still be in the pew, but his mind would be wandering down more interesting paths.

I realize that Paul, in writing to the people in the congregation in first century Corinth, boldly declares that he was basically boring, not at all creative and in no way using his intellect and academic learning when he came to preach the Good News:

> I was unsure of how to go about this, and felt totally inadequate—I was scared to death, if you want the truth of it—and so nothing I said could have impressed you or anyone else. But the Message came through anyway. God's Spirit and God's power did it, which made it clear that your life of faith is a response to

God's power, not to some fancy mental or emotional footwork by me or anyone else.[26]

Scholars pretty much agree that Paul was not nearly as adverse to using "human wisdom"[27] and "plausible words of wisdom"[28] as this text might suggest. Paul used all his training, background, and intellectual ability when it came to making a case for the Gospel. Whatever tools he had, he used them. When addressing the philosophers in Athens, he grabs their attention by starting with: "Men of Athens, I notice that you are very religious in every way, for as I was walking along I saw your many shrines. And one of your altars had this inscription on it: 'To an Unknown God.'"[29] That demonstrates being observant in life to be relevant and grab attention. He may not have been a storytelling preacher, but he was not afraid to be creative. I think in 1 Corinthians he is too quick to draw a line and build a fence between human wisdom and God's wisdom. All wisdom, the ability to think carefully, and the gifts of imagination and creativity come from God and were meant to be used in the preaching of the message God wants our people to hear.

I have been helped immeasurably in my preaching, both in being creative and in learning how to communicate by the stories told and the writing styles found in novels, TV shows, and movies. Encouraged by a mother who loved to read, I have read fiction since as far back as I can remember. One of the only limits placed on my reading was, when still under the influence and guidance of my parents, the books I read had to be either Christian (Danny Orlis taught me fundamentalist Evangelical theology) or not harmful to my Christian faith. Hardy Boys, Bobbsey Twins, and a host of other fiction was fine. The other limit was how much we read. Life was about more than sitting in my room and reading. At some point, the rule was made that I was not allowed to read more than one book a day. That meant a 128-page Moody Press book[30] was a bad choice for Sunday afternoon.

Back in the eighties, I would sometimes say that nothing had helped me as much in my preaching as the fiction of John Steinbeck. Though

26. 1 Cor 2:3–5. *The Message.*
27. 1 Cor 2:13. NRSV.
28. 2 Cor 2:4. NRSV.
29. Acts 17:22–23. NLT.

30. I realize this reflects my baby boomer age and the powerful influence *Back to the Bible Broadcast* and, in particular, its youth division had on my life.

I have read Steinbeck, Graham Greene, Margaret Lawrence and other, more recent writers of literature, I tend more towards the bestsellers. I have read and continue to read and enjoy and learn from the wonderful storytelling skills of Michael Connelly,[31] David Baldacci,[32] Peter Robinson,[33] Louise Penny,[34] Jeffrey Archer,[35] John Grisham,[36] Richard North Patterson,[37] Lisa Scottoline, and others.[38]

Though not as obvious a tool to help my preaching, I love reading spiritual memoirs. I keep my eyes open for them. Recently a friend gave us *Leaving Church* by Barbara Taylor Brown. Nadia Bolz-Weber's *Pastrix* is not to be missed. However, be forewarned, the first word in the book is "S***"[39] and by the second page of the introduction she refers to a "f***ing fairy tale."[40] For some, that may be carrying language relevance too far. I loved and gave away as gifts Sara Miles' *Take This Bread*. And, given the influence Eugene Peterson has had in my life, I read *The Pastor* as soon as I discovered its availability. I have also read *Hannah's Child* by Stanley Hauerwas and, as you will notice in chapter 1, Ted Schwartz's *Laughter is Sacred Space*. These memoirs feed me and therefore feed my preaching. They also help my interpretation of the memoirs that make up so much of the Ancient Writings and the telling of stories as a way of preaching and/or including stories in my sermons.

There was no TV in our home growing up (and we had to hide the radio when Grandpa came to visit). I have probably made up for that since. The VCR and PVR (or DVR) have been a real boon. Now, thank you, God for Netflix, and thank you for a partner who shares my love

---

31. I started with the Lincoln Lawyer series and then continued with the Harry Bosch novels when the two story lines merged.

32. Particularly the Amos Decker series, starting with *Memory Man*.

33. I've read every one of his Alan Banks mysteries.

34. Her Inspector Gamache novels are best read in order, starting with *Still Life*.

35. Stay away from his prison trilogy. The ending of the third volume of *The Clifton Chronicles* helped me preach the Easter sermon from Mark's version one year.

36. Grisham's work is uneven. However, some of the novels are excellent as entertainment and examples of storytelling.

37. Many of Patterson's novels are written around social issues.

38. For an example of how a novel can help with Biblical interpretation, see Brueggemann, "The Creatures Know."

39. Bolz-Weber, xv.

40. Bolz-Weber, xvi.

for shows and movies. Friday night, unless it's the CFL[41] season, is often movie and pizza night at our house. Fiction writers and movie makers are storytellers of today. If we are going to be creative preachers, we had better be storytellers. Therefore, we should all allow ourselves to be taught and entertained by much of what is available on our TV screens and the fiction sections of our local libraries.

Even better, visit garage sales and used book stores and build a fiction collection. This way, you can read the books at your leisure and have them on hand if you need to refer to them again. (And, a guilty pleasure on my part, I buy at least one book, often more, when I visit an independent book store in Canmore, Alberta or when Sylvia wants to eat at Prairie Ink, a restaurant attached to the McNally Robinson bookstore in Saskatoon, Saskatchewan. Yes, there are also online booksellers and there are times I simply cannot resist ordering the next volume by one of my favorite storytellers.) You will not be the preacher you can be if you do not read novels and watch movies and TV shows.

In the pages that follow, I share with you various examples from my own attempts at creative preaching. Though some sermons and series were planned specifically with the creative style I used, most of the time the creativity "just happens." That is, I sit down to write the sermon and ideas come to mind for how I will shape and write it.

As a result, I am unable to tell you how to be creative or how to choose what kinds of sermon styles to use because I have no idea, except that having been exposed to creativity, it is with me. I share these sermons not as the best there is in preaching. There are many fantastic preachers out there. Nor do I share these because I think you should preach these in your pulpit. You should preach your own sermons. I share these hoping that in reading them, ideas will pop up in your own mind and, having been exposed to my creativity, you will be inspired to write your own creative sermons.

I have had significant editorial assistance in bringing these sermons to publication. At the same time, they are close to what they were when I headed to church on Sunday mornings. When I was preaching regularly, I did not have the time to do a lot of polishing. I have a friend who, when he was a pastor, would usually preach his sermons to an empty building three times between writing and Sunday morning. Most of my sermons, providing all goes well, are written by Friday supper time. I

---

41. Canadian Football League, Canada's professional football league whose season runs from mid-June to the last Sunday in November.

turn my manuscript into preaching notes on Sunday morning between 7:30 a.m. and 9:15 a.m. Before I was sick with cancer and chemo, I was better at handling early mornings and I would usually arrive at the office between 6:30 a.m. and 7:00 a.m. Then, on occasion, the sermon could get a major rewrite at that point. That rarely happened since because I did not have the energy for that much work on a Sunday morning. My point is that in regular preaching, there are obvious limits to how much work you can put into each sermon each week. Accept those limits, in terms of polish. Unless a crisis happens, do not accept those limits in terms of preparation, relevancy, and creativity.

I share these sermons in no particular order. I start with the sermon that gave me the title for this collection. It seemed to make sense to do so. After that, the ordering is fairly haphazard.

Some of you will think these sermons, especially a few of them, long. I am not much in love with twelve to fifteen-minute sermons. Those are verbal blogs. Creative preaching, particularly if it includes storytelling, takes time. Good storytelling may take lots of time. Why do movies often run two hours and novels that keep you up at night run to three hundred pages? It is because good, imagination-grabbing storytelling takes time. Sure, there are great short stories around, but even those take time. How long should a sermon be? I might be inclined to answer the way one of my professors in university answered when asked how long a term paper should be "As long as a piece of string. If it's not long enough, it just doesn't quite reach. If too long, you have loose ends dangling around all over the place."

Recently I read an online article by Justin Trapp on the length of sermons.[42] His organization surveyed some of the better known Evangelical preachers in America. The ten preachers surveyed averaged forty-two minutes, from John Ortberg at Menlo Church, Menlo, California at thirty-two minutes and Timothy Keller at Redeemer Presbyterian Church in New York City (thirty-seven minutes) to Rick Warren at Saddleback in California (fifty-seven minutes).[43] Trapp goes on to say: "The one thing about each of these preachers, though, is their messages are well-organized, incredibly diverse in the way they present the message, and they appeal to all the many different ways people learn."[44]

---

42. Trapp, "How Long Should."
43. Trapp, "Average," para. 4–10.
44. Trapp, "How Long Should," para. 10.

My aim is twenty-five minutes. If you are not creative and the congregation is not engaged, five minutes is too long. If they are engaged, depending on how hard the benches, they may be wanting more after thirty minutes.[45] Finally, it depends on you, your preaching style, and your congregation.

One more thing about my own sermon writing: forty years later, it is still hard work. For me, writing a sermon takes a ton of energy. When I was pastor at Zion Mennonite, I had an administrative assistant in the office with me, Tuesday to Friday. All too often on a Friday morning, she would notice me walking around, sometimes even pacing in the hall. She would ask, "Ray, are you procrastinating?" and I would have to answer, "Yes." The energy outflow required to write was so much that it seemed a daunting task to start writing another sermon. Pulling together the ideas from the text, the things I have discovered in my research, the connections I want to make with life today, and being creative all at the same time takes, for me, tremendous focus. I take fairly detailed notes when I research but rarely go back to them once I write, unless there is a specific quotation I am interested in. Usually I know my main points when I start, but not always. I do my best thinking while writing, and so the sermon takes shape as I write. Sometimes I drive the sermon; sometimes it drives me. Every now and then, I get lucky. I have an idea for the introduction before I start the research. I sit down and write the intro—so I won't forget it—and when I finish writing, I call home and tell Sylvia that I have a problem: "My sermon is done but I haven't done my research."

And yet no matter how difficult and how much energy it takes, every week when I sit down at my computer and call up the text in three parallel versions on Bible Gateway, I get excited and then again, when I sit down to write the sermon. Another opportunity to translate the Ancient Writings into the twenty-first century and have them, through me, become God's Word for the congregation for that week.[46] Could there be a more exciting adventure and a more worthy calling?

Finally, something about the title. In chapter 1, I explain how I came upon the phrase I use in the title. I want to say a little bit more about the importance of that phrase. As the sermon in chapter 1 shows, it is for

---

45. When I was in university, I had a political geography professor whose classes were fascinating. When he would end the lecture after fifty minutes, I would look at my watch and think, "What? Already?"

46. When did or do the Ancient Writings become God's Word? For a discussion of this question, see Appendix B.

me a label for discipleship. It is a description of how to read the Ancient Writings. It is what we need to do if we are going to preach. It is what we invite our people to do every Sunday as we get up, set our notes or manuscript on the podium if we use them, pause for a moment to invite curiosity, offer a silent prayer, and then begin to speak God's Word for God to God's people. Earlier in this introduction, I briefly referenced that I believe the Bible to be essentially story and that it is crucial preachers learn to read story and be storytellers in their preaching. I want to come back to this now and expand on it.

The Bible is not a manual for living, not a book of theological propositions, not a collection of pithy, even inspirational sayings hidden amongst a whole bunch of useless, and maybe even boring, stuff. It is a library,[47] a collection of writings that as a compiled volume tell the story of people searching for God, meaning, purpose, and belonging in an often chaotic history more reminiscent of Wilderness than Park. In their search, the people often lose their way, and then seem to manage to find it again, sort of. Finally, that search reaches a kind of climax when God realizes God has no other recourse but to go live among people and show them who God is. Jesus shows up, and history, understanding of God, meaning, purpose, and belonging are never the same again.

In 2016, still dealing with the limitations placed on me by chemotherapy, I watched a lot of TV. A friend told me about *White Collar* and I dove right in, binge watching the series on Netflix. When the last episode ended, it was like I went through separation anxiety. Neil Caffrey and Peter Burke had become so much a part of my life and I theirs that it was like I was losing a couple of special friends. That is what it means to jump into the story. We find a home there and it is increasingly difficult to separate it from our story. That is, I believe, how the Bible was meant to be read.

In a workshop, I have occasionally read the story of the healing of the paralytic man found in Mark 2:1–12 to the audience. Then I tell them I will read it a second time. Before I begin, I want them to choose one of the characters in that story and pretend they are that character. I read the story and then we talk about what they experienced. That is a way of jumping into the story. It is a way of the story becoming real to us. It is

---

47. Along with Peter Enns and Rob Bell, Brian McLaren makes a similar point in *A New Kind of Christianity*. See especially chapter 8, "From Legal Constitution to Community Library," 78–86. The Bible is, writes McLaren, a "portable library of poems, prophecies, histories, fables, parables, letters, sage sayings, quarrels, and so on." (79).

important that we as preachers experience that reality of the Story if we are going to help our people experience it.

In her book, *Inspired*, Rachel Held Evans says:

> Renowned New Testament scholar N. T. Wright compared Scripture to a five-act play, full of drama and surprise, wherein the people of God are invited into the story to improvise the unfinished final act. Our ability to faithfully execute our roles in the drama depends on our willingness to enter the narrative, he said, to see how our own stories intersect with the grander epic of God's redemption of the world.[48]

Walter Brueggemann, in one of his books on preaching, *Cadences of Home*, makes a similar point when he says that "the preaching of [the Biblical] texts is . . . the enactment of a drama in which the congregation is audience but may at any point become *participant*."[49] The goal is that "in the preaching moment the congregation may see itself as among the characters in the drama."[50] The goal is, having jumped into the story, from within the story the preacher can invite the people of the congregation to join her/him in that story, like a father encouraging a young son or daughter to jump into the pool.

Brueggemann says, "Such a mode [of preaching] holds the potential of showing the congregants that their lives (and life together) also constitute a drama being enacted and a story being told, in which they are characters with work to do, options to exercise, and loyalties to sustain or alter."[51]

Since the entire Ancient Story is about finding God and meaning in a chaotic life and history, our own stories will always find a place where they fit. As we write our story in that Ancient Story, our story takes on a different hue and meaning and God is seen, experienced, and understood differently. For all the philosophical and theological ink spilled in trying to make sense of God, people, and history, it is really only as we jump into the story that meaning and understanding will come. In Story, I am convinced, we also become more comfortable with not understanding and discovering that meaning is hard to grasp. If our story fits the Grand Story, it's okay.

---

48. Wright, "How Can," para. 26–30, as quoted in Evans, *Inspired*, xx.
49. Brueggemann, *Cadences*, 33. Emphasis mine.
50. Brueggemann, *Cadences*, 33. See also Brueggemann, *Texts*, 64–70.
51. Brueggemann, *Cadences*, 34.

When I was at Swift Current Bible Institute,[52] I taught the course that all students had to take in semester two of year two. It was a course that attempted to help students pull together their studies and experiences in two years of Bible school into something meaningful, something that fit with their earlier life, something that was part of God's Story, and something that could continue to shape their life's narrative. One of the assignments each year was to write their life story as if it was going to become one of the books of the Bible. My hope was that the exercise would open up their minds to what the stories in the Ancient Writings that speak God's Word to us actually were and, at the same time, help them see how they were part of God's grand narrative and dream for the world.

I also hoped it would do one more thing. Borrowing one more idea from Wright, our story is also a continuation of that Ancient Story. The Ancient Story was nowhere near complete when John of Patmos wrote the final line of his fantasy story: "And they lived happily ever after."[53] Okay, he didn't write that line, but he should have, no doubt would have, had he read as many fairy tales as we have. What we call the Old Testament is chapter 1 of that story. A really important second chapter was completed when Dr. Luke reached Acts 28:31 and John of Patmos signed off with Revelation 22:21 (without that final, so important sentence). However, a whole new chapter 3 had just barely begun. The New Testament makes the point in various ways. Maybe the best way, given the importance of story, is by Mark. His gospel really has no ending. It just stops.[54] I think Mark's point is that the story is far from finished. It continues and it will never end until The End. The writing of this third chapter is up to us. To write it and to write it accurately, we will have to jump into the story, first

---

52. One of the many small Bible schools that popped up on the Canadian prairies during the 1930s, it closed in 1996.

53. Unfortunately this idea is not original with me. It is part of a wonderful and humorous story by Jonas Jonasson, *The 100-Year-Old Man*. In the story a bit of a shyster and crook gives his buddy a couple of dollars for a pallet of Bibles with a printing mistake destined for recycling. The small time crook is going to sell them as good Bibles. However, his curiosity gets the better of him. What might the printing mistake be? So he digs out his Lutheran confirmation Bible and begins reading with Gen 1:1, comparing the two Bibles. It's not till he gets to the very end of Revelation that he discovers the mistake. The printer had added one more verse, the quoted line.

54. Later editors did not like that and so they gave us a couple of endings to choose from. However, the original, or at least our copy of it, just ends.

into chapters 1 and 2 so we understand the story, and then into chapter 3, for we can only write it if we are in it.

One morning on my way to another period of writing in my office, I stopped at a friend's office, two floors down. Our conversation led me to think of what may be one of the best examples of people jumping into the story to make sense of and bring hope to their story. On the way to work, he had heard an interview with a professor from Harvard. The scholar had made the point that when African American slaves wrote and sang their spirituals, it was *all* code and *only* code for their dreams of escaping slavery.

I think that is too simplistic of an interpretation of what went on. At the same time, equally simplistic, is the view that their songs were *only* about their Christian faith based on Ancient Stories. I think this was an example of jumping into the story. Their experience of slavery and hope for rescue drew them to the Ancient Story of Exodus and deliverance. Their own experience helped them understand the Story. The Story then, as they connected with it, gave them hope for their own rescue, deliverance and homecoming in the Promised Land. *This* was about *both*, deliverance from physical slavery and a story that was a metaphor for the spiritual journeys. Transformation of their situation would be *both* a physical transformation of slavery to freedom and society's move from oppression to freedom, as well as a spiritual change in society and culture.

While all that was going on, deliverance and transformation were also spiritual realities in their personal lives and a possibility in the lives of their oppressors. That spiritual transformation in the lives of the oppressors would result in a change in society and the practice of slavery, which would result in physical deliverance from slavery. So they jumped into the story in the songs they sang, the way they responded to their lives, and the way they did what they could to resist the oppression and work with God, like Moses and Miriam and Joshua, to overthrow oppression.

There was simply no drawing of lines between one story and another. They were completely in the Exodus story and the Jesus story. Those stories made sense to them because of their situation. The Ancient Story and their own poetry also helped them find meaning and hope in what would otherwise have been a truly hopeless situation. This is a way in which all stories merge. This is jumping into the story.

We see this same kind of jumping into the story happening within the Ancient Writings themselves. The Ancient Poets of the Hebrew Psalter and the Ancient Folk Singers and Protest Singers (otherwise known as prophets) show in their poetry and preaching that they had jumped into the story and were finding their home there in the story as they reviewed the current historical story and sketched a new script for the future story. The lines blurred in language used and in metaphors adopted. There was no separation between the ancient Exodus story and their current historical situation—especially once they were in Babylon—and the future story they were hoping for.

Walter Brueggemann points to this in his study of 2 Isaiah,[55] especially 54:1–17. Brueggemann understands 2 Isaiah in general and the text from chapter 54 in particular to be an example of how jumping into the story, though not using the phrase, can create a reassessment of the current situation. Brueggemann asserts, "*Re-entry into the memory* requires and permits a rereading of the present reality."[56] In summarizing how a message of hope for freedom is drawn from the memory held in Story, and pointing to "black literature" as another example, he says, "Such larger freedom is a possibility for exiles, but *only where the slave narratives are re-entered and claimed as ours*—even in a foreign land."[57]

John of Patmos follows 2 Isaiah's example as he writes his fantasy version of the Good News of Jesus. For example, the dragon of Revelation 12 is Egypt, Babylon, King Herod at the birth of Jesus, and the Roman emperor at the time of John's writing of the book. The many stories become one Story and the one Story fits the many stories. John of Patmos had jumped into the story.

In my own Anabaptist/Mennonite tradition, Menno Simons[58] is a good example of jumping into the story. In his discussion of the persecution of the Anabaptists in sixteenth-century Holland, he jumped into the story and placed himself and his fledgling flock into the story so thoroughly that he can describe their persecutors and their actions as "Ananias and Caiaphas, together with all the scribes, conspire to the death of Christ . . . Herod, with all his lords and princes, scorns and

---

55. Brueggemann, "Only Memory Allows Possibility" in *Hopeful Imagination*, 89–130.

56. Brueggemann, *Hopeful Imagination*, 120. Emphasis mine.

57. Brueggemann, *Hopeful Imagination*, 130. Emphasis mine.

58. Menno Simons was a Catholic priest in sixteenth-century Holland. After studying the Bible and hearing about a violent uprising of Reformers near his hometown, he left the church to join the Anabaptists (re-baptizers) in 1535. Shortly afterwards, he was persuaded to take on leadership of the scattered Anabaptists in the Netherlands. His leadership was so determinative for the group that his name became the name by which the various Mennonite churches would be known.

mocks him . . . Pilate and all those to whom the service of the sword pertains sentence Him to the stake, to fire, to sword, and to the water."[59] They identified with Jesus so closely and they were involved in the story so thoroughly, that, aside from bringing salvation by Jesus's death and not theirs, they were in the Jesus story.

So jump into the story.

However, be forewarned. Like Soren Kierkegaard's "leap of faith," this is a dangerous jump. It is fishing for people while standing in your boat, teetering on the very edge of the falls. Christian discipleship—following Jesus—is not for the faint of heart. Jesus warned us: "If any of you wants to be my follower, you must give up your own way, take up your cross, and follow me."[60] In Jesus's day, if you were carrying your cross—that is, the cross beam of the cross on which you were to be executed—it meant you had been convicted of a capital crime, most likely treason or insurrection, and you were about to die a horrible death, already having been whipped within an inch of your death. Jumping into that kind of story is not a jump that should be made lightly.

When we jump into the story as a preacher, we jump into a dangerous story, telling a dangerous story. We are speaking the Word of God. That Story is a dangerous weapon. The Ancient Theologian writing what we now know as Hebrews said, "[T]he word of God is alive and powerful. It is sharper than the sharpest two-edged sword, cutting between soul and spirit, between joint and marrow."[61] We better not wave a sword like that around carelessly for people are liable to get hurt. It must be treated with care, caution, and respect. Even then, blood may get spilt and people may be "mortally wounded."

Eugene Peterson says God's "powerful Word is sharp as a surgeon's scalpel."[62] That's a good image for our day and age. A sharp surgeon's scalpel is a crucial instrument in the operating room. Though I did not see it being used and its immediate aftereffects were painful, I was very thankful for a sharp surgeon's scalpel when Dr. Khori had to remove eighteen inches of cancerous colon from my body. However, such a sharp instrument in the wrong hands or used carelessly or used with a wrong

---

59. Simons, "The Cross," 582. For a fuller interpretation and discussion of the connection that Simons and other Anabaptists saw between their story and the entire Biblical story, see Friesen, "Theology of the Martyrs," 76–118.

60. Matt 16:24. NLT.

61. Heb 4:12. NLT.

62. Heb 4:12. *The Message*.

diagnosis—I recall the story of a doctor who removed a woman's only functioning kidney when he saw what appeared to be a weird growth—can do a great deal of damage.

What Barbara Brown Taylor says about being an Episcopal priest is, I think, equally true about being a preacher: "Being a priest seemed only slightly less dicey to me than being chief engineer at a nuclear plant. In both cases, one needed to know how to approach great power without unleashing great danger and getting fried in the process."[63] So too, when we jump into the story to preach. Crosses to carry, falls to run over, scalpels to wield, swords to unsheathe, power to unleash. We best be careful and do our preaching with a great deal of enthusiasm and imagination, but also with great care.

Jumping wholeheartedly into the story and preaching it in a way that is alive today can also be dangerous to a preacher's career. Menno Simons was a fugitive from the moment he decided to jump into the story. When Martin Luther began reading Romans and decided to jump into that story, he was soon on the run. He left Catholic territory and was safe only because he helped the German princes in their own attempts to be free of Catholic political domination. Romans has gotten me into trouble as well. I have been asked to leave congregations because I preached the "scandal of grace" and God's call, through Jesus (Matt 22:34-40) and Paul (Rom 13:8-10), to radical love as the only foundation to ethics that matters.

Jump into the story by all means! There is no life quite like it. But, be forewarned. Stories have ways of taking on lives of their own and who knows how the story may play out with you in it.

Happy preaching! And remember, preaching is a sacred responsibility. "Do you have the *gift* of speaking? Then speak as though God him[/her]self were speaking through you."[64] If you don't have the gift, don't miss a good opportunity to shut up. If you do have it and you've been called by God and your congregation to preach, I think you have every reason to put your best creative effort, and the full power of your imagination, into it.

---

63. Taylor, *Leaving Church*, 31.
64. 1 Pet 4:11. NLT.

Chapter 1

JUMP INTO THE STORY

IT WAS A SPRING Tuesday or Wednesday morning and time to get working on Sunday's sermon. I was using the lectionary that spring to guide my preaching and the text for Sunday was John 21:1–19 (Year C). I knew the story. I also knew I had a creative sermon on file, one I had preached several years ago (like maybe nine years ago) in a different congregation. However, thanks to the foibles of technology, the digital version of that sermon had been laid to rest in some cyberspace graveyard. I had a paper copy, but it was in a filing cabinet twenty minutes away and I wasn't about to drive to our country church and back for a copy of that sermon.

I was going to have to write a new sermon. Somehow, a "here are three things you can learn from this story" sermon held no interest for me. I knew if I could barely get myself to write it, it would be tough for the congregation to listen to it.

I had, since the late nineties, heard live productions of Ted & Lee's wildly funny and deeply profound presentations of *Fish Eyes* and *Creation Chronicles*.[1] That same spring, I was reading Ted Swartz's autobiography, *Laugher is Sacred Space*. A few days earlier, I had read a piece from the closing scene of *Fish Eyes*, the story from John 21. In it, Peter and Andrew, out fishing, are trying to understand what Jesus is shouting to them:

> ANDREW: Caaaa . . . Caaa . . . Cashew. Nuts. Cashew nuts. Cashew nuts on the other side. Cashew nuts?

---

1. These are two-man drama productions telling the New Testament and Old Testament story respectively.

PETER: Cashew nuts?

ANDREW: Did you bring a snack?

PETER: No, I didn't bring one.[2]

There's more and it's hilarious. I remember how hard I laughed when I saw the whole production in St. Louis back when the General Conference Mennonite Church and the Mennonite Church had a joint, binational conference there.

I knew I was no Ted & Lee, so I couldn't be as funny as they were. But, ideas were starting to dance around. I could still do Peter and Andrew. But who would be my Andrew? I couldn't think of any of the men in our congregation who would consent to join me Sunday morning, even if I wrote the script.

And then I had another idea. There was no male I could arm-twist into working with me, but . . . I knew a female who, according to God and the Bible was supposed to be my partner and helper in time of need. This was a time of need. Would she dare decline? And, besides, as my co-pastor at Emmaus, she had a professional duty to help me, didn't she? How could she say no? Actually, I know how she can do that, but that is for another time. Fortunately she said "Yes."

The possibilities were born. I couldn't do Peter and Andrew, but I could do Peter and Martha. That meant I couldn't set it, timewise, on the beach that morning. I would have to choose another time and possibly place. But that was no big deal. I could have Peter tell the story, and my fingers started dancing on the keyboard.

I was about two-thirds of the way through writing the piece when the phrase "jump into the story" popped into my mind. Wow! It was like fireworks went off in my imagination. Some might suggest they burned some of my circuits, but forget them. I was excited. I went back to what I had written and rewrote a few pieces to make the use of the phrase work throughout the sermon. It seemed like the perfect phrase to describe discipleship. Jump into the Jesus story. Jump into God's story. It fit for me in so many ways.

Soon, I saw its larger implications. As a preacher, that is what I was called to do every week: jump into the story. Muck around in it sometimes. Be surprised by it often. Find my place and our congregation's place in it week by week.

---

2. Schwartz, *Laughter*, 122.

So that is how *Jump into the Story*, the sermon, came to be born and got written.

JUMP INTO THE STORY

John 21:1–19

Third Sunday of Easter, Year C

Peter is sitting on the dock fishing, with rod & reel

MARTHA: (*calls out from back of the church walking up the aisle*) Hey Peter, try casting on the other side of the dock.

PETER: (*as he turns toward the sound of the voice*) Try casting on the . . . Martha! Martha! How the heck are you? (*runs toward her and hugs her*) So good to see you! You're looking great.

MARTHA: Thanks. You are looking right well yourself, for an old man.

PETER: Hey, careful now. You got time to sit a bit? Of course you have time to sit. You can't be by the Sea of Galilee and not have time to sit a bit. Here, let's grab these deck chairs. Wow, this is quite something, you coming by. It's been a while.

MARTHA: It has, for sure.

PETER: How you been?

MARTHA: Good. Good. And you?

PETER: Same. Good.

MARTHA: How come you are out here? I thought you had given up fishing, or fishing for fish at least.

PETER: Not given up. Just traded it in. But sometimes, when the stress and stuff get to me, I find coming out here for a while and catching a few fish is the best therapy around. This fishing for people sounds nice, but it is tough. You think a twenty-pound jack can put up a fight? You should try landing a one hundred fifty-pound Jewish convert. It's like you need a massage every time you snag one. So, a few times a year, I come up here to sit back, catch a few fish, and relax, renew, and think back to those days. You know, I can go a whole afternoon without a nibble and it's okay. Memories flood my mind and it's like I'm back there, well, back here but back there again, reliving what were some pretty wonderful times.

MARTHA: I bet you have a lot of memories.

PETER: Oh boy, do I ever. And when you called out—you know, that was good, "try casting on the other side of the dock." Really good. With your voice so low, almost like a man, it's like in a moment I was back here, after Easter when Jesus told us to cast our nets on the other side of the boat.

MARTHA: Did you know it was him when he called out to you?

PETER: No, had no idea. Far as I could make out, it was some stranger.

MARTHA: But you listened to the stranger.

PETER: Yeah. On the Sea of Galilee, in the early morning, there are times the sun hits the water just right and reflects off the shiny scales of the fish just below the surface. You have to be at the right angle to see it, and so sometimes someone on shore can see the fish and you don't notice them from the boat. So we cast our nets on the other side.

MARTHA: And caught some fish.

PETER: And caught some fish. You could say that again. It's like the fish were jumping right into the net, we caught so many. I still remember, we counted them, 153. The most Andrew and I or any of the guys we knew who fished on the Galilee had ever caught in one cast.

MARTHA: And that convinced you it was Jesus.

PETER: Actually it was John who first recognized him. John said later that it was like "déjà vu all over again." It was like he was back in time to the first time it happened.

MARTHA: This had happened before? I didn't know that.

PETER: Yeah, about three years ago. And so when it happened now, John just knew it was Jesus.

MARTHA: And you believed him?

PETER: I did. As soon as John said it, it made sense. Of course it was Jesus.

MARTHA: And then?

PETER: We got to shore, as fast as we could. It was so good to see Jesus.

MARTHA: You had seen him before, hadn't you? I mean after his death?

PETER: Oh yeah, we had. That first Sunday, when Mary Magdalene found the empty tomb in the morning, she came and told us she had seen Jesus. John and I ran to check it out. We told the others what we saw, but had no idea what it meant. And then, that evening, Jesus himself showed up where we were hanging out. We were afraid. Nothing made sense and we had no idea what to do next. A week later when Thomas was with us, Jesus "popped in" again. So we had seen Jesus, twice, and sometimes we actually believed he was alive, but then he would disappear, and it all seemed like mass hallucinations. Now, here he was on the seashore, telling us how to fish, cooking breakfast, and somehow it just sealed the deal. Jesus was alive.

MARTHA: That morning really brought you around?

PETER: Yeah, yeah, I think it did. There just seemed no question that Jesus was alive. Resurrection had happened. That meant everything had changed. And everything was the same, more the same than ever. It meant that all we had heard Jesus say and seen him do, that was more real than ever. All we had experienced with Jesus was really real. And, it was meant to be real forever, not just for the few years we were with him. I think that's what hit me that morning, even though I didn't know what it meant. I couldn't have, not what it meant nor what it would mean for me.

MARTHA: Wow.

PETER: And then, of course, there was the conversation he and I had.

MARTHA: Yeah? I don't know if I've ever heard this part.

PETER: After breakfast, Jesus asked me three times if I loved him. I remember getting a little annoyed at him by the third time. Imagine getting annoyed at a guy who a few weeks ago had been crucified, "dead and buried," and now is alive and just cooked breakfast for you. But, I admit, I got annoyed. Each time I told him yes, of course I loved him. And each time he told me to feed his sheep and lambs. And then he told me what I probably remember most, and will never forget. That thing, I think, more than anything, has gone with me all these years and what has kept me going. He said, "Jump into the story."

MARTHA: He said what?

PETER: Jump into the story.

MARTHA: Jump into the story?

PETER: Jump into the story.

MARTHA: Yeah right, he said that.

PETER: Well okay, maybe he didn't say it quite that way, but that's what he meant. He said, "Follow me," but I knew he meant, "Jump into the story."

MARTHA: I'm listening.

PETER: Well, to understand, I think you have to go back to the first time he said this to me. After Easter, here on the shore of the Sea of Galilee, wasn't the first time, you know. He had said it before.

MARTHA: Told you before to jump into the story?

PETER: Well, like I said before, the words he actually spoke were, "Follow me" but what he meant was, "Jump into the story."

MARTHA: I'm all ears.

PETER: It all goes back to when I first met Jesus. I actually met him through Andrew, you know. One day, late afternoon, Andrew comes barging into the house like a blankety blank lunatic, shouting about this guy he had met that he wanted me to meet. Woke me from a most beautiful nap and this dream I was having about my wife.

MARTHA: Not sure I want to hear about this dream.

PETER: Don't worry. No sweet dream stories. I woke up and I was annoyed—do I have a problem with getting annoyed? Maybe. I thought I needed my rest to go fishing again, but Andrew wouldn't let me be. He told me I had to meet this guy. They had agreed to go for a pint or two and he wanted me to join them.

MARTHA: And you did.

PETER: I did, and it was an amazing evening. I had never had a conversation like that in my life. He talked about what he was planning, the ideas he had. It blew me away the way he talked about God. It sure wasn't what the local rabbis and synagogue keepers were saying. They talked about God too and thought they had wonderful ideas, but they could put you to sleep in no time flat. Not this guy. And, at the same time, he was interested in us, asked us about fishing, life in Capernaum—he said he was thinking of getting a house in Capernaum and making it his home base. He asked us about our hopes and dreams, our plans, for ourselves, our families.

MARTHA: And the pints kept flowing?

PETER: Yes. No. I mean, you know, I have no idea. No one was paying attention to how much we were drinking. I can't tell you if I had six or if I nursed one all evening. I sure wasn't drunk, except maybe on what Jesus was saying. We were completely focused on Jesus and what he had to say. And we talked about nothing else for the next couple of weeks. While fishing we focused on fishing, but while cleaning and mending nets, we would talk about what

Jesus had said. Wondering if what he had said to us could really be so. Wondering if we would ever see him again.

MARTHA: You obviously did.

PETER: We sure did. A few weeks later Andrew and I, along with our buddies, James and John, were sitting on the shore, cleaning and mending nets. It had been a good night of fishing. The sun was nice and warm, but not uncomfortable. And, again, like every other day, we were talking about the things Jesus had said. We were in the middle of our conversation, barely paying attention to the nets, much to the chagrin of Zebedee, James's and John's father, when Andrew suddenly whispered, "I think it's him!"

MARTHA: Meaning Jesus?

PETER: Yeah. We all looked up and sure enough, there was Jesus strolling along the shore, coming right towards us. When he got close enough he shouted, "Hi," and Andrew and I, of course, shouted back. He walked over and greeted James, John, and Zebedee. We introduced them. John and James were excited about meeting Jesus after all they heard us say. Zebedee was a little more reserved. He could be a bit of gruff old goat at the best of times, and I had noticed he had not been quite so taken with our conversations about Jesus as we were. Jesus turned back to the four of us young guys and said, "Lads." Maybe that was the other thing that morning after Easter that clued us in, when Jesus called us "Lads." Anyway, Jesus said, "Lads, come with me if you think you can. I have something I want to run by you, a proposition for you."

MARTHA: Did you have any idea what he was talking about?

PETER: None, but we hesitated only a moment and then said, "You bet." We just left our boats and nets. Zebedee was kind of taken aback when his boys just took off and left him with the work. "What about these nets?" he shouted after them. They just waved at him and said they'd be back later to finish.

MARTHA: And the proposition?

PETER: Jump into the story. Let me explain.

MARTHA: Please do. You really have me curious.

PETER: We went to the Goat & Camel and Jesus offered to buy a round. We chit-chatted about fishing, the weather, and the latest rumors about what the Romans were up to. When our cups arrived, Jesus turned serious and said, "I have a story I would like to tell you."

MARTHA: He was a great storyteller. I sure do remember that.

PETER: He was, and this afternoon was no different. We were mesmerized. I told you Andrew and I hadn't been able to stop talking about the things we heard that first night. Well, obviously Jesus had not stopped thinking about it, and he had worked out the details, and it was a fantastic story. That day in the Goat & Camel he told a story like none we had ever heard. God was at the center but this God was a lot different from the God we heard about in the synagogue on Sabbath when we still used to go. In fact, I remember John interrupting at one point and asking, "This is the Lord God, *our* God, you're talking about?"

"It sure is," Jesus replied. "The very same." He talked about this new world that was going to be. Oh, still the same olive trees and Sea of Galilee and fish, and goats and camels and so on, but life in the world, it was going to change. No more Roman armies. No more war and poverty. Sick people healed. Lame people walking. Guys in jail set free. Religion and its rules, gone! Guilt and threats of punishment, gone! Healed relationships, healed families, transformed communities. He had it all worked out.

As he talked, I could see it all playing out in my imagination, scenes like I had never ever imagined—suspense, conflict, conflict so fierce it would take all your courage, tough times and struggle so difficult it would take all the strength a person had, but always the beauty of peace and the vibrancy of life running through it all. And then at the end he looked at each one of us for a moment and then said . . .

MARTHA: (*waiting*) Yeah?

PETER: He said, "I want you to jump into the story." He said, "I've told you my story, but it's not complete. It needs people, all kinds of people, to bring it alive and make it a real story, a true story. That's why I need for you to jump into the story. The script has parts especially designed for each of you. Without you, something will be missing. I need for you to jump into the story.

MARTHA: What did you think?

PETER: That he was nuts. That this guy had gone completely loco. That the sooner we got back to our boats and our nets and our fishing, the better.

MARTHA: But?

PETER: But, there was something about what he said, something about him, the look in his eyes, the way we seemed to matter to him, that we couldn't resist. I think what it really was, was three or four things. One, this was something new, new with regards to God, new with regards to the world, new with regards to people, something new that seemed so much more filled with life than what we had heard in the synagogue growing up.

Two, it fired our imagination. In a sense, by firing our imagination, it set us free, free to be and do what we had never imagined. Did we understand it? We had no idea! But it grabbed our imaginations and wouldn't let go.

Three, it was the fact that he wanted us, fishermen and not religious types, guys who liked their beer and could cuss a blue streak, that fascinated us.

And four, there was this sense of joining an adventure, not just an adventure like trying something new or going someplace you haven't been before. Jesus promised us an adventure, not just with a capital A, but with every letter capitalized: ADVENTURE. Even today, after years of living that adventure, I can't explain it much better than that. This was going to be big. It would mean our whole lives, shake us up to the very core, be more dangerous and more exciting than any Sea of Galilee storm, and somehow just be BIG, big for us, big for people, big for the world.

MARTHA: Hard to say no to something like that.
PETER: Right. We couldn't.
MARTHA: And?
PETER: We didn't.
MARTHA: And?
PETER: And it was all of that and more. We had no idea what we were getting ourselves into, but it was worth every minute of it. Those three years with Jesus were simply incredible.
MARTHA: And then Jesus said it again: "Jump into the story."
PETER: Right. After breakfast on the seashore and our conversation, his final words to me were "Jump into the story." On the Friday of his death, we thought the story was over, had been badly conceived, poorly written, and now with an awful ending. But then came Easter, and, well you know all about that. Now Jesus was telling us, the story still is. It's only barely begun. The three years we had with him weren't the story, they were just the prologue. This is where the story really begins.

And so, I want you to jump into the story. And again, I had the same sense I had the day I left my boat and nets. One, Jesus was willing to work with me, a fisherman who had really messed up bad. I was nothing much to start with—just a cussing, drinking, synagogue-skipping fisherman. During the three years with Jesus, I don't know how often I messed up and didn't get it. Then I denied him the night he died. And he still wanted me in. That was something I wanted to be part of.

MARTHA: This Jesus thing was something for anyone and everyone.

PETER: Right. So I wanted in.

MARTHA: And two?

PETER: Two, there was something about what Jesus was about and the kind of world he kept talking about the three years we were with him, and the kind of God he introduced us to—so different from anything we had been taught—and the possibilities for real life, and peace and justice and forgiveness and love. I realized at some point over breakfast that I had caught the vision again of what could be in our world, and I wanted to be part of it. My imagination was beginning to hum and I liked the sound of it.

MARTHA: And three?

PETER: Three: ADVENTURE, in capital letters. Adventure like nothing anyone else could promise. I knew when Jesus said "Jump into the story" to me the last time that I had no idea what would happen if I said yes. But I didn't care. This was, I was convinced, the only adventure worth living, the only adventure that could both promise and deliver.

MARTHA: And you weren't afraid?

PETER: Afraid? I was scared sh— . . . I mean, you bet I was afraid. But I was even more afraid of what I would miss if I didn't join with Jesus. Life outside the Jesus story just did not seem worth it compared to what could happen inside the story.

MARTHA: So you jumped into the story. You decided to follow Jesus.

PETER: I did.

MARTHA: And now, looking back if you had to do it all over again?

PETER: I would jump in again. It's why I have poured all my energies since that day into telling others to jump into the story, to follow Jesus. Sure, there are other stories around. But this one has four things I would not give up—the potential for a new world, something that fires the imagination, a part for me, a fisherman, and adventure. What more could you want?

MARTHA: So your message to anyone else would be?

PETER: Jump into the story.

MARTHA: Jump into the story.

Chapter 2

Jesus's Autobiography

In January 2013, I began reading Norman Mailer's book, *The Gospel according to the Son*. It is a novel written as if it is Jesus's autobiography. I didn't like it. I simply could not identify the Jesus in Mailer's "autobiography" with the Jesus as I understood him from the Gospels. I experienced a similar unhappiness when I tried reading Anne Rice's *Christ the Lord: Out of Egypt*. I have yet to see a movie portrayal of Jesus's life that I can honestly say I liked. Martin Scorsese's *The Last Temptation of Christ* may come the closest, in my mind, to being realistic, although it seemed to be the one most hated by Evangelicals.

After tossing aside Mailer, I thought that it might be a fascinating project to rewrite the Gospel stories and tell them in the way Jesus might have told them if he wrote an autobiography. Sure, it would be Ray Friesen's Jesus that would come through. But then, what we have in our collections is Matthew's version, Mark's version, Luke's version, and John's version. Why not Ray's version? At one point I started to make plans to spend a month in Bethlehem and work on the project. I thought it might be easier to "get into the spirit" if I was in Palestine, lived in Bethlehem, and traveled to Jerusalem and the Galilee a few times. Things happened and the trip did not.

However, I decided to try my hand at this retelling nonetheless, actually before the idea of traveling to Bethlehem. I use the lectionary texts during Lent in odd years. The year I read part of Mailer's book was such a year, so I decided to preach the Gospel stories during Lent and preach them as if we were listening in on Jesus thinking about what he was writing in his autobiography. I sat at a small table with quill and scroll to create some more interest—reality? It was fun. I rewrote five stories (someone else preached one of the Sundays) and the exercise helped me get into the stories in ways that had not happened before.

The worship materials published by our denomination that year were produced around the theme, "Ashamed No More." That influenced both the titles of the sermons and the content.

ASHAMED NO MORE: NO MATTER WHO

John 12:1–8

Lent 5—Year C

During Lent, we have been imagining that five years ago, Lyl Fraser, an archaeologist at Birzeit University in Ramallah (where her sister, Raeja, teaches political studies), discovered a scroll purported to have been written by Jesus himself. I asked you to imagine that in five years of study, scholars are increasingly convinced that the scroll is authentic. Further, I invited you to pretend that through the modern marvels of time travel and technology, we could go back and watch Jesus write the scroll and listen in to his thoughts as he wrote. How this has been unfolding has been that Jesus noticed us, and turned from his writing to speak directly to us. Today we come upon Jesus reflecting on another time or event in his life. We "catch up with Jesus" a week or so before what will be the weekend of his death:

April, 29 CE. Six days before Passover. It's late and a lot happened tonight. However, I'm restless. There is a lot on my mind, mainly because of what happened tonight. Maybe if I write for a while I'll be able to settle down and get some sleep.

I will die. There, I wrote it. I will die. I know we all die sometime, but I will die soon, before my time as it were, before my life is really over. In fact, now that I am face to face with it, I may as well admit it, I suspect I will die this coming weekend, during the Passover celebrations. Seven days from now I may be dead, and I also realize, it won't be pretty. I will die.

For several months now, I have had the growing sense that this will happen. Much of the time I tried to push the idea away. Some days that worked. Some it didn't. A couple of times it seemed so real I actually said something to the twelve guys I like to call apostles, once or twice to the whole group, once to Peter, James, and John. That was wasted energy. I thought maybe if they heard it and talked with me about it, it would be easier. I should have known better. A couple of times they just looked at me with these blank looks. They obviously had no idea what I was saying. I thought "will die" was pretty simple and straightforward. Maybe they just couldn't get themselves to believe it. I was having trouble with it, why wouldn't they? Finally, the one time, Peter just came right out and said what I think all the others were thinking: "It's not going to happen, Jesus. You've got it all wrong." Good old Peter. He tries hard, I know, and wants desperately to get it all and be tuned in to it all, but sometimes I don't know whether to laugh or cry. That time I was probably a little hard on him. I had been thinking about this dying business for a while. By the time I said something I was pretty uptight and what I needed was some support and comfort, not this "in my face" put down. So I snapped at him and called him "Satan." As soon as I saw the look on his face, I knew I was wrong. I didn't apologize to him right away—I guess I was too wrapped up in what I was thinking and the overwhelming dread I felt at the thought of dying. Later I did apologize. He accepted my apology, but it was a few days before we were okay. Another lesson: be careful how you talk to people who care for you.

Until now, when I talked about dying, it always seemed a long way off, and more often than not was more of a philosophical discussion than something that I really, really knew would happen. Always the thinking was driven by the question: How can I convince the people that God is a God of love, acceptance and forgiveness, a God of second chances? Gradually it dawned on me that only if God let people do whatever they wanted without retaliation, even kill God, would people get it. Only as people got to heap all the shame and suffering and evil and wrong on God without God offering resistance and without any threat of punishment would the message have any chance of getting through. Anything short of that, and people simply would not get it. Even my disciples, the twelve and the others who traveled with me or came to see me at the various places I preached, were not getting it. Everyone that was, except for the publicans and sinners. They were tuning in.

God was going to have to suffer and die. Gradually I realized that that is what God was going to do through me. I was the one who was going to have to suffer and die, without retaliation, without lashing out, without revenge or resistance. It was a hard idea to come to terms with, and I never quite did. Oh, like I say, I thought about it, even talked about it, but always it was an idea, a growing idea, but an idea.

And then tonight, it hit home, with a reality that left me with the wind knocked out of me, bent over in pain as it were, like I had been kicked in the stomach. I finally have to admit it. I will die this week, and it won't be pretty. I wish it weren't so, but I realize, this was probably the plan from the beginning. I just didn't know it. God let me come to it slowly, gradually, at a pace I could handle. Tonight, I guess God decided to let me know, make it clear, let me know without a doubt. Here I've been grumbling about others not getting it. Tonight I finally got it. I will die, soon, this week, within the next few days.

I wonder what they—whoever decides to write my life story, I'm sure someone will—I wonder what they will make of what happened tonight. What happened created quite a stir, to say the least, and if the reality of dying wasn't so front and center, I might laugh. Even now, I can't resist a smile. Though there was still grumbling, regularly, by scribes and Pharisees, most people had gotten used to me hanging out with publicans and sinners. But tonight, I think tonight may have gone past the line, pushed things over the edge. I wonder if anyone will have the guts to tell the story the way it happened. Peter and Matthew love telling stories and are good at it. They may try to collect some stories once I'm gone. Peter, of course, would have to dictate them to someone. He's good at telling stories, but couldn't write a sentence if his life depended on it. Even though Peter's a "rough & tough" fisherman and Matthew a publican, I suspect even they may try to tone it down a bit when they write about tonight, take out or even change a detail here and there. I suspect if pastors tell this story a few years down the road, they will want to clean it up a bit. I think the biggest change they will make is they won't say who the woman really was, or they might even go so far as to give her a name to make it look like it was one of the disciples, a friend rather than a . . . but I'm getting ahead of myself. I think they might be tempted to have her pour the perfume on my head rather than my feet. It would be nice to be around to see what they do with it. I wish they could just tell the story the way it happened because I think just the way it happened is absolutely important. But I also realize people can only handle things at a pace that works for them. As long as the story gets told. Maybe in bits and pieces it will all eventually get out and people will get the whole thing. In the meantime, I can tell it here. Maybe someone will keep this scroll and the story will get told. It needs telling everywhere stories about me are told. This story needs telling. So, let me tell it.

I was invited to supper at Simon's place, here in Bethany. Simon was a Pharisee. Several years back when he got leprosy, he, like everyone else with the disease, had to leave the synagogue, his community, his home, and his family, and go live in a colony where only lepers were allowed. Two years ago, ten of these lepers met me on the road and asked me to heal them. I did. Simon was one of the ten and after the priest declared that he was in fact healed, he moved back home and rejoined the Pharisees, though he never quite fit after that. Like Nicodemus, he took me and what I was teaching seriously and kept coming back to learn more. Tonight, on the second anniversary of his healing, like he did last year, he invited me along with a bunch of other people to supper to celebrate.

It was during supper that it happened. One of the women—everyone knew her as one of the town's better known "women of the night"—this "sinner," standing with others around the outside wall,[1] walked over to where I was lying, dropped down at my feet, and began to weep quietly. I could feel the tears falling on my feet, and then felt her hair, long and full and flowing, as she used it to dry my feet. People around me stared and were scandalized. I could tell they were expecting me to pull my feet back and tell the woman to stop. It was when she kissed my feet that Peter blanched, John pretty much lost it, and Simon, my host, growled.

Should I have let it go this long and this far? There would have been lots of reasons to stop her, even scold her, because she was making it look like I was ready to do business with her. But she was as much loved by God as was Simon, the Pharisee, and for me to stop her somehow seemed to me to go against everything I had been trying to teach the people. And I couldn't help remembering Rahab, my ancestor, ancient King David's great-great-grandmother. She was a brothel keeper and, as brothel keeper, helped God's people. Who was I now to judge this woman, doing the only thing she knew to let me know how much she cared for me? So no, even on second thought, I'm glad I did not stop her. Simon, John, and the others will recover.

1. In Jesus's day, people did not sit at tables for supper. Instead, the food was placed on mats in the center of the room. Guests lay on their left elbows, leaving their right arms free to handle the food. Feet would therefore all be sticking to the outside, easily accessible. When a special guest came to supper, many of the people of the village would gather at the house and line the walls. They would not eat, but would be there to listen to the conversation. Hence, this prostitute was able to sneak in with the crowds and Jesus's feet would have been easily accessible to her.

It's what she did next that was the kick in the gut for me, the one thing that almost makes me wish I had stopped her. She opened a bottle of expensive ointment called nard and poured it on my feet. The smell of it filled the entire room. As the smell filled my nostrils, I knew where I had smelled it before—when we buried Grandma and Grandpa, and then again, five years ago, when we buried Dad. The ointment this woman was putting on my feet was really more of a perfume used to kill the smell of dead bodies. This woman was telling me what until now had been only an idea—I was going to die and die soon. She knew. I realized then, that she "got it." She understood. All of the religious people, and all of the male leaders, and all of my own disciples had no clue, no matter how often I told them. But she got it. Pharisees all believed they were much smarter and wiser than ordinary folk, and certainly than women. Among my disciples, the men all thought they were smarter than women and thought that's why I had picked twelve men to be apostles. Well, none of them got it, but this woman, this "woman of the night," did get it and tonight God was using her to get a message to me. I was going to die and die soon. It was part of God's plan.

The criticism was quick. Simon told me that if I was really a prophet, I would know both who this woman was and that what she was doing was unacceptable. I needed no special revelation from God to know who she was—I had seen her at lots of the parties with publicans and sinners I had attended in Bethany. I was tempted to tell him, "Remember Rahab," but I didn't. Others criticized this waste of an expensive perfume. It could have been sold and the money given to the poor. As if they cared about the poor! They were just looking for ways to make themselves look better and add to this woman's shame. So typical of religious, pious types. Let's heap the shame on others and make ourselves look good. Since religious folk know deep down inside that they aren't all that good, they need that much more ammunition to make others look bad.

As for me, I was reeling. I knew what this meant. And I had to say it, both to shut up the grumblers and to say it to myself. I probably sounded kind of clumsy. I think I said something like, "She has done this for my burial." It probably wasn't very helpful, not one of my more articulate moments. The disciples around me just looked at me with that strange, blank look I was almost used to by now. The other visitors looked puzzled. I didn't care. I just wanted to get out of there, away from the stinking piety and self-righteousness, and away from the people who just did not get it, away even from my friends. I needed to be alone.

And so here I am, alone. I've told the story. I've said what it means. I am finally more honest with myself than I have ever been. I will die, and I will die soon, probably this coming weekend. Why? So that people will finally get the message in this story. No, not the message God gave me—that I will die—but the message God has for them. My death will hopefully finally speak so clearly to the people that they will get it, even the religious types and the pious types and the burly fishermen, that God is a God of love, acceptance, forgiveness, and second chances.

Along with its message to me, what happened tonight has the same message as my death will have. I hope, when people hear this story after I have suffered and died, they will get it, the overall message and the finessed details that come out in a story like this.

I hope people will realize that:

1. *God is a God of sinners and second chances.* God will use whoever is available. God doesn't care what their past has been. In fact, it seems God specializes in partnering with those with a shady, dark past. The more shameful the past, the more excited God is to wipe out their shame by making them God's partners in the great dream of God, making sure everyone knows God loves them, accepts them, and forgives them. So tonight, the best candidate for God's work was a prostitute. In that moment when she fell at my feet, her shame was gone. God was working with her and she had the highest status possible—partner with God.

2. *Men, men, men.* Sometimes I think the male half of the human species is the most hopeless creature God made. They think themselves so important. They think themselves so smart. They think themselves so wise and skilled. I have this uneasy feeling that in the church that will follow my time on Earth, men will again and again try to take over and shut out women. And yet, tonight proved again, *it was a woman who got it and partnered with God, while all the men were clueless and actually got in the way.* How often hasn't that been the case during my time on Earth? It's the women who are God's hope in this world, not the men. I wonder if the men will ever learn this.

3. *I realize that what the woman did tonight had sexuality written all over it, and that made everyone uneasy.* But that's all she had. Misused by men and an outcast from polite society, her sexuality was all she had. And she gave what she had, did what she could, borderline

though it was, I will admit. But God used it, partnered with her just like Yahweh partnered with Rahab and her brothel twelve hundred years ago, with Esther in Babylon, and has partnered with people through the centuries and will through the coming centuries. It's not high religion and great theology that will win the world for God. *It's people giving whatever they have to offer in their partnership with God, and God turning what they bring into the best gift of all.*

If people will learn and remember that from this story, my dying will not be wasted. May it be so.

Chapter 3

SAME TEXT, DIFFERENT SERMON

OVER A LIFETIME OF preaching, most of us undoubtedly preach several times on many texts. This is certainly true if you follow the lectionary—once every three years, though you have a choice each year as to which of the four texts will be your focus. And then of course there is Christmas, Palm Sunday, Good Friday, Easter, and Pentecost. Christmas gives us two versions (Matthew & Luke); the stories around Holy Week four versions (all four Gospels), but Pentecost only one (well, maybe two, if you take John's "giving of the Holy Spirit" as an authentic "Pentecost" story). So being creative becomes important. Also, there are some stories and/or texts that just beg repeated preaching. For Evangelicals, John 3:16 is one such text. (I noticed today that in Year B of the lectionary, it pops up twice.) Micah 6:8 might be one for Mennonites. Luke 15 and the Prodigal Son is certainly another one.

Aside from preaching through Luke every eight years, the Prodigal Son story also shows up, for me, every six years in the lectionary. What I have included in this chapter is two very different—in terms of style—sermons on that famous story. The first one, you will notice is part of the autobiography Lent series I preached in 2013. The second one was first preached ten or fifteen years earlier.

One spring, in planning my summer preaching, I asked people to nominate stories they would like to hear a sermon on. That summer, the Prodigal Son got nominated. (This was long before the "autobiography" sermon that is included here.) Summer Sundays, it seems to me, also call for an extra effort in the area of creativity. Brunch on the patio, a round of golf, a weekend in the campground, a day at the beach—all these and other things beckon with at least as much attractiveness as a morning in church. So, as preachers, we should make sure people will not feel the hour or so at church was wasted. If content doesn't catch them, maybe sermon style will. If both do, well then you've got a home run.

That summer, Sylvia and I decided to preach the requested story in the way shown in the second sermon in this chapter. It is another one of our dialogue sermons earlier in our career when they were rare. This one was subsequently preached at a few other places.

ASHAMED NO MORE: PARTY ON

Psalm 32; Luke 15:1–2, 11–32

Lent 4—Year C

During Lent, we have been imagining that five years ago, Lyl Fraser, an archaeologist at Birzeit University in Ramallah (where her sister, Raeja, teaches political studies), discovered a scroll purported to have been written by Jesus himself. I asked you to imagine that in five years of study, scholars are increasingly convinced that the scroll is authentic. Further, I invited you to pretend that through the modern marvels of time travel and technology, we could go back and watch Jesus write the scroll and listen in to his thoughts as he wrote. How this has been unfolding has been that Jesus noticed us, and turned from his writing to speak directly to us. Today we come upon Jesus reflecting on another time/event in his life:

I think it's probably, no, not probably, it is the best story I ever told. It came to me one early morning as I watched the sun rise, sitting on a hilltop all alone. The people traveling and camping with me, including the twelve guys I called 'apostles,' were still sound asleep. This happened a fair bit when we were on the road. I like the quiet of the early morning. It was the best time to think and pray. Always my prayer was: How might I get the people to catch on to a new understanding of God, get a new vision for what life could be like, what God wanted it to be like? How can I do what God sent me here to do?

That morning, sitting on the hilltop, watching the sun rise, praying, and thinking about the day ahead, the question moved front and center again. I had just spent several days with people and had not had a lot of time to reflect quietly. Evenings I would drop into my bed roll, dead tired. This made getting up early in the morning difficult. This particular morning, something woke me and as I opened my eyes, I noticed dawn was beginning to break on the eastern horizon. Before I could think about snuggling down into my bed roll again, I got up. I sensed the beauty of the morning all around me and was not going to waste it. I stretched, and stepped carefully over the sleeping bodies around me. I stumbled over James's walking stick, just about stepped on Andrew, and then for sure I would have landed on Peter. You can imagine what would have happened if Peter woke to the oomph of me landing on him—the whole camp would have been awake in seconds, the air blue with "fisherman talk." That would have been the "end" of the morning. Fortunately, I didn't step on Andrew nor land on Peter and I got out of camp without waking anyone. I walked up the side of the hill behind our camp and, in about fifteen minutes, arrived at the top, just in time to watch the sun rise.

The last few days had been tough, fun at times, but tough. I spent a couple of evenings partying with what the religious folks called "publicans and sinners." Oh, could those religious folk carry on about the "publicans and sinners." "Publicans and sinners" could include quite a bit. However, most of the time it meant men who were tax collectors working for the Roman Empire, traitors cheating their fellow countrymen. Most of the women were prostitutes. The men had, according to the religious types, betrayed our faith and our people by working for the Romans and by cheating when they collected taxes. The women had betrayed love and marriage and home. I agree, they were not necessarily nice people and you really might not want your daughter marrying a publican or your son marrying a sinner. So, when you hear "publicans and sinners," think about the people most regular people don't like and look down on, even despise, and talk badly about. However, publicans and sinners were a lot of fun to be with. There was a freedom they had since they didn't have to worry about their reputations. Their reputations were shot long before this. What made them particularly fun to be with was that they were really interested in what I had to say. They knew they did not stand much of a chance with the standard view of a God who rewarded good people and punished the bad. They were bad, they made no attempts to deny it or think otherwise, and with your standard God, they were in deep, deep trouble. So they liked what I was saying about God. They got it, and got it pretty quick, and even as the beer and wine flowed, the music played, and people danced, they would ask questions and beg me to say more about this new God, or new understanding of God. When I was with them, I felt like I was doing exactly what I had been sent to do and it was working.

The religious folk on the other hand, especially the leaders—the scribes and Pharisees—they could really get their loin cloths tied in a knot when they saw me having a great time with these "publicans and sinners." Scribes are scholars, spending their time studying the Torah and teaching it. Some worked day after day copying Torah from one scroll to another. These guys know Torah—God's Word—backwards and forwards. Pharisees are religious leaders who pump all their energy into religion and right living because that is how they think they will get Messiah to come. They believe that if for a split second every Jewish person lives right, Messiah will arrive. You could see why they didn't like publicans and sinners because publicans and sinners messed up their plan for Messiah to arrive. These two groups—the scribes and Pharisees—got so angry with me, they had trouble even hearing what I would say in my teachings. Understand? Not a chance. And therefore the question that haunted me daily and was front and center that morning: How could I get people to understand what God is really like? What I needed, I thought, was a story. Just the right story might get past the anger and self-righteousness and know-it-all conviction of the religious folk, the scribes and Pharisees.

And so it was, as I was thinking about this that early morning, watching the sun rise, the idea for a story came to mind. It started innocently enough as stories do. And then, also as stories do, it took on a life of its own. It seemed all I could do is follow it to the end. Parts of it surprised even me. But I liked it. I liked it even the first time through. I rubbed my hands in excitement. This had the potential to be good. I went back over it and I rethought a few parts. Then I went over it a few more times, until it all fit and I had the sense I had a good one. This story would get their attention. I figured it would get everyone's attention—religious leaders, ordinary folk, and my friends, the "publicans and sinners." I now had a story for the next time I needed it.

The chance came sooner than I thought. That very afternoon, in fact. A fairly big crowd had gathered, with, as usual, the Pharisees and scribes near the front of the crowd where important people like to be. Everybody turned to the side at the sound of loud, raucous laughter and, sure enough, a group of publicans and sinners came walking up, joking, laughing and helping themselves to what they had in their little jugs. A rowdy bunch. Immediately, the Pharisees and scribes started grumbling. I could hear them: "See, we knew it. This guy eats and drinks and hangs out with publicans and sinners. And he thinks he can teach us about God?" There was more, but I didn't bother listening. I had heard it all before. I raised my hands. The joking and laughing stopped immediately and soon the grumbling folk shut up too.

"Let me tell you a story," I said. "A certain man had two sons." I need to say something here. I realize there are only men in this story. That means it's less than a perfect story. This may sound lame to you women out there, but a story should never try to do too much, and I really wanted this to get to the target. I knew if I included women, people would follow other tangents, and I could not afford that, not this time. I needed to keep it simple. There were also a couple of twists in the story and for that I needed a man. Actually, given the realities of the culture I am in, I had to use a male for each of the three characters. I did tell another story, similar to this one, with a woman representing God. You should have been around when I told it, but that's for another time.

"A man had two sons. The younger son told his father, 'I want my share of your estate now.' So his father agreed to divide his wealth between his sons."[1] You should have seen the looks on people's faces, publican and sinner or Pharisee and scribe, or just the ordinary folk. Before I could continue, someone—I think it may have been Peter—came and whispered in my ear, "Jesus, you can't say that. No one will believe your story. No son would ever ask his dad to pretend he was dead and divide the estate. And if a son did, the father would never give it to him. He would disown the son and the son would get nothing, not now, not when the father died. Your story simply isn't believable. You better start again."

I gently pushed Peter away, or as gently as you can push away a burly, irate fisherman. "I know what I am doing," I said with a slight smile. "Trust me." Peter turned, but I could tell he was not convinced.

I continued the story. "A few days later, this younger son packed all his belongings and moved to a distant land, and there he wasted all his money in wild living." Now the people were nodding. Exactly. Any son who would wish his dad dead so he could have his money would do exactly that, waste the money and his life on wild living. Ungrateful wretch! Wicked son. Stupid father. The people still had trouble with what the father had done, but they knew how the story would continue. With the son leaving, the father would tear his robe—a sign of mourning, a

---

1. Where Jesus is telling the story here and in the rest of the sermon, Jesus is reported as using the text from the *New Living Translation*, with a few editorial changes to help the flow of the story. The story is found in Luke 15:11–32.

sign that to him, the son was dead. That son did not exist anymore. They would hold a funeral for the son. After the necessary days of mourning, the father would go back to farming as if the son had never existed. That is how things were done. The people did not know I had another surprise for them.

I continued the story. "About the time his money ran out, a great famine swept over the land, and the son began to starve. He persuaded a local farmer to hire him, and the man sent him into his fields to feed the pigs. The young man became so hungry that even the pods he was feeding the pigs looked good to him. But no one gave him anything.

"When the son finally came to his senses, he said to himself, 'At home, even the hired servants have food enough to spare, and here I am dying of hunger! I will go home to my father and say, "Father, I have sinned against both heaven and you, and I am no longer worthy of being called your son. Please take me on as a hired servant."'"

The crowd burst out laughing. "Yeah right, you'll go home and ask to be a servant. You're dead. You wanted your dad dead. Well, to him you are dead. Get real. You are stuck in the pig pen." Well, at least the people were with me. This is where I had that other surprise for them. I continued, "So the son returned home to his father. And while he was still a long way off, his father saw him coming. Filled with love and compassion, he ran to his son, embraced him, and kissed him."

I didn't think people could have been more horror struck than they were when I started the story. Well, I was wrong. This was simply incomprehensible to them. Immediately, I noticed Peter was back at my ear. "Jesus, have you gone crazy? No father would ever sacrifice his dignity and honor this way, not by welcoming the son back and definitely not by running out to meet him. That has never happened. Will never happen. No self-respecting man would dream of doing such a thing, no matter how much he loved his son! If you want to save this story, you better apologize for even suggesting it, and then give the story a decent ending." Again, as patiently as possible and as gently as possible, I pushed Peter aside. "Don't worry," I whispered. "I can handle this. I know what I'm doing."

And then I held up my hand for silence—Peter wasn't the only one talking about the impossibility of my story. I held up my hand for silence and when all was quiet, gave them the punch line. "The father wouldn't even let the son speak, but said to the servants, 'Quick! Bring the finest robe in the house and put it on him. Get a ring for his finger and sandals for his feet. And kill the calf we have been fattening. We must celebrate with a feast, for this son of mine was dead and has now returned to life. He was lost, but now he is found.' So the party began."

That, my friends, is how God feels about publicans and sinners. That's how God feels about anyone and everyone who has messed up in life. God specializes in people who mess up and God's only response to them is "Welcome home! I've been waiting for you. Let's party!" That's why I spent so much time partying with publicans and sinners. This was God's party already started, here and now. No guilt. No shame. No fear. No, nothing but love, acceptance, and forgiveness, and no one cares what you have done nor how often you have done it.

Welcome home. Party on.

I really hope once I am gone, the people will remember this and will carry on the party. Imagine if there was always, somewhere, a party going on where publicans and sinners were welcome and having a whale of a time—dancing, laughing, meeting friends, making friends. Yeah, sure, and some beer and some wine—these are God's gifts for the party.

I wonder what I might call this 24/7 party for publicans and sinners, this party with no fear, no guilt, no shame. I'm not sure it needs a name, but a name would be nice. If we just say "The Party," it could mean other parties, parties that get destructive and have less to do with God's party. I know, I'll call it "church."[2] I have to remember to tell Peter, James, Mary, Joanna, and the others about this name. Church—has a nice ring to it. Short. To the point. Church: Party Central. Church: Where the music and dancing never stop. I like it more and more. Church: Where everyone knows your name. Maybe I should call it "Cheers." That would work too, but I'll stick with "church." Church. Welcome home! Party on!

The other thing I need to remind them of is there are those who will think this Church is a shameful place, what with publicans and sinners and a 24/7 party, and music and dancing. What I want Peter and the others to remember is how shamefully the father in my story acted and how shamefully God is prepared to act to make the 24/7 party happen.[3]

---

2. There are those who would suggest what Jesus describes doesn't even remotely reflect what the church is today—uptight, opposed to partying, judgmental, and condemning toward publicans and sinners. The church, these people would say, with good reason, is more appropriately used for scribes and Pharisees. Jerry Cook, in his book, *Love, Acceptance & Forgiveness*, describes, I think, what Jesus had in mind. A detractor referred to that church in Portland, Oregon, as "nothing but a bunch of garbage collectors." (back cover)

3. In 2 Cor 5:21, another lectionary text for this Sunday, Paul writes: "For our sake

It's time to throw caution to the wind and act out God's love. Never mind what religious folk think. Honor is highly overrated. It is being willing to be seen as acting shamefully by religious people that sets us free to offer people, especially publicans and sinners, a party where shame is gone, guilt is gone, fear is gone, and love rules supreme. God, through the church, being shameful to show all shame has been taken away.

Welcome home. Party on.

THE LOVING FATHER

Luke 15:11–32

RAY: Luke 15:11–32
SYLVIA: There was a man who had two sons.
RAY: It could have been two daughters.
SYLVIA: Pardon me?
RAY: It could have been two daughters. The man could have had two daughters. I know such a man.
SYLVIA: I suppose, it could have been two daughters.
RAY: It could, and daughters can be stubborn and go their own way and want all the money that they think is coming to them.
SYLVIA: I suppose.
RAY: If your dad was here, we could ask him. I bet he could tell us.
SYLVIA: Okay, okay. But in this story it was two sons.
RAY: All right. I just want you to know, it could have been two daughters.
SYLVIA: There was a man who had two sons. They lived on a farm, a large farm, a farm that had done well. The man knew the value of hard work. He was a good manager and a shrewd—in the good sense of the word—a shrewd businessman. He planned carefully. He did his research, checked the Internet, kept his eye on the future markets, listened to all the projections, and used the best seed stock and cattle breeds. Through hard work, sound management, and his share of good luck, his farm had become a large successful farm that required both his sons and a crew of hired men to run it.

[God] made him to be sin who knew no sin, so that in him we might become the righteousness of God." I think this could appropriately be paraphrased, "In Jesus, God exposed [God's own] self to shame, the shame of the cross, so that we might realize our freedom from shame."

RAY: The two sons had learned about hard work. The older son in particular looked with pride on all their dad had accomplished and all they had helped achieve since they were included in the operation. He loved the farm and looked forward to a lifetime of working the soil and caring for cattle. He could see himself settling into the main farmhouse when his dad was ready to move to an acreage, raising a family, and being happy with life in southwest Saskatchewan.

SYLVIA: The younger son loved the farm, and life in Swift Current was nice, but there was more to life than seeding wheat, pulling calves, renting movies on Saturday night, and going to church on Sunday. He loved his dad and his brother, but he also wanted to see the world. The two years in Saskatoon studying agriculture had given him a taste for city life and he was itching for more. He wanted to see the world, experience things, expand his horizons, taste life.

RAY: See, I told you they could have been girls.

SYLVIA: What? Oh, never mind. Just get on with the story. The younger son wanted to taste life.

RAY: So, one day, a few weeks after seeding, while Dad and the younger son were travelling to Swift Current, the younger son said to his father, "Dad, I like the farm and all that, but I feel stuck here. I want to see the world. You're about ready to retire. Could you divide the farm between me and my brother and give me my share now, in cash?"

As the younger son, his share was one-third of the farm.

Dad looked over at his son. If the son had been looking at Dad instead of focusing on the road, he would have seen the sadness in Dad's eyes. Dad loved both his sons and wanted what was best for them. In his mind, best meant the two boys working on the farm together, living on the farm, close to home, and raising their families in southwest Saskatchewan's beautiful farming country. But he knew refusing his son's request and forcing the boy to stay home was no solution. The boy wouldn't be happy and what kind of togetherness is forced togetherness.

With a wistfulness he could not hide, Dad replied, "I thought you might come up with an idea like this. You know I'd love to keep you on the farm, but I'm not going to force you to stay. Summer is a busy time, I don't have to tell you that, but after harvest, if you still feel the same way, we'll take a look at the numbers and see what we can do."

SYLVIA: A smile spread across the boy's face. "YES!" This was going to be good. He would be free! FREE! With his pockets full of money, the open road before him, and the bright lights of the city beckoning him, he would live.

In late October, Dad and the boys sat down and began to work the accounting. It would create some cash flow problems the first few years, but an operating loan should help with that. They would have to sell about half the livestock, but the herds could be built up again. They divided the estate, made the necessary arrangements, the younger son signed off on the land and any future claims on Dad's estate, and the deal was done. Two days after Christmas, the younger son threw his bags into his car and he was gone, off to a "distant country." Ah, life!

RAY: What's a distant country?

SYLVIA: A place far away from home, where no one could report home, where none of the adults from church could find him and gossip about him, where he could live, without caring what others thought, and a place where there was lots of excitement and fun. Places he had heard about, places like Vegas and San Francisco and New York and Atlantic City.

RAY: That's a distant country, all right. It's a long way from a Wymark farm to the bright lights of Vegas and the offerings of downtown New York.

SYLVIA: When he got there, he began to live—the casinos, the lounges, the friends, the parties. This was life like he had never known and it was fun. Fun, fun, fun.

RAY: And then, things changed. Without work to earn more or sound investments to keep the principal intact, money will eventually run out. And New York and Vegas know how to make your money run out.

SYLVIA: How would you know?

RAY: I've been told. Never been there, but I've been told.

SYLVIA: Just checking. What happened to the younger son?

RAY: By remarkable coincidence, his money ran out just about the time his friends had pressing business elsewhere and no time for him. The motel evicted him, his credit card was maxed out, and nobody in the city needed someone to feed cattle. Nobody seemed to be hiring for anything.

The younger son found himself alone, sitting in a shelter for the homeless, his friends gone, and no one who would even talk to him. By now he was HIV positive, both his arms were covered in needle marks, his whole body was shaking from withdrawal, and he was hungry. Where could he steal enough for one more fix or even a cheap bottle of wine? Where were the soup kitchens in this town? Oh, why had he ever left home?

SYLVIA: Home! Home! Who would have thought that he would ever long for home again? Home, with its bright sun and beautiful blue skies. Home, with its house and garden, the barns and corrals. Home, where there was always enough to eat.

Would Dad take him back, not as a son but as a hired man? Maybe. It was worth a try. Maybe he could find a local church that would give him a bus ticket home. He would send a letter to Dad, letting him know when he would arrive at the bus depot in Swift Current. Maybe Dad would at least care enough to send one of the hired men to pick him up. If not, he could always beg the RCMP for a night at the York, and leave Swift Current. the next morning. He had no idea how or to where, but he would cross that bridge when he came to it.

He found the church, sent the letter, and the next morning he was on his way home, or was he? Was he going home, or just to southwest Saskatchewan?

RAY: And what of the father and older son? They had gotten the operating loan and had rebuilt the cattle herd. The farm was doing well. But the father's heart was not in it. He kept thinking about the son who had left. Every day he checked the mail—no letter. In the evenings, he would look at the phone as if willing it to ring—no calls. Some days he would look down the road, as if hoping for a certain car to be pulling in the drive.

His friends and neighbors all thought him stupid for having given the boy the money. They knew the boy could not be trusted with that much. He had been nothing but trouble in school and Dad should have known better. Oh, they didn't say it straight to the father's face, but the first few weeks after the son left, coffee row certainly had no shortage of conversation material.

As month followed month, they began to worry about the old man. There was no energy in his walk. He rarely showed up at coffee row or the curling rink. Didn't seem to care for lunch at Houston's and no longer attended coffees and breakfasts at the rink. They tried to tell him to focus on the farm and the son at home. Forget the worthless one who had left.

But the father couldn't. It was his son who had left. He loved his son, both his sons. His arms ached to hug the boy he had rocked, read to, taught to ride bicycle, and trained to operate tractor and combine.

SYLVIA: Two years had passed, but still the ache remained. As seeding and calving finished for another year, the father wished again he could share the satisfaction, enjoyment, and feelings of accomplishment with both his sons.

Slowly he walked to the post office, opened his box and took out the mail. As he leafed through the stack of flyers, bills, and government mailings, his heart skipped a beat. The one envelope was addressed in a script that seemed vaguely familiar. Could it really be? With an excitement he hadn't felt in a long time, he opened the letter. It was! His younger son had sent him a letter. No matter what it said, his son had finally sent a letter.

RAY: The father began reading. "Dad, I've not been the son you dreamed of," it started. Dad didn't care. How was the boy doing? That's what mattered. Quickly his eye scanned the page to where he saw a date and time. The boy was coming home by bus! Dad checked his watch. Today! He was coming home today! In an hour the bus would be in. This called for some quick action.

Dad grabbed his cell phone and called home. He told them to get the steaks out of the freezer and to prepare for a barbecue. Steak, baked potatoes, salads, and chocolate pie for dessert. It was his boy's favorite. "Call the neighbors and tell them to come over for a party!" he said. Then he had a bunch of calls to make—his brothers and sisters. They had to be told. "And make sure you tell your kids and have them come too!" he added. "Are we going to party!" Then there were his closest friends. So what if they had doubted him and his decisions. They had to be there for the celebration!

SYLVIA: Just as the father parked his truck at the bus depot, the bus pulled in. He hurried to the unloading area. Then he saw him.

His boy. He didn't even see the gaunt face, the shaking hands, the tears in the eyes, or the limp. Before the boy could say anything, Dad had him in a great big bear hug. "It's so great to see you! I missed you! How have you been?"

Then he held him at arm's length and looked him over. "Looks like we need to put some meat on your bones. Well, we'll start tonight. Having a big barbecue at the house. Where's your suitcase?"

"I don't have one, Dad," the son replied. "This is all I got left."

"That's okay. Travel light, I always told your mom. Travel light. We'll just go over to the Co-op and get you some clothes. Big party at our place tonight."

RAY: They did. Clothes at Co-op, a pair of new boots and a hat at Swift Shoe, and then they were on their way home.

When they turned into the driveway, they noticed cars were starting to gather. Everybody cheered and welcomed the boy and father. Soon the music was playing and the steaks were sizzling. This was a great day!

SYLVIA: The older brother had spent the day working the summer fallow. As he pulled into the yard and headed toward the Quonset, he noticed all the cars and the people. When he shut off the tractor he could hear the music. What in the world was going on?

One of the hired men walked by just as he came out of the Quonset and the boy asked him, "What's with all the music and the people?"

"Your brother has come home and your dad is throwing a big party."

A scowl appeared on the boy's face and his insides burned with anger. He stalked over to his 4x4. He wasn't going to have anything to do with welcoming his deadbeat brother, the lazy bum!

Just then his dad noticed him getting into the pickup and hurried over. "Have you heard, your brother's home? Grab a quick shower and join us for the party."

The older son cut him off. "Look Dad," he said. "All these years I have worked with you. We paid off the operating loan. We rebuilt the cattle herd. I busted my butt for this farm while my brother over there wasted the money you gave him on drugs and gambling."

RAY: How did the brother know how the younger boy had spent his money? Maybe, though his body had stayed on the farm, his mind had also been in "the distant country." The older brother continued.

SYLVIA: "There ain't no way I'm going to welcome him home, let alone join the party. After what he's done, I don't know why you would celebrate."

With the same sadness that had filled his eyes two years ago when his younger son wanted to leave, the father looked at the older one. "Son, we've worked together all these years. Everything I have is yours. We've had a great relationship. And now, now your brother is home. He was gone, lost, we didn't know where he was, and now he is found. He was like dead and now he's back, alive. If there ever was a reason to party, this is it!"

(pause)

RAY: And so?

SYLVIA: And so what?

RAY: What happened next? Did the brother join the party? Were the brothers reconciled? Did they farm together again? What happened next?

SYLVIA: That's it. That's the end of the story. Well, not the end really, but that is where the story stops.

RAY: That's the story. And what a story. There's more than enough there for us to learn from.

SYLVIA: For sure. For me there are three things in particular that I noticed.

One, both of the boys messed up. Often the story is called the story of the prodigal son. It's not really about one son. It's about the father, and more on that in a bit. But it's not one son, it's two. And they both messed up.

This tells me that there is more than one way to mess up. What the younger son did was not right. He made choices that were wrong. Sin really had a hold of him. It made the father very sad. But what the older son did when his younger brother came home was no better. His refusal to celebrate the brother's homecoming was just as sinful and made the father just as sad.

RAY: Hold it. Stop just a minute. Doing drugs and living immorally is wrong, right?

SYLVIA: Right, we all know that.

RAY: But are you saying that pointing the finger at people who live that way, or making snide comments about them, is just as bad?

SYLVIA: I think that's what Jesus was trying to say.

RAY: Then all of us are a pretty sad lot. What hope is there for us?

SYLVIA: That's the second thing I noticed in the story. The father loved both his sons and wanted both of them close. God loves everyone. How we live and the choices we make do nothing to change that love. God loves everyone in this building. That includes people who have lived faithfully. God loves them. But God loves them no more or less than he loves the people involved in drugs and prostitution in downtown Vancouver. God's heart is just brim full of love, more than enough for everyone. There is nothing God likes better than if people love in return. It doesn't matter what they have done.

RAY: That means I can never get away from God's love.

SYLVIA: That's right.

RAY: Even when I do things that make you wonder why you ever loved me?

SYLVIA: That's right. God's love includes everyone equally. There is absolutely nothing we can do to change that. God has always loved everyone, will always love everyone, and will always welcome anyone and everyone no matter what they have done.

RAY: We all mess up, in different ways, and God loves everyone, no matter what they have done. That's two things you noticed in the story. What's the third?

SYLVIA: The story has no ending.

RAY: Yeah, I told you that. Seems weird, it has no ending.

SYLVIA: That's an important point. It has no ending because the ending gets written over and over, every day. We are the ones who write the ending. The ending is in how we respond to the story. If we point the finger and talk negatively about those who make lifestyle choices different than we think they should, we write a sad ending. When we welcome people with open arms, no matter who they are and what they have done, we write a happy ending.

We judge and criticize others, shut people out of our circle of love, acceptance, and forgiveness, the older brother gets in the truck, and drives away. The family circle will remain broken, shattered, its shards lost in the dust.

On the other hand, if we welcome anyone and everyone—those who think differently, those who act differently, those who are different, those who make unhealthy and, to us, disturbing choices—when we welcome them into our circle of love, acceptance, and forgiveness, the older son gets out of the truck, takes his shower, and joins the party. He even has a handshake, maybe a hug for his younger brother. He is proud to have Uncle Jim notice how his kids have grown. The party just gets better.

You see, God has left the ending in our hands. We can take this love of God and share it with people. We can accept and forgive, freely, and celebrate the reconciliation that happens, and the ending gets written, just like heaven intended it. What happens with the ending is up to us.

RAY: What happens with the ending is up to us. That's a big responsibility. But, in light of the fact that I've also messed up, sometimes like the younger son, sometimes like the older, and in light of the fact that God loves me, no matter what I do, I guess it's a privilege to be able to write the ending, a happy ending. It's a privilege to be able to write a happy ending to the story by offering love and forgiveness and acceptance to everyone I encounter.

Chapter 4

The Twelve Little Guys

For all the balance I tried to have in my preaching, I realized at some point that I had never preached a series, barely even a sermon, on the Minor Prophets. I might have touched on or even used some of the more famous texts—Hosea's story, Ash Wednesday and Palm Sunday texts, Habakkuk's song of hope. At Zion, Amos 4:12 greeted us every Sunday morning as we entered the sanctuary: "Prepare to meet thy God." I had never preached on it and had, in fact, near the end of my time at Zion, and certainly at Emmaus, made it clear I believed we did not have to prepare to meet God because we never could. However, that was okay because God was prepared to meet us, the way we are. I recall cringing at a funeral where the preacher, a former pastor, was telling the people they best get ready because the day was coming when they would die and have to answer to God. Then he turned around and drew attention to the verse on the front wall.[1] I shied away from the Minor Prophets because it seemed to me that Charlie Farquharson was right when, in his rewrite of the Bible—*Olde Charlie Farquharson's Testament: From Jennysez to Jobe and After Words*—he summarized all the prophets in one line: "You're doin' it all wrong."[2]

---

1. The verse created increasing controversy while we were at Zion. When, as part of a thorough review and evaluation of our pastors and congregation, a task force was appointed specifically to deal with the controversy, its recommendation was to create a committee to deal with the verse on the front wall. (I'm not kidding. This actually happened.)

2. Harron, *Olde Charlie*, 158.

Still, the twelve Minor Prophets were there, beckoning me to preach on them as well, equally as much part of the Ancient Writings that speak God's Word to us as any of the other Old Testament books, or at least many of them. As I thought about that, it occurred to me that the Old Testament is really about covenant and therefore the Minor Prophets, whatever else they were, were about covenant. Maybe if I took that approach as I read them, they could speak to me and through me to the congregation. It also occurred to me that one thing that seemed like a good symbol of covenant, given our use of the word "covenant" at weddings, was dancing. And so I decided to call my series: *Dancing with God by the Twelve Little Guys*. Given the realities of the calendar, I had to stick to eight of the twelve: Hosea, Joel, Amos, Jonah, Micah, Habakkuk, Zechariah, and Malachi. I no longer remember how I decided which ones to omit. To stick to the theme, each of the sermon titles had the word "dance" in it. A third to a half of each sermon was a story. The Hosea story was the Hosea story. All the others were contemporary stories that I hoped would somehow help the people to connect with what I saw as the main theme of the prophet. The prophets and titles were:

- Hosea: The Wedding Dance
- Joel: An Inspired Dance
- Amos: Everyone's Invited to the Dance
- Jonah: The Reluctant Dancer
- Micah: Dancing the Three-Step
- Habakkuk: Dancing with Abandon
- Zechariah: A Dance of Reconciliation
- Malachi: Dance with Who Brung Ya!

Here are two of those sermons. It was hard to decide which ones to include. I picked the ones so that I could tell you that two years later, when I preached the series on country songs, I used most of this sermon with some adaptations, to preach the sermon around Taylor Swift's song, *Breathe*. In the *Breathe* version, Daryl and Jesus listen to the Swift song as they are driving in Daryl's truck and then have a conversation about it. And yes, after preaching the *Breathe* version, one person in our congregation told me he thought he had heard that sermon before. He can be trusted to do that when I repeat sermons or parts of sermons. That is a compliment because it means he is listening. And no, it is not an academic used to listening to lectures, but a mechanic who tries to live his life faithful to Jesus.

I included a second in which the "God" character is a woman.

DANCE WITH WHO BRUNG YA!

Malachi

Daryl was excited and couldn't help whistling as he showered, shaved, and got dressed. After doing his three weeks at the Syncrude Plant in Fort Mac, he was home, and he and Bev were going to the Lover's Dance in Neveah. Anyone could attend the dance—young couples, those married for many years, even singles, anyone who loved to dance—but the evening had a special lover's theme, and if there was one thing true about Daryl, it was that he loved Bev. Every time he was in Fort Mac, the first two weeks were bearable, but by the third, it seemed excruciating to be away from Bev for so long. That made being able to go to the dance this year all that more special. The past two years, he had been away.

Daryl loved to dance, the band this year was one he really liked, and of course, there was always the fact that he and Bev got to dance as much as they wanted. Being away from Neveah for three weeks at a time, he appreciated every chance he got to attend community events and connect with his friends. Many of those friends would be at the dance, creating a great opportunity to catch up on each other's lives. And then, of course, it was an evening with Bev. *Okay*, he admitted to himself, *this was really all about dancing with Bev*. This could be any dance, with some DJ playing music he didn't much like, in any town, without any of his friends. An evening out with Bev made all else fade into insignificance.

Bev and Daryl had lived together for a couple of years and then, five years ago, they got married. Their love for each other was strong and their times together wonderful, not without disagreements and occasional arguments, but that was normal for every couple. Being gone twenty-one days out of thirty was hard for both of them, and sometimes, the first few days after he was home, things could be awkward as they adjusted from Daryl gone 24/7 to Daryl home 24/7. But they worked it out. The last few times he had been home, Daryl had wondered if things were changing between them. But he decided it was just him—there were still times he found it hard to believe Bev really loved him (his old insecurities coming through)—and so Daryl decided it was nothing. Besides, he would always give Bev the benefit of the doubt.

When Daryl and Bev arrived at the dance, the band was already playing and several couples were dancing. Daryl and Bev chatted with some of their friends, and then they joined the dance. Daryl was sure his heart could not have taken much more. After a few fast dances, Bev settled into his arms for a slow dance. It seemed to him that her love for him was as strong as his was for her.

After several dances, they, as was common at the Neveah Lover's Dance, they decided to split and dance with some of their friends. They had a strong relationship and had always encouraged and supported each other in maintaining both male and female friends. Dancing with others was all part of having a great time with friends. A few dances with others, then an occasional dance with each other. The evening went by quickly.

However, tonight something seemed different. The nagging doubts Daryl had pushed aside came back. Bev seemed so busy dancing with others that it was as if she had forgotten Daryl was home. Daryl realized Bev had to attend dances without him, but would she really forget that he was home and that the two of them had come together tonight? He tried to simply mark it down as his own jealousy and kept visiting with friends and joining in the occasional dance. After Bev's third slow "wrapped in each other's arms" dance with Tom, Daryl started to worry. When the dance ended, he decided to make his way over to Bev to ask her to dance with him again. Before he could get there, he saw Tom and Bev share a laugh and then head toward the door. By the time Daryl got to the door and looked outside, all he could see were the taillights of Tom's car headed down the road with two heads silhouetted in the front seat.

Daryl stood still, in shock, with tears forming in his eyes and the hurt in his heart turning to anger. Then he headed for his car, got in, and pulled out of the parking lot with a spray of gravel and a roar of the engine. He didn't care if the stones hit other cars. He didn't really care about much of anything as his car fish-tailed and he almost hit an oncoming super B. How could he have been so stupid, get sucked in? His thoughts were a mess, his heart was shattered, and his eyes were filled with tears. He had been betrayed, made to look the fool. He had been dumped, publicly humiliated. He would go home, get his suitcase, and never show up in Neveah again.

As Daryl approached the next intersection, he turned to his right to see if any vehicles were coming. He nearly had a heart attack. He hit the brakes and looked again. There was someone sitting beside him in the car.

"Who the %$^%# are you and what the &^%$&* are you doing in my car?" Had Daryl looked closely he might have noticed the man looked strangely like a cross between Morgan Freeman and George Burns.

"I am God," the man said.

"Yeah, bull . . . !" and then Daryl stopped himself. If this was really God, he should probably watch his language. There's no way it could be, but why take the chance. So he started again, "Pardon me! You are who?"

"I'm God. You know, like 'in the beginning God created,' and 'for God so loved the world,' and 'Our Father who art in heaven.' God. That's me. And as for why I am in your car, I figured you needed someone who could understand how you felt. I've been there. Hurts like, well, I guess if I'm God I should watch my language. Hurts like crazy, doesn't it?"

"How do you know how I feel? Oh, okay, I guess if you are God, you know everything. You saw what happened tonight? What Bev did to me?" By now Daryl was parked on an approach to his dad's durum field and God, or whoever this was, had his full attention.

"I saw," God said. "I saw, and it made me mad. That was mean, cruel, uncalled for, and low. I know what it is like to get unceremoniously dumped at a dance."

"You?" Daryl exclaimed. "Dumped? At a dance? When? By whom? Why would anyone want to dump God?"

Why would anyone want to dump God? Now there's a good question. As God sat in the car with Daryl, God knew this was not the time and place to discuss that question. Daryl needed a listening ear, someone who would walk with him in his pain. But God also knew the question was an important one for people to think about. And so, earlier this week, I got a phone call from the Almighty, asking if I would say a something to you folks about God getting dumped. How could I say no?

Five to six hundred years before Jesus was born, Malachi was upset with the Jews because—it was his contention—they had dumped God. God loved them. God had done far more for them than they could ever have expected or even imagined. And still they had dumped God and danced with someone else. For Malachi, this was particularly evident in their *laissez faire* attitudes toward worship, in their disregard for the sanctity of marriage, and in their skimping, cheating, and cheaping out on their offerings. God had brought them to the dance and God had had to leave alone, heartbroken, because the people did not seem to care about or be really interested in God.

What about us? Have we dumped God? Are we dancing with the one who brought us to the dance or has God, again, had to leave the dance all alone, heartbroken?

On Thursday, when Chris and I had lunch to supplement the baptism classes he is taking by participating in adult Sunday school, I asked him to share some of his big questions. One was: "Once I get baptized, will I have to change my lifestyle?" It's an excellent question, one far too many people ignore, and a question that gets us right to the heart of our sermon today. Let me explain.

In baptism we make a commitment, or, in a sense, two commitments that really make up one larger commitment. One of those is a commitment to God. It's like this. When Jesus died on the cross, God demonstrated how much God loved us.[3] It was, in effect, God declaring loudly and clearly that God wanted to take us to the dance. In baptism, we accepted that invitation, jumped in God's car with God and went to the dance. Now the expectation is that you will dance with God.

Let me move from the dance metaphor to marriage. With Jesus's death on the cross, God proposed to us. God said, "I love you so much that I want to live with you for the rest of your life." In baptism, we said yes to the proposal and married God. Baptism is a lifelong commitment to be in a relationship with God. When you enter that relationship, do you have to change how you live?

Chris,[4] let me ask you this: When your dad and mom decided to be a couple and then made it permanent by getting married, did your dad have to change his lifestyle? Don't answer that and give away family secrets, but let's all think about that for a bit. In a sense, no. He continued to be a good mechanic. He continued to love car racing. He probably still listens to the same music. I suspect he still has the same sense of humor. So he didn't. And yet in another way, he did. For one thing, no matter who he went out with before and how many girls he dated before—and a handsome young man like your dad may have dated a few—once he was married, I suspect your mom had something to say about him spending

---

3. Rom 5:8: "But God demonstrates his own love for us in this: While we were still sinners, Christ died for us." NRSV.

4. Given how small the congregation was in which I preached this sermon, addressing Chris this way was appropriate. In a larger congregation, that might not be acceptable.

time with other women. But also, he no longer wanted to spend time with others. He loved your mom too much. In that sense, his lifestyle changed. He was now committed to doing only those things that fit with his love for your mom, only those things that helped their marriage be a better marriage. Okay, Teresa, I know he's not perfect, none of us guys are, but you know what I mean.

The same thing is true after baptism. After committing yourself to God for the rest of your life and joining God in a partnership, we are now committed to living true to that relationship. Anything that breaks relationship with God, God asks you not to do and because you love God and appreciate what God has done for you, you don't want to do. Those things that fit with a relationship with God, that fit with being in partnership with God, and that fit with the dream God has and help you be true to that dream, those are things you do, that you are committed to, and that you want to do.

What are those things? That is really the question we focus on every Sunday in sermons and Sunday school. With the help of Malachi, let me point to three things this morning:

1. *Take worship seriously.* Three weeks ago, when we interviewed Sara Wenger Shank for president of AMBS, she made what was for me a very interesting comment. I don't remember the exact words, but she said something to the effect that "All of life is to be grounded in worship and lived out of our worship of God." Our worship of God roots our lives in God, shapes our character, defines our mission, reminds us of who we are, and sets our life agenda. Without regular and faithful worship, we lose our moorings. We are set adrift. To be too casual about participating in worship is to ignore God at the dance when God was the one who brought us.

    This worship takes at least two forms. One, it includes public worship together with others like this morning. It also involves private, personal time spent in Bible reading, meditation, prayer, and reflection.

2. *Take relationships seriously.* I've said this other times, so I want to be brief here, and simply get it on the record again. Nothing matters to God as much as relationships. Everything about God is about relationships. We are faithful to God and our baptism vows when we are faithful in our relationships, faithful in how we act in relationship,

and faithful in how we reconcile and heal when relationships have been broken.

3. *Take our money seriously.* When the Jews of Malachi's day did not give enough when the offering plate came by, Malachi was unequivocal: "You are robbing God!" How we handle our money, how we earn it, how we spend it, and how much we share and give determines how faithful we are in our relationship with God.

Jesus, in the Sermon on the Mount said, "You can't worship two gods at once. Loving one god, you'll end up hating the other. Adoration of one feeds contempt for the other. You can't worship God and Money both."[5]

You have to choose, says Jesus. You can't love God and your money. You can't dance with God and dance with your money. You have to make a choice. If your commitment is to your money, you've dumped God. The way to dump money and be true to God is to use that money to share when the offering plate comes by, giving to share with those in need through MCC, or extending the work of mission through Mennonite Church Canada or Camp Elim, or helping with the ministry of Emmaus. Be generous—very generous—for every dollar given is one more act of telling God "I'm all yours."

In conclusion: That night of the Neveah Lover's Dance, after Daryl and God finished their conversation, Daryl felt better. However, he knew he needed time to think and sort out stuff. He also realized he and Bev would have to have a serious heart-to-heart. Was his marriage over? Could he and Bev get past this, if they both set their minds and hearts to it? Would Bev even want to? Did he want to? There were going to be a lot of questions to work through. Maybe they could start tomorrow. Maybe next time he was home from Fort Mac. Maybe, who knew what and when?

Fortunately for us, God keeps coming back, inviting us to the dance again. No matter how unfaithful we may have been in the past, God's invitation to us today is "Let's dance!" And we are given another chance, no matter how many chances we may have blown, to dance in faithfulness with the Lord of the Dance.

---

5. Matt 6:24. *The Message.*

A DANCE OF RECONCILIATION

Zechariah

Focus: Zechariah 1–8

Beth sat in the semi-darkness of the rec room, had been for an hour or more, as the shadows lengthened and the room grew dark. There seemed no reason to get up and turn on a lamp or overhead light. Sometimes she wondered if there was reason to do anything. It wasn't like there wasn't any good in her life—she loved her children, she had a great job, her friends meant a lot to her, she lived in a great house with a wonderful yard, but (and there was always that but, had been for too long)—but the one relationship that meant most to her was slowly destroying her. She and Paul had been married for twenty-three years now. It would be exactly twenty-three years next month. Sometimes it felt like an eternity, an unending hell.

Their marriage had started out so well. Their courtship had been great, their wedding a wonderful celebration of love and commitment, their honeymoon all she dreamed it would be. Even the first few years had been great. But then—and she could never point to a particular time or event, she just knew it had happened—things had changed. She and Paul spent less time together. Sometimes he had to work late, sometimes he went off to do his own thing, sometimes he was out playing hockey or having a beer with his buddies. It was like other people or things were more important than she was. Even when they were together, they talked less. She tried, God knows how hard she tried, sharing her life, asking him questions, showing interest in the things she thought mattered to him, doing things he wanted to do, watching the shows and movies he liked. And still he grew more distant, less affectionate. When she saw him with his friends, he would laugh and tell stories and be having a great time. At home he was quiet, even sullen at times. When he laughed at something she said, it felt like he was treating her like a child. When she asked about his day or his time with his friends, he rarely had anything to say, like nothing ever happened, no stories, until someone else was with him. Any suggestions she made that they go for counseling were mocked or met with an angry silence.

Two months ago, she found out he was having an affair, might, in fact, have had several since they got married. She had insisted that he move out of the bedroom. Since then, she had wondered what to do. All her attempts to get him to change, to do something about their marriage had failed. She had been angry, she had complained, she had told him how she felt about what he did, she had begged, she had pleaded, she had yelled, she had cried. None of it seemed to have made any difference. Now she sat in the growing darkness that matched the growing darkness in her heart and spirit. Should she finally say enough is enough and tell Paul to leave, see a lawyer, and file for divorce? It seemed the easiest, maybe the only, way out. And yet, and yet, something inside urged her not to go there. She knew she still loved him. All the things he had done, the betrayal and pain, had not killed the love she first had for him when they were going out and the love that grew as they got to know each other and were first married.

Their children, Denise and Sam, at twenty-one and nineteen, were old enough and smart enough to know what was going on. They had been for years. Each in their time had asked her why she stayed in the marriage. Her answer had always been the same: "Because I love your dad and because I committed myself to him." But she realized the follow-up question they had asked, each in his or her own way, haunted her: "Is that enough to stay when Dad treats you the way he does?" But if she left, could her kids ever believe in love and marriage? But could they believe in it if she stayed, given the state of hers and Paul's marriage?

By now the room was dark, the only light coming from the time readouts in the entertainment center. They told her it was 9:23 p.m. She realized she had not had supper, but her stomach was too uptight to feel hunger. In light of her struggle, food seemed inconsequential. Crying might have helped, although she wasn't sure with what, but she felt like she had long ago run out of tears. Was it really over? Was there nothing more she could hope for?

Beth's situation was perfectly mirrored in another rec room in another place. The view out the window in this other rec room was better, much better, and the surroundings more posh, but none of that really mattered to God as she sat in the gathering darkness and agonized over her failed marriage to Israel, not one person, but a people she had chosen for a special and unique partnership, for a marriage for which she had great hopes, but a marriage that had gone bad, very bad.

God, like Beth, had tried everything. Through the prophets, God had begged with the people, yelled at them in anger, pleaded with them, cried, and even kicked them out of the bedroom, but nothing seemed to make any difference. It seemed like there was nothing left to do but give up on the people, the relationship, the partnership, the project. But what would the rest of the world think of God and love and God's plan if God just gave up on the people? Could they ever believe in God? But what about now, given the state of the relationship and the way the people were treating God? Could anyone believe in God if what was continued? What ought God to do?

And then God had an idea. There was one more thing God could do, one more thing God could try, one more way of trying to change the situation. It was going to be radical. Nothing quite like it had ever been tried before. Any other gods in the neighborhood would have said it made no sense and would have advised against it. Even the people would say it was a foolish act. And yet God figured she had nothing to lose. She had nothing to lose, but even more, she had an inkling that this one thing might well be the most powerful thing she could try. She was going to do it, and it would be absolutely amazing, unlike anything ever seen or done, and the effect and impact astounding.

But if God was going to do this, God would somehow have to let the people know that it had been done, for only if they knew could it have the desired impact, and only if someone told them would they know. To make sure that happened, God decided to do two things. She would start with one, and then follow it up with the second.

The first thing God did was choose a man called Zechariah to take the message of what God was doing to the people. Doing so turned Zechariah into a prophet—a person who speaks for God. Zechariah did not know he had been chosen by God, except that one morning he woke up and realized he had had an amazing dream, a dream like none other, a dream that would take some thinking about. The next night, he had another, and then another, and gradually, as he recalled the dreams, reflected on their meaning, and heard God whispering in his ear, Zechariah got the idea and realized that God had given him a special message and chosen him to proclaim that message to the people. And preach it he would, with all the enthusiasm and energy he had, for the message he had was truly the best message anyone could ever hope to preach.

The message: God was going to forgive the people and transform them into God's project to demonstrate to the world the wonderful things God was going to do.

And so Zechariah began: "Thus says the Great God, Lord of the Heavenly Armies: Return to me and I will return to you. Change how you act and I will forgive you. Be true to your relationship with me and I will be true to you."

Zechariah was just getting his heart into it when God stopped him. "Sorry, Zech," God said, "but that is not the message."

"It's not?" Zech asked in surprise. "But that's what all your prophets having been saying, again and again. 'Change your ways and God will forgive.' I've heard it. I've read it. Every Sabbath the rabbis say it, 'If you change your ways, God will forgive.'"

"That may be true," God replied, "but I'm giving you a new message. The new message is God is forgiving you."

"That's what I said," Zech replied, a little defensive and mouthy to God, it seems, but that was Zech. "Change your ways and God will forgive."

"I know," said God. "I heard what you said." God could have been impatient by now, but believed too much in the project to give up on Zech. This had to work. "I didn't say I will forgive if the people change their ways," God continued. "I said, 'I will forgive.' Period. Exclamation mark. I will forgive. I am not going to wait to see what the people will do. This is not about them and what they do. This is about me, and I WILL FORGIVE. Can you repeat that after me: GOD WILL FORGIVE?"

Zech felt a strange stirring deep inside. This was something unlike he had ever heard before. God would forgive! Not because the people changed their ways. Not because the people deserved it. Not because, well not because of anything other than that God wanted to do so. As Zech let his imagination get around that idea, he began to see the possibilities and the dreams he had seen and the whisperings he had heard not only made new sense, they became bigger and more awesome. God was going to work. It was all going to be at God's initiative. God would forgive. God would turn the people into God's special project. It was all going to be at God's initiative, by God's action taken because God decided as an expression of God's faithfulness.[6] This was going to be God's project dependent on God's action growing out of God's forgiveness. From now on, people were going to change, but not out of fear, not so they could earn forgivingness, not so they might be loved by God. People were going to change and grow out of the forgiveness and love they would first experience from God. Reconciliation between the people and God, the rebuilding

---

6. Ollenberger, "Zechariah," 800. "Indeed, God's decision to save . . . derives solely and absolutely from the character of God . . . God's graciousness toward Jerusalem and Judah is rooted in God's identity and not in any action that Judah has taken."

of the marriage that had failed, the creating of a whole new partnership between God and the people would all be done at God's initiative and by the action of God.

Zech's imagination could barely capture the pictures God painted for him. This was not going to be just some spiritual experience that left everything else the same. Instead, the people's situation would change. They had experienced army oppression, captivity, poverty, fear, famine, death, disease, and terrible living conditions. All that would change. Life in the world was going to be made new. Elizabeth Achtemeier, in her commentary, paraphrases Zechariah's vision in 8:4 and 5 by saying:

> The Kingdom of God . . . will be like a public park, where the elderly can sit together and talk and bask in the sun, and little children can play in contentment and safety with nothing to threaten them—no pervert lurking in the shadows to lure one of them away with candy; no drug dealer waiting to peddle his poison to innocents; no child bruised or warped by abusive parents or stunted by poor nutrition or inadequate education; not even a bully among the group to terrorize the younger and weaker.[7]

And there was going to be more. When the rest of the world was going to see what God had done and was doing for the people, they would all be interested in the same thing. They would be so interested that ten people would grab one person and say, "Please, let us go with you. We have heard God is with you and we want what you have."[8]

All of this was because God was going to try forgiveness without qualification and transformation without condition.

I said earlier that there were two parts to God's plan. One was choosing Zechariah and sending him out with a message after filling his imagination with pictures that blew him away. The second thing was sending Jesus. God realized that telling people was not enough. People would also have to be shown. And so Jesus came to show us the forgiveness of God and what life inside God's project was like. And then God created the church to have one more go at showing the world the transforming power of this forgiveness, what people who are forgiven by God are really like, the love, acceptance, and forgiveness that they extend to others, and the community and life that was really possible because God forgave.

---

7. Achtemeier, *Nahum—Malachi*, 136.
8. My paraphrase of Zech 8:23.

Unfortunately, that project has not turned out so well. Like Beth and Paul's marriage and like God's and Israel's partnership, God's partnership with the church started well and showed great promise. But like Paul and Israel, the church too has betrayed the partnership, broken commitment, and all in all made quite a mess of things. And still God's message is "I will forgive. Not after you do certain things, but rather I will forgive first, and then invite you back to the dance, back to the partnership, back to the marriage."

As I thought about that yesterday, I couldn't help thinking about Emmaus and its pastors specifically. We too have a history of not doing things so well. Sylvia and I have twice had to leave congregations because things did not work out. This congregation used to be much larger. Over the years, many people have left because of broken relationships, because of things that were said and done that were much less than what God hoped for. Even today there are people who do not attend here because of broken relationships.

God's message to us is the same as it was to Israel through Zechariah. "I forgive! I will take the initiative to start again. I will not give up on the project, the partnership. My dream is that through you, people will see and experience my love and forgiveness, my life and peace. My dream is that through you, people will see what the Kingdom of God really looks like."

That is God's invitation. That is our hope.

Chapter 5

STORY SERMONS

I SHARE THE SERMON that follows for two reasons—the series it was part of and, primarily, the way I decided to preach one of the topics.

In 2014, at its annual meeting, Emmaus Mennonite Church adopted a new constitution. Included in that constitution was a list of thirteen statements that we believed defined and described the kind of faith and spirituality we were trying to nurture at Emmaus. This list follows after the sermon.

A year later, in spring 2015, I decided to preach my way through that list. After preaching two sermons, one on the Bible and one on Jesus, cancer and chemotherapy waylaid me, and my preaching was done for a while. However, I had not given up on the idea of preaching that series of statements to help us as a congregation understand what it is we said we believed. I returned to preaching in mid-January 2016. By the fall, I decided to give these thirteen statements another whirl. Limited by the calendar, I had to combine a few of the statements to fit them all into a ten-sermon series.[1]

When the time came to preach on generosity, it seemed to me that if the topic was going to capture the imagination of the people in any way, it would require a new approach. Generosity was part of the character of our congregation and its people and part of the emphasis every Sunday when an usher walked down the aisle and back again to the front with an offering plate. So I decided to tell a story inspired by the Matthew account

---

1. A copy of the whole series is available from the author. It is titled *Faith for Today & Hope for Tomorrow*.

of a rich man who is told by Jesus to sell all he has, give all his money to the poor, and come and follow Jesus.

I followed a similar format with another sermon later, bringing back the character of Josh and telling of Josh's conversion as, I think, Matthew encourages us to understand it.

ENOUGH!

A Faith & Spirituality that Instills Generosity

Matthew 19:16–22; 2 Corinthians 8:1–15; Matthew 25:31–46

Wide awake the moment he opened his eyes, Jim jumped out of bed to engage another day with all that it had to offer him. He gave his wife a quick kiss on the cheek to show his love and to remind her it was time to get up and make coffee—she needed more time to get herself going in the morning. While she went to the back yard to light the cooking fire and make some coffee, he washed at the basin and then headed to the cupboard. He helped himself to one of his wife's wonderful pita breads baked yesterday and then grabbed the cup of coffee she extended to him, gave her another kiss, this time on the lips, and headed out the door to meet the day. Another day filled with potential and possibility. Another day to grow his business. Another day to enjoy his success. Life was great!

As he walked to his first meeting of the day, a question that had been increasingly nagging him slipped back into his mind, like a dark cloud on the horizon moving in to cover the sun. His Master of Business Administration (MBA) had set him up for life and his skills and business acumen had delivered on the MBA's promise. He could have almost any job he wanted. His commission checks kept growing. Money would never be an issue for him and his family. But there was one thing the MBA had not done. It had not filled what sometimes felt like an emptiness, almost like a hole, at the very core of his being. Most of the time dollar signs hid it from sight and excitement at the potential and possibilities he faced everyday buried the nagging doubts, sometimes almost fears. Dollar signs might hide it, but money did not fill it, he discovered. No matter how much money he poured down that hole, it was like it had no bottom. The money just disappeared. Deep in thought, not about work, but about these nagging doubts that had kept him awake at three in the morning when all was quiet and dark and the only sound had been his wife's easy breathing, he stumbled over the first beggar sitting in his path as he turned the corner and almost landed on the two sitting beside the first.

"&^%$ beggars! Go get a job! Freakin' left-wing city government! Why couldn't they get rid of these lazy, good-for-nothings? Keep them out of the way of hard-working people who earned their money and deserved to walk down the street without being bothered by them or breaking something and getting a concussion by falling over them."

Jim righted himself, kept walking, and returned to his former musings. Then a thought occurred to him. Last night, over a mug of wine, his friend Andy had told him about a guy he had recently heard speaking on the beach on the weekend, a guy Andy called Josh. This Josh guy had some remarkable things to say, different than anything Andy had ever heard a rabbi say, different than anything preached in the synagogue on the Sabbath. Apparently this guy was stirring up the excitement of a lot of people and the anger of the *&^&* religious leaders—self-righteous b*****ds. If the phony religious types were mad at him, he couldn't be all bad, Andy had suggested. Jim agreed. Andy had said something about Josh offering a new way of living wholeheartedly, at peace and content. Jim should go hear him sometime. Maybe today was as good a time as any, mused Jim. He had no meetings after lunch. He would check around where the Josh guy was going to be today and go have a listen, maybe even ask him a question or two. H***, maybe this Josh guy would have an answer to these nagging doubts that seemed to be more persistent with each passing month. Andy seemed to think so.

Across town, another young man got out of bed. Also instantly awake, he too had much on his mind, but it wasn't making money that was occupying Josh's thinking this morning. It wasn't even on his agenda. Survival was more like it. Street preaching, political activism, and being a spiritual guru simply did not pay all that well. And a degree in Social and Political Thought on your resume didn't seem to attract employers. It seemed you had to choose between changing the world and growing your economic status. You couldn't do both at the same time.

Over coffee and pita bread for his breakfast, (it seemed rich and poor were the same in one way—what they had for breakfast) Josh thought about where he might go today and what he might say to the people who, by now, inevitably seemed to gather wherever he went. His gig might not pay well, but it did attract the interest of a lot of people, especially poor people. They listened intently to what he had to say, and most days he saw a lot of heads nodding as he spoke, and not from being sleepy either. There was another group that seemed interested in his every word, but they did not hang on his every word, nor did they nod in agreement. They were mostly "frothing at the mouth," angry as h***, well angry as heck, angry as all get out, and no matter how religious they were, Josh thought he had heard them swear occasionally, when they thought no one could hear them.

Josh had just returned to what he might say today when the door swung open with a bang and Pete, Tom, Matt, and some of the rest of his friends burst in.

"All set, Josh?" they almost shouted. *Sure, why not,* Josh thought. He could always think about what to say as they walked, or maybe he would just wing it. Even better, maybe someone would have a question and he would take off from there. At least then he would know he was talking about something that someone found interesting.

By early afternoon, Josh and his crowd seemed to have staked out a street corner on the edge of the town square. By now all of Josh's regulars—men and women, including Joan, Maria, and Simone—were there with him. Around them, a crowd was beginning to gather and Josh was thinking what story he might tell. Repeat one from yesterday on the hill outside of town, or give them a new one to mull over? He was about to start when he noticed a young man, about his own age, pushing his way through the crowd as if on a mission. Josh stopped momentarily, and then the man—we would have recognized him as Jim, the MBA from this morning—gave one last elbow dig and push and stood in front of Josh. Jim looked up and his eyes met Josh's. That was a little unsettling, even for a self-confident MBA grad and money trader like Jim. Josh raised his eyebrows as if to say "Yes?"

Catching his breath, Jim spoke. "Excuse me, sir. I don't mean to be rude, but will there be a chance to ask questions at some point?"

"Sure," Josh answered, a smile toying at the corners of his mouth—just what he had hoped for. "How about right now?"

"Great," Jim answered. "I'm not quite sure how to say this but I'm wondering, how can we live, like, um, like, how can we live in tune with God, feel like we are in fact in partnership with God and God is pleased with us? Live without guilt and fear and sleep without being haunted at night?" It was a little bit more than Jim had really meant to say, but now it was out.

"What does the Torah say? What did you learn in synagogue school and what do your rabbis keep telling you?" Josh asked.

"There seems no end to what they try to tell us. What specifically?"

"Well," said Josh, "Respect all life—don't kill. Keep your marriage vows sacred. Be honest—don't steal and don't lie. Honor your parents—take care of them as they get older. And love your neighbor as yourself."

Jim was quiet for a moment. How honest was he going to be with this man, this stranger, and all these other strangers listening in? H***, he had come this far, he might as well go for broke. "I've done all that, Josh," Jim answered. "Meticulously, and still, I wake up at night with a haunting emptiness inside and live my day barely able to hide that same emptiness by focusing on work."

"You're serious, aren't you?" Josh asked.

"Never been more serious in my life," Jim replied.

"Okay," said Josh. "There is one more thing."

Jim waited. This was it. This was what he had come for. Finally, the answer to his life, his haunting, his fears, his, well maybe his everything.

"You need one more thing," Josh said. "Sell everything you have, give that money and all your savings to the poor, and then join my movement to create a changed world, a new society, a whole new way of living, doing business, developing community, and creating peace."

Jim's heart nearly stopped. His jaw dropped. "Are you sh******, I mean, kidding me? Sell everything? Give it all away?"

Everything he worked for? Everything that made him the success and man he was today? Everything he had provided for his family, often by working late nights and long weekends? How could this guy be serious? Who in his right mind would listen to him? What had Andy been thinking when he told Jim to go listen to this Josh dude? Okay, Andy was a bit of a left-wing nut, but this? This? Sell everything and give it to the poor, those lowdown, no-account beggars he had tripped over this morning? No wonder the poor people liked this guy. If his ideas ever caught on, the poor would never have to work. They would laugh at the rich suckers who had busted their butts to get where they were and then gave it all away, and suddenly everyone was equal.

"As if!"

And with that, Jim turned away. He didn't know whether to swear at this man's sheer stupidity or cry at the dashed hopes of his heart. *I guess there really is nothing to cure the haunting,* he thought. A few more beers on Friday and Saturday night, and simply focus on work, and hope he learned to sleep through the night. Sell all and give it away, as if!

By now you recognize Josh or Joshua, the Hebrew name for Jesus. And we have all heard the story and Jesus's answer to life's haunting that he gave to Jim. "If you really want to live, without fear, without haunting, without emptiness, without being driven to try to achieve what you will never achieve, there is one thing left to do. Sell everything you have, give all the money to the poor, and join me in my mission to change the world, reorder society, develop community, and create peace."[2]

As I suggested in my sermon several weeks ago, the one about how we read the Bible, it seems no matter how committed we are to the Bible as God's Word, to the truth of the Gospel and the importance of doing what Jesus said, we pretty much ignore this verse. Others may be binding on every one but this one, well we respond to this one in much the same way that Jim did. We are just not prepared to go there. And yet, it's there. Jesus said it to Jim and three of the Good News Storytellers—Matthew, Mark, and Luke—have it in their collections, suggesting they thought it important to creating a full picture of who Jesus was and what it meant and means to live the Jesus way, to experience abundant life and partner with God in healing people's inner lives, changing the world, reordering society, building community, and creating peace.

What could Jesus have meant? Did he really want us to be that radical? Let's back away from the saying's most extreme interpretation, allowing for Jesus's use of first-century hyperbole—like when he said another time to cut off our hand if it does something wrong—and tease out what Jesus might have wanted Jim to catch and still wants us to learn. Let me suggest three things. No doubt there are more.

1. *Giving money away destroys its power and breaks its tight-fisted grasp on our hearts.* Subtle though it may be, money has tremendous power and can make us do, it would seem, all sorts of things. I know, some of you would say it is "the love of money [that] is the root of all kinds of evil."[3] True enough, but if you hold on to it and/or buy all kinds of luxuries with it when others need the help it would provide, me thinks you love it. Jesus himself, in his famous sermon, suggested Wealth and God were competing powers, competing authorities in our lives. We have to choose one or the other. And, the only way

2. My paraphrase of Matt 19:21.
3. 1 Tim 6:10. NRSV.

to break money's power is to give it away. As long as we hang on to it, it will hold on to us and shape our lives and characters, and all too often, make us do things we will later regret. And it leaves us empty. Money does not buy happiness nor contentment nor peace of mind and heart, nor does it get rid of the haunting at three in the morning and just underneath the surface the rest of the day. If we have more than enough, we are in trouble. Our generosity is needed, so we do not have more than enough.

2. *When we give our money away to the poor, we help those who need help.* We do a lot of good in the world, and God knows our world needs a lot of good done that money could do. As if Syria wasn't enough, or Haiti after the 2010 earthquake, Haiti after Hurricane Matthew could use and will need every penny—nickel, I guess[4]—that we can find. Jesus's story in Matthew 25 makes it clear that is our mission in life—feed the hungry, put clothes on the backs of the shivering, and build houses for those who have lost theirs. Absolutely simple. And no wiggle room. Our mission in life is to provide for those who need stuff. And there is no easier way of doing that than donating through our church to MCC.[5] Our generosity is needed so others will have enough.

3. *Us giving what we have away and the poor receiving what we give moves us towards everyone having enough and no one having too much, a reordering of society's economic structures.* Yep, that sounds like Marxism and communism and on that one thing, Marx and his interpreters and followers got it right. That is exactly how Paul interprets Jesus's expression of what God is and what God wants and Jesus's teachings on economics for us. God's intention is that with our commitment to the Way of Jesus, we will give until we are all equal, until everyone has enough and no one has too much. Absolutely, make all the money you can. As long as you do so honestly, fairly, and with justice for all, there is nothing wrong with making millions. But don't make the millions for yourself and your family. God's intention in giving you hundreds, or thousands, or millions, is that you will share those hundreds, thousands, and millions with

---

4. In Canada, the government has abolished the use of pennies. Cash transactions are all rounded to the nearest nickel.

5. Our denomination, Mennonite Church Canada, is a partner in Mennonite Central Committee, a global relief, development, and peace advocacy organization.

others until we all have enough and no one has too much. That is God's dream for the world.

That is what it means to have generosity as part of our faith and spirituality.

Faith & Spirituality at Emmaus Mennonite Church

Emmaus Mennonite Church exists to offer to, and nurture in, people a kind of faith and spirituality that is:

1. Centered in Jesus
2. Energized by the Holy Spirit
3. Informed by the Bible
4. Grounded in the belief that relationships matter more than anything and that the Biblical story and the message and person of Jesus and the dream of God are all about relationships
5. Nurtured in the context of community/family with particular emphasis on public worship, times of fellowship, and dialogue with each other
6. Welcoming of everyone
7. Humble enough to freely admit that other spiritual traditions and other ways of interpreting Christian spirituality may well be equally part of God's relationship to humankind and the world in which we live.
8. Committed to engage all Christian and other-than-Christian faith traditions in respectful dialogue with the goal of learning from each other.
9. Convinced that God's peace is a peace to be experienced in relationships locally, nationally and internationally
10. Respectful of creation as God's gift to us to be nurtured and cared for.
11. Generous with all we have so that all people may enjoy the fruits of God's creation and live well.
12. Dedicated to advocate for, and work toward, justice for all
13. Expressed in service to our community and its people

The ten sermons and the topics they covered (in parenthesis) are as follows:

- "It's Story Time" (#3)
- "History's Pivot" (#1)
- "Superpower for Super Heroes" (#2)
- "From Beginning to End" (#10)
- "Enough" (#11)
- "SC Courthouse or UG Coffeehouse" (#4 & 5)
- "Looking for Jesus I Encountered Allah" (#6, 7 & 8)
- "It's a New World Come or Coming?" (#12)
- "Which Cross Will We Embrace?" (#9)
- "You are Invited to be 'Most Important'" (#13)

The original two sermons preached in the series were "Jump into the Story" (Bible) and "God for Dummies" (Jesus).

Chapter 6

ANCIENT WRITINGS AND TWENTY-FIRST-CENTURY GURUS

Though we both grew up with the same tradition (Evangelical Mennonite Conference [EMC]), even the same congregations (first Blumenort near Steinbach, then Treesbank near Wawanesa), and then got married and attended and/or pastored at Aberdeen Church in Winnipeg (also an EMC congregation), Sylvia and I still, unapologetically, have nurtured our faith and spirituality in different ways and by reading different books and authors. Even as we did that, we were able to learn from each other. I am deeply appreciative of all that I have learned from Sylvia, whose commitment to self-education in a few different fields surpasses mine by at least a mile. Her only formal training beyond high school is two years of Bible school (Steinbach Bible College [also EMC].) However, she is widely read and continues to put me too shame as she reads a book that teaches her and I entertain myself with a Michael Connelly murder mystery.

Sometime between 2006 and 2010 or so, she was fortunate enough to be asked to develop and teach a government-funded life-coaching program that she called "Making Dreams Come True." She worked with small groups, three to four women at a time, to help them gain or regain their self-esteem after it had been severely damaged by a variety of life experiences. Among others, she used the writings of contemporary spiritual and personal development gurus like Louise Hay and Wayne Dyer. While reading one of Dyer's books, at Sylvia's encouragement, I realized that Dyer was saying many of the things taught by Jesus and the Ancient Writings. However, Dyer's audience, though not necessarily less spiritual, was definitely less religiously partisan than your average Christian congregation.

In 2010, I read Mark Batterson's book, *In a Pit with a Lion on a Snowy Day*.[1] It occurred to me as I read it that if we used the book as a guide, particularly what might be called his seven "Characteristics of a Lion Chaser," Sylvia and I could do a sermon series that would bring together the things from Dyer, Hay, and others that she was teaching in her program, the teachings of Jesus, and some of the teachings in the rest of the Ancient Writings. And so, an eight-sermon series was born. I had written some of Sylvia's lectures and so was fairly well-acquainted with her materials. With her books and conversations with her as a resource, I wrote the script for each sermon and then we would present them together as conversations between the two of us that the congregation was invited to listen in on. We were paid maybe as high a complement as any when one young adult, who had started attending our church with his wife and two children, said to his mother-in-law over lunch, "It was difficult not to pay attention."

I was originally going to call the series "Will You Live 'til You Die?" as in the important question is not when will you die, but will you live until you die. Council thought only old guys like me would be interested in that question, so we called it "Living the Adventure."

One more thing. We happened to notice an offer on the Internet for a very good deal on copies of Batterson's book, so we bought copies, making it possible for people to read the book week by week as Sylvia and I preached the series and we discussed it in Sunday school. Yeah, Batterson is more Evangelical than I am, but he still has lots of good things to say.

What follows is the introductory sermon to that series.

LIVING THE ADVENTURE

2 Samuel 23:20–23; John 10:7–10

RAY: Sylvia, have you ever been in a pit with a lion on a snowy day?
SYLVIA: No, but I've been in the kitchen with a bear on a Saturday morning.

---

1. I was drawn to it when I saw the title after having earlier read his *Wild Goose Chase* and appreciating it.

RAY: I'm sure it was a gentle, fuzzy bear, warm, nice to cuddle –

SYLVIA: Stop, Ray, I think that's more than the congregation needs or wants to hear.

RAY: Just trying to be helpful, so the people here will understand what you mean.

SYLVIA: I'm sure! Now what was your question?

RAY: Have you ever been in a pit with a lion on a snowy day?

SYLVIA: It's still a question that is hard to take seriously, and, if it were meant seriously, it's a question to which you know the answer. You think if I had been in a pit with a lion on a snowy day I would now be here, working with you on this sermon? You'd be here by yourself. So, why the question?

RAY: Don't sell yourself short. I know you are small, but I also know you, and I'm not sure that lion in the pit would stand a chance against you.

SYLVIA: Okay, okay. Why the question?

RAY: Earlier Fred read a strange and rather interesting, though very brief, story from the collection in what we know as 2 Samuel. It's barely a story, really. It consists of three verses that outline the exploits of a certain man, Benaiah. Among the list of exploits of this brave man is the brief detail that on a day when snow had fallen, he went and killed a lion in a pit. That story inspired Mark Batterson to write a book called, *In a Pit with a Lion on a Snowy Day.*

SYLVIA: Yes?

RAY: Reading that book gave me the idea for this sermon series. See, in Mark's book, Benaiah's encounter with the lion on a snowy day becomes a metaphor for life. We would like life to be easy, like a walk in a meadow of flowers. You know, like Psalm 23 says, "God lets me lie down in lush meadows"—I can see them in my imagination: grass, flowers, shade trees, butterflies, birds, and sunshine—and, like the Psalm says, bubbling mountain brooks that sing their praises and quench my thirst.

SYLVIA: And so since July you have been pining for our campsite in Kananaskis,[2] wanting to go back to the mountains and campfires, and days spent reading your favorite books.

RAY: Yeah, exactly, that's the life I would like.

---

2. A tourist area in the Canadian Rockies that includes wonderful campgrounds and fantastic hiking opportunities.

SYLVIA: But you know life is not like that. Psalm 23 also mentions dark valleys, rocky mountain paths where it's hard to see your way, easy to trip and fall, cold, and haunted by death. You can't have life without those valleys as well.

RAY: Precisely. And though I wish I could camp forever in the Rockies, I had to come back to life in Swift Current.

SYLVIA: I know Swift Current is in a valley. Are you suggesting it's a dark, haunted valley?

RAY: No, no, not at all. Swift Current is a great place. But, for us, Swift Current is a metaphor for everyday life. This is where we live, our friends live, where we work. And though Swift Current is a great place to live, this is where we encounter those lions, on days that are already overcast and the ground is covered with ice and snow.

SYLVIA: Your question, then, have I ever been in a pit with a lion on a snowy day, is really a question that asks, "Have I ever encountered tough times, maybe had a lion sneak up on me, or suddenly show up on the path ahead, when I least expected it?"

RAY: Right, and then you had to decide what you would do, run from the lion or chase it into the pit and deal with it.

SYLVIA: Well, then, in answer to your question, that bear I mentioned earlier, there are times he has seemed more like a lion . . .

RAY: Sylvia!

SYLVIA: Okay, all jesting aside, yes, I have, we all have, and that's why I think this sermon series is so important.

RAY: That's what I thought when I read Batterson's book, but then something else occurred to me.

SYLVIA: You and your ideas!

RAY: No, wait, you'll like this. Reading Batterson's book reminded me of some of the books you have talked about and suggested I read, including Wayne Dyer's book, *Excuses Begone!*, a book we read together, or actually, you read to me while we were traveling last summer. There seemed all kinds of connections between what Batterson was saying and what Dyer says, not only in *Excuses Begone!* but also in *Inspiration* and *The Power of Intention*.

SYLVIA: Okay, I get it. There are other books as well. Mary Anne Radmacher wrote *Lean Forward into your Life*, Rhonda Byrne published *The Secret* along with the DVD, and Louise Hay has several books including, *You Can Heal Your Life*.

RAY: Seeing the connections between what Batterson was saying based not only on the 2 Samuel story about Benaiah, but the entire Story of God as captured in Scripture and the books we just mentioned, I realized that, in your work at DreamForest Life Coaching, you pull a lot of this together and teach these ideas to women who have seen their fair share of lions on snowy days—fierce lions, on cold, stormy days, in deep, dark pits. What you teach them has helped them look at their lives differently, right? And given them the courage to turn their lives around?

SYLVIA: It has. You know me, I didn't need any convincing, but my experience at DreamForest, seeing the changes in women's lives, has made me even more convinced that how we look at life, how we *think* about life, our *attitudes* and *mindset*, can make all the difference, not just on nice days, but when encountering a lion on a snowy day.

RAY: So it occurred to me that if we could take the things you teach in your program, use Benaiah's encounter with the lion as our metaphor, and track down other stories in God's larger Story in Scripture, we could help people in our congregation think about life as an adventure.

SYLVIA: I like that. When Benaiah first encountered the lion, he could have decided to run from it, couldn't he have?

RAY: He could have. I think I would have. Whether real life lions or metaphorical lions, they scare me and I am inclined to run.

SYLVIA: In that case, there may be something for you to learn in this sermon series.

RAY: I think so. Maybe no one else here needs to hear these sermons, but I know I need to preach them.

SYLVIA: Benaiah could have decided life with lions was just too scary and he could have run the opposite direction. But he didn't. Instead, he gave chase. Then, when the lion fell into the pit, Benaiah could have said, "That's it, my job's done. Besides, with all this snow, the sides and bottom of that pit will be slippery. I'm going to leave." He didn't. No matter the snow and ice, slippery footing, and a lion that probably outweighed him by three hundred pounds or more, Benaiah jumped into the pit and took on the lion.

RAY: I call that attitude!

SYLVIA: Real attitude! But good attitude. I would say Benaiah decided life is an adventure and he wasn't going to miss any part of it nor back down from anything. He was going to take life on, full stride, and live it. Nothing was going to stop him from living!

RAY: That reminds me of one more thing that I think will be important to our series.

SYLVIA: What's that?

RAY: Jesus.

SYLVIA: Please say more.

RAY: There is that second text that Fred read earlier, the one from John's Good News Story Collection. It's a piece out of a sermon that Jesus gave. The part Fred read ended with Jesus saying "I came that they might have life, and have it abundantly."[3] I like how Eugene Peterson translates this. In *The Message*, he has Jesus saying: "I came so they can have real . . . life, more and better life than they ever dreamed of."

SYLVIA: Oooh, I like that. "More and better life than they ever dreamed of." Making dreams come true, and more. What you are suggesting is that Jesus came to make it possible for us to live life as an adventure, to chase lions rather than run from them, to dream and follow the dream, to live, here and now.

RAY: Exactly. People have often thought of Jesus as the way to heaven, with little reference to how we live here. In John's Good News Story Collection, or what some people call the Gospel of John, Jesus talks a lot about life, but never about going to heaven, with maybe one exception. What Jesus talks about is how to live here, now, abundantly, as if life is an adventure that we take on boldly and courageously.

SYLVIA: This moves the whole idea of "in a pit with a lion on a snowy day" beyond just taking on trouble in life.

RAY: For sure.

SYLVIA: I like that. I think God has a dream for our whole world, but also a dream for each one of us. God's dream inspires our dreams, but I think God pushes them even further, stretches them until they take our breath away. It is God's dream, then, that shapes our adventure for whatever happens in our lives and whatever we

---

3. John 10:10. NRSV.

encounter in life. God dreams that into the dream and dreams adventure and courage and excitement and enthusiasm for us.

RAY: Yes. Yes. God's story, a bold, sweeping story that pushes back the horizons and catches us up in its grandeur and adventure, speaks that dream to us. But then God also dreams each of us into that story and has dreams for us, each one of us. These dreams invite us to take life on as an adventure, an exciting adventure.

SYLVIA: A big adventure. We can be tempted to dream too small, barely dream at all. God invites us to dream big, as big as God, for it is always us and God together in those dreams.

RAY: And Jesus came that we might live that dream.

SYLVIA: Yes, and live it boldly, without fear, enthusiastically, without pulling back. I think God wants us to embrace the dream and then take on life as an exciting adventure. If we do this in the right way, life becomes something we love to live, love it so much that we don't want to go to bed at night and can hardly wait to get up in the morning.

RAY: We're halfway there.

SYLVIA: Pardon me?

RAY: We're halfway there.

SYLVIA: What do you mean?

RAY: You said that when we live the adventure, when we embrace God's dream, then we can live so that we don't want to go to bed at night and can hardly wait to get up in the morning. Well, I think we are halfway there. I don't want to go to bed at night and you can't wait to get up in the morning. Now we just have to work on the other half.

SYLVIA: And how would you suggest we do that?

RAY: This is what we want to hunt down in this sermon series, by checking in with the contemporary gurus you've met in your research at work, by listening to the Ancient Story of God, and by connecting with Jesus who said he came that we might live more and better than we ever dreamed of.

SYLVIA: Can you be more specific?

RAY: In the book, *In a pit with a lion on a snowy day*, Mark Batterson refers to seven characteristics of lion chasers. These same seven characteristics, in various forms, show up in the literature we mentioned earlier. So we will go with these seven. Call them Characteristics of Lion Chasers. Call them Principles for Living the Adventure. Call them God's Way of Living the Dream. Call them seven Attitude Boosters. Call them Dream Catchers. Whatever the label, the point is that these seven ways of approaching life can make an amazing difference in our lives.

SYLVIA: Like they did for Benaiah.

RAY: Like they do for the women you have taught.

SYLVIA: Like they did for Jesus.

RAY: And, at the risk of embarrassing you, like I think they have for you. I can't think of a bolder lion chaser that I know of than you. In that sense, I think this sermon series will be your testimony, your story that can be an inspiration for all of us.

SYLVIA: Thank you. I have experienced it making an amazing difference in my life and have seen it change others in amazing ways. I think there is one more thing we should highlight. We mentioned it earlier and we'll come back to this in a future sermon. However, I think it's important we say it here as we wrap up.

RAY: What is that?

SYLVIA: This change we want to make in our lives, living the adventure, starts with how we think.

RAY: It does. You saying that reminds me of something Jesus said.

SYLVIA: What is that?

RAY: In Mark's Collection of stories about Jesus—this is the first-century Mark, not Mark Batterson—Jesus's core message is summarized like this: "Repent, and believe the good news." The word "repent" has often been understood to mean "Change how you live."

SYLVIA: Yes?

RAY: It does mean that. But over the last year or so, I have increasingly become convinced that in this particular place, it may refer, first of all, to change how we *think*. That is, when Jesus says "Repent," he means "Change how you think." When Jesus then adds, "Believe the good news," he is saying, "Think this! Think this good news I am bringing. Change how you think! Think this new, great stuff!" That will then translate into a different way of living. In our case, it means living the adventure, going from surviving to thriving and from boredom to excitement.

SYLVIA: That reminds me of something Wayne Dyer says. In his book, *Excuses Begone!* he says that it is a "scientifically verified idea that your beliefs have the power to rearrange and change the material world."[4] Earlier in the same book, quoting Tom Perez, Dyer says: "In this world anything is possible when you put your mind to it. I know that your mind can work miracles."[5]

RAY: That's incredible. How we think determines the kind of life we have and the kind of world in which we live.

SYLVIA: It does. You know how you have accused me of thinking I can change reality? Well, it seems it's so.

RAY: Point to you! And then we have Jesus saying, "Repent! Change how you think and believe the good news!" As we read that good news, we notice it's about a new world and a new life, about living God's adventure in God's world. And all of it starts with how we think.

SYLVIA: So we have to rework our thinking.

RAY: And we'll do that in this series, starting next Sunday with how we might think and act when it seems the odds are against us.

SYLVIA: But in the meantime, we can start living the adventure today, now. We can each be a lion chaser, living the adventure. Let's go for it!

* * *

The other titles in the series were:

- "How Big is God"
- "Where Angels Fear to Thread"
- "Doing Cataract Surgery"
- "A Wild Goose Chase"
- "I'm Just Me"
- "Playing to Win"
- "Just Do It"

---

4. Dyer, *Excuses*, 26.
5. Dyer, *Excuses*, 8.

Chapter 7

SING ME A SONG ABOUT JESUS

IT WAS EARLY TUESDAY morning (not all my preaching crises come on a Tuesday) and I had no idea what I was going to preach come Sunday. Usually my preaching plan is laid out well ahead of time, often as much as a year. Now, here it was the Tuesday after Easter and I did not have a series planned to get me through to June 30. Sure, I could always go to the lectionary, but for me, unless I had a specific reason to do so other than pure planning, that did not seem like a good option.

A further complicating factor was that it was 2011, the year I generally worked six and seven days a week between my pastoral responsibilities and my mediation practice. Along with my private files, I was a contractor for three other agencies and one of them required a weekly trip to Regina, a trip that could last two or three days. This morning I was on my way on one of those trips. There wasn't going to be a lot of time for planning and dreaming. When the scheduled time for sermon prep arrived, I'd better be ready to prepare.

On these out-of-town trips, I always had a case of CDs with me and if I was not listening to CBC, I was listening to music, classic country music. That morning it was Johnny Cash. Suddenly, an idea popped up from somewhere. It would be fun to do a series on sermons around the songs people listen to. It could be an invitation to have them listen to songs in a whole new way. I would invite them to nominate songs, any songs, as long as they were NOT religious songs. "The Old Rugged Cross" and "Because He Lives" were too easy and did not create the opportunity to learn to listen to the music "out there" in a new way.

I knew I had just the song to start the series this coming Sunday—Stompin' Tom Connors' "The Singer".[1] In that song Stompin' Tom sings about the importance of song in the life of a people, not just individuals but a people, a collective.

What I would do is include a bulletin insert in each bulletin inviting nominations and hopefully at least a couple of people would hand theirs in before they left that morning.

I wrote my manuscript, preached my sermon, and collected the inserts. I don't remember if I got more nominations than I needed. Whatever the case, I ended up preaching sermons built around the following songs: "Folsom Prison Blues" by Johnny Cash, "Sunday Morning Comin' Down" by Kris Kristofferson (hey, this is southwest Saskatchewan), "Breathe" by Taylor Swift, "Seven Spanish Angels", sung by Ray Charles and Willy Nelson, "What a Wonderful World" from Louis Armstrong, and "One Tin Soldier" originally sung by, of course, The Original Cast. I know, the last two were almost cheating for a Mennonite preacher, but we went with it.

I have included two of the sermons from that series: "Folsom Prison Blues" and "Sunday Morning Comin' Down". An interesting story about the second of the two sermons. A few years after preaching it, I was attending the one hundredth anniversary of the Salvation Army. A local singer, who prided himself on being able to sing almost any classic country song known, performed a few numbers. "Sunday Morning Coming Down" was one of them. He introduced it by saying that after one concert, he had been criticized by a member of the audience for singing that song when the theme was gospel. He told us he had told that man and was telling us that he thought Kristofferson's song was also spiritual.

The next day when I got to the office, I printed off a copy of my sermon and sent it to him as a way of affirming both what he had said and his ministry. He called me a few days later with the emotion still in his voice. He had started crying a couple of times during the course of reading the sermon because of the way it had connected for him. We as preachers live for phone calls like that.

For each of the sermons, I printed the words of the song in the bulletin. Then for all but two, I played the song off a CD at the start of the sermon. In the case of "What a Wonderful World", I used the song as something to develop worship around, rather than preach, because we

---

1. Connors, "The Singer," *A Proud Canadian*, track 20.

were back at that same camp on the lakeshore. In the case of "Breathe", I played the song partway into the sermon because about one-third of my sermon was a story in which a jilted lover and Jesus were traveling in a truck (again, this is SW Saskatchewan) away from a dance and having a conversation. In retrospect, as I get more involved in the publishing industry and learn more about copyright and use of intellectual property, I realize I may have pushed the boundaries a little bit. So, I encourage you, before you preach this kind of series, get the details of what is allowed and what is not. It is important, if we as preachers and congregations are to have integrity, that we honor copyright laws and the rights to intellectual property.

It is for those reasons that I have not reprinted the words to the songs in this book. You will also notice that in the sermon on "Folsom Prison Blues," I refer to other songs, but have not quoted the specific lyrics from within the song. For the same reasons. My understanding is if you simply preach a sermon, it is okay to quote lyrics. However, if you record or video your sermons, you better check the rules. If the songs mentioned in these two sermons are not known to you, they are easily available on YouTube for you to listen to (and don't ask me how YouTube gets away with what they do).

"FOLSOM PRISON BLUES"[2]: STRUGGLING WITH LIFE'S CHAINS

This song, written and sung by Johnny Cash, could be heard as Cash's autobiography. No, Cash never shot a man in Nevada or anyplace else for that matter. The only time he was in Folsom Prison, or any prison of note, was when he went there to sing for the inmates. His ex-con image was part of the myth that sold records, not part of the reality of Johnny Cash. And yet the twentieth-century musical legend lived the "Folsom Prison Blues" much of his life, imprisoned by bars made of drugs and alcohol, chained to the ball of a bitter childhood, and haunted by demons and ghosts that rarely gave him a moment of real peace.

The links in his ball and chain were forged early by a father's alcoholism and drunkenness that "inflicted precisely the sort of damage that could lead a boy to believe that a devil was loose in his house, indeed in his own blood. And such was Cash's belief," writes Patrick Carr, co-author

---

2. Cash, "Folsom Prison Blues," *With His Hot*," Track 11.

of *Cash: The Autobiography.* Carr continues: "[Cash] saw himself quite clearly as a battleground between good and evil, God and the devil, the black dog he often mentioned in liner notes and interviews and the white light he saw in his moments of greatest transcendence." This battle was one in which Cash engaged "consciously and intensely, often viscerally, on a daily basis throughout his life."[3]

Later in his life, Cash apparently devoted an album to that battle. His *American Recordings* CD features a picture of Cash with a haunted look, a dog on each side, one black with a stripe of white, the other white with a little bit of black. The album includes songs with the "Folsom Prison Blues" theme, the sense of being imprisoned by one's history, by one's character, by one's weaknesses, and/or by one's choices. "Delia's Gone" is the song of a man who, like the one in "Folsom Prison Blues", kills. This man is not haunted by the freedom others enjoy while he is cooped up in prison. This man is haunted by what he has done and the person he attacked. Every night while he sleeps, he hears Delia's footsteps circling his bed. There is no getting away from her and his awful deed. The music itself has that haunting quality and I find if I listen to the song, it stays with me in my head, the line acknowledging Delia's death repeating itself over and over until it almost drives me crazy.[4]

Another song more obviously speaks to what it feels like, this inner haunting that expresses itself in destructive choices, with the title, "The Beast in Me":[5]

For Johnny Cash, it wasn't just his father's destructive influence on his life that forged the links in his chain and built Folsom's walls. It was also his own choices, like the man in Folsom Prison who was well aware why he was in prison. It was no one else's fault but his. Spending days and weeks on the road, touring from town to town, away from home and family, and young girls idolizing the new star, his marriage began its spiral downward. Singing and traveling with little time to rest, amphetamines soon became the crutch that got him through. For Cash, genetically predisposed to addictions, drugs—illegal, prescription, and

---

3. Quotations taken from Carr, *Cash: The Legend.* The four-CD collection, along with written materials, has no page numbers. Most of the information about Johnny Cash's life used in this sermon comes from that collection, interpreted, of course, by my own readings of Cash's autobiographies and watching the movie, *Walk the Line,* directed by James Mangold.

4. Cash, vocalist, "Delia's Gone," *The Sound of Johnny Cash,* track 7.

5. Cash, vocalist, "The Beast in Me," *Johnny Cash,* track 3.

alcohol—were like a prison sentence given to a man, at other times, for shooting someone on a whim. He lived with addictions much of the rest of his life, occasionally managing to free himself from the vice-like grip, once for a period of thirteen years. Others could be seen enjoying the train ride of life; he was caught by life itself.

Added to all this was the Christianity that Johnny Cash, his family and friends, and many of his colleagues had learned as children and grown up with in the American South. Whether or not they needed it, fellow singer Jerry Lee Lewis would never fail to remind them that their lifestyles were sure to send them straight to hell, straight to that land where, to quote another song sung by Cash, they had to work the devil's cattle ranch with nary a break or any hope of the work ending.[6]

Cash's self-chosen yet demon-haunted spiral into self-destruction, into not only Folsom Prison but the Blues that came with the cell, almost ended his life in 1967 when he attempted suicide.

Though one of the more famous people "living behind Folsom's bars and trying to survive its Blues," Johnny Cash was by no means the only one, nor the first. A man Cash admired—Johnny went so far as to write a novel based on this man's life[7]—expressed a similar sense of life and its destructive grip two thousand years earlier, maybe not as poetically but at least as desperately. Paul, the missionary preacher, in his letter to the house churches in Rome in what seems almost a moment of weakness, lets the readers of his letter look into his soul and see there not the pious holiness of a saint, but the deep, dark struggles of a man caught—by his history, his character, his weaknesses, his baggage, and his struggle, singing the Folsom Prison Blues long before California's Folsom was built or Cash ever strummed a guitar:

> The trouble is with me, for I am all too human, a slave to sin. I don't really understand myself, for I want to do what is right, but I don't do it. Instead, I do what I hate. But if I know that what I am doing is wrong, this shows that I agree that the law is good. So I am not the one doing wrong; it is sin living in me that does it. ("The beast in me"[8])
>
> And I know that nothing good lives in me, that is, in my sinful nature. I want to do what is right, but I can't. I want to do what is good, but I don't. I don't want to do what is wrong, but I

---

6. Cash, vocalist, "Ghost Riders In The Sky," *The Sound of Johnny Cash*, track 5.
7. Cash, *Man in White*.
8. Cash, vocalist, "The Beast in Me," *Johnny Cash*, track 3.

do it anyway. But if I do what I don't want to do, I am not really the one doing wrong; it is sin living in me that does it ("The beast in me"[9]):

I have discovered this principle of life—that when I want to do what is right, I inevitably do what is wrong. I love God's law with all my heart. But there is another power within me that is at war with my mind. This power makes me a slave to the sin that is still within me. Oh, what a miserable person I am! Who will free me from this life that is dominated by sin and death? *(In "Folsom Prison Blues, Cash sings about being haunted by others' freedoms even as he rots in prison.)*[10]

Paul had his own demons to live with, guilt that may have haunted him. He had originally been caught in religion's prison, bars of rules and required beliefs that can be as strong and destructive as a father's abuse, alcohol, and prescription pills. He had to live with the memory of people he had killed, not just to watch them die, but to wipe out this new community of Jesus that was turning Paul's world upside down, a community that also offered him the very hope he needed. He doesn't tell us about other things that haunted, held him in their vice-like grip, but the haunting despair of Romans 7 suggests they may well have existed.

I don't know where you identify with the stories of these two men. I don't know what the walls and iron bars of Folsom Prison are made of in your life. Depression that can drag you down into deep dungeons of blackness. Alcohol that twinkles in the glass, but rots in your soul. A history of abuse—physical, emotional, or sexual—that you thought was history only to release its demons on your spirit and life at the worst possible times. Guilt that ravages your body and spirit, threatening to destroy a world you have neatly put together, hoping you could get on with life. You feel like the Hebrew poet: "When I kept it all inside, /my bones turned to powder, /my words became daylong groans. /The pressure never let up; / all the juices of my life dried up."[11] Pornography, its pictures strangely alluring and revolting at the same time; its impact on your personal life and your marriage only destructive even as its grip tightens.

Folsom Prison's iron bars, locked gates, razor-barbed fences, clanging gates and guard towers come in many forms. As you sit behind those

---

9. Cash, vocalist, "The Beast in Me," *Johnny* Cash, track 3.

10. Rom 7:14a–24. NLT. With connections to Cash lyrics in parenthesis and italics.

11. Ps 32:3–4. *The Message.*

bars and look out, it seems that everyone else is having a great time, riding the train toward fun and you wish that train could be yours so that you could move along in life, far away from the demons that haunt you, the iron bars that stop you, the ball and chain that hold you back.

Is there any train that can take you away from this prison? Paul insists that there is. After bemoaning his wretchedness and asking, in desperation, if there is anything that can save him, he bursts into testimony: "Thank God! The answer is in Jesus Christ our Lord."[12] It's an answer he came back to time and again in his writings. There was something about what happened in Jesus that rolled that darkness away. Was it as simple as believing in Jesus and everything was great and healed? No, by no means. In another letter he wrote, Paul was clear that we "work out [our] salvation with fear and trembling."[13] It was Jesus, most definitely, but is was also a long and difficult journey. Cash's life and music offer us a glimpse into the complexity of that journey.

Cash expressed the same longing for redemption that Paul did. In a song recorded during the seventies, "Keep me from Blowing Away."[14]

Like Paul, Cash too, found Jesus to be this lifeline. The story of Jesus went with him his whole life. From the day he started recording, he wanted to record gospel songs, for he found something in their message that made a difference. He visited the Holy Land and then made the movie, *Gospel Road*, a telling of the Jesus story I find compelling, a telling that engages my imagination, and touches my life. Late in life, Cash sang a song that testified to what the story had done in his life, in a song called simply "Redemption"[15]

That story can make a world of difference, but not just as a story. It is the reality in and behind the story that makes the difference, the reality of love, God's love discovered in Jesus. Cash found that love in the story and experience of Jesus, a love that was strong enough to overcome the earlier fears, the demons that threatened his survival, the guilt that haunted him, and the addictions that gripped his life. He discovered that love was truly the strongest and most redemptive force that had ever entered our universe[16] Cash found that love in Jesus and he found it in another person,

---

12. Rom 7:25a. NLT.
13. Phil 2:12. NRSV.
14. Cash, vocalist, "Keep Me From Blowing Away," *Bootleg Vol. IV*, disc 2, track 8.
15. Cash, compower and vocalist, "Redemption," *American* Recordings, track 11.
16. Cash, vocalist, "A Thing Called Love," *A Thing Called Love*, track 3.

a woman who stuck with him through thick and thin. In these two, he discovered and experienced the love that freed him from Folsom's awful life sentence.

That same love—"God's love and peace discovered in Jesus, experienced in community and expressed in daily life"[17] —can have the same freeing, life-giving impact on our lives. We sense the love as we read and/or hear the story of Jesus. We begin to know its reality as we encounter the living Jesus of the story. We experience that love in a person close to us, a partner, a friend, a brother or a sister, a parent. We experience it in a community that accepts us the way we are, a community where we can let our struggles show. We are not judged for the struggle, but joined in the struggle so we do not have to struggle alone.

That is the love that Paul said made the difference in his life. This is the love that Cash sang of again and again, a love that made all the difference in his life. Already in the seventies, when he was barely halfway through his struggle with Folsom's fierce grip on his life, he sang, as he looked at others around him, desperate for hope and transformation, of how love had made the difference in his life.[18]

Cash, like Paul, knew what it was that made the difference in his life—love. He knew what it was that could and did break down Folsom's destructive walls—love. He knew where to find that love—in God through the person and story of Jesus and in a person committed to him, no matter what, and in a community that accepted him the way he was. Because of God and a person who loved him, Johnny Cash did ride that train a little further down the line and, bit by bit, had that whistle blow his blues away. Because of that same love, we too can live freed from Folsom's life sentence and live a love-filled life.

"SUNDAY MORNING COMIN' DOWN"[19]: "FROM LONELINESS TO SOLITUDE"[20]

I can identify with the feeling, the loneliness of a Sunday morning on a downtown city street. In the early seventies, I attended and lived at MB

---

17. I used this particular phrase because it was printed on our bulletin every Sunday morning as a summary of our mission statement.
18. Cash, vocalist, "If Not," *Man in Black*, track 4.
19. Kristofferson, "Sunday Morning Comin' Down," *Kris Kristofferson*, track 12.
20. This phrase is borrowed from Henri J.M. Nouwen in *Reaching Out*. It is the

Bible College in Winnipeg, and played in a gospel band. I still vividly recall one Sunday morning. We had played a concert the night before and it was up to me to get the rental van back to the agency early on Sunday morning. It was a beautiful morning and so I decided to walk the two miles or so back to the college residence. There was very little traffic and very little noise. There were few people around and in a city of six hundred thousand that feels strange. It feels lonely. In the city, you can be lonely even when the sidewalks are crowded, but it's a different kind of loneliness when it feels like you are the only person up and around in a city of thousands. As I walked over the bridge across the rail yards, I stopped and watched a slow-moving train passing underneath, headed west. Loneliness washed over me. Life felt overwhelming. It seemed so easy to go underneath the bridge, hop the train and get away from everything. If you had asked me what I wanted to get away from, I might not have been able to tell you. I just wanted to get away. Away from life, I suppose, without dying. Away from loneliness into another loneliness. Away from, well, like I said, just away.

And so, I identify with the Singer as he wakes up, looks for an unlaundered shirt that he can still wear, and stumbles out into the loneliness of a Sunday morning. Life the morning after the night before can be wonderful. It can also be lonely, empty, and haunting as you wonder what it's all about and what it's all for and is it really worth it. Last night, good or bad, is gone, leaving you nothing but the leftovers which are rarely good, tomorrow is an unknown mystery, and today is empty when there is no activity demanding your attention and taking your mind off the emptiness. In the song, it sounds like the Singer had a great evening playing guitar and singing his songs—why wouldn't Sunday morning be a great feeling? And yet, here too, I can identify. Monday mornings can be difficult after a great Sunday. Even if the sermon went well, you complimented me on it, and Sunday school discussion was lively, Monday morning hits with a sense of "Now what?" The sermon, no matter how good, has been preached. It's over, done with—no solace there. What will the week bring, and how can I ever write another sermon? Does anyone understand how I feel? Who can share my moments of dread, emptiness, anxiety, and uncertainty?

I too have looked for something to wear, not really caring much what it looks like, been tempted to have a beer for breakfast, wondered if

---

first of the three movements Nouwen describes in the book.

a smoke would take the edge off the empty, and proceeded into the day, alone even as there were people around, noticing not the happy smiles—who wants happy smiles when you are feeling this way—but noticing instead the kid living with his own pain and anger that has him kicking anything in sight that is kickable. Not only are you alone, but life sucks! And misery loves company, though shared misery can be a lonely experience still, for no misery is ever like your misery.

Loneliness can take many forms. You know how and where you experience it. The specifics may be different in your life than the Singer's or mine, but I suspect the feelings communicated in the song are feelings you can identify with. The temptation, when those feelings hit, is to do something, anything, to try to get away from them. Hop a freight to Calgary. Smoke a joint and get stoned. Have a couple of beer for breakfast. And then there are those "more responsible" ways of escaping. Get busy cleaning the house and bake stuff for the freezer. Fix the car and work in the yard. Go shopping. Watch a Rider game on TV. Turn up the volume on the iPod with earphones firmly in place. Go for coffee with a group of people. Go to a meeting. Surf the 'Net. The opportunities to escape are many, to drown out or get away from the loneliness and the emptiness.

Our Singer is tempted by those same escapes. He lights a cigarette, though the taste from last night's smoke fest is sour in his mouth. He has a couple of beer and as he hits the streets, he wishes he had a joint or two to help the day. But then, something changes. He did not have enough beer to deaden his mind. The weed wasn't available and the nicotine he barely noticed. The quiet streets, unhurried pace, empty sidewalks, and uncluttered mind create space for him, the space to begin to notice things, more things than a boy who shares his misery.

First there is something in the air, a smell he can't quite place. His nose twitches, he looks up, and turns his head to follow the smell. There it is now, stronger. And then he recognizes it, a smell suspiciously like the smell that used to come from Mom's kitchen on a Sunday morning on towards lunch. The smell takes him back to home (that's my guess), and Mom cooking up southern fried chicken and biscuits. Home, and the love and warmth he experienced. Home, and the arms that held him close and told him he was not alone. Home, and its sense of wellbeing and life, life without having to smoke, drink, and turn up the music to endure. Memories can create loneliness, but they can be a good loneliness, filling the loneliness with something good, with life, with warmth, and with love. Memories you had forgotten were there. Memories that remind you that there is another kind of life; you are not limited to this empty, dirty-laundry life you find yourself in.

The memories and smells begin to override the taste of old cigarette smoke from the night before and the emptiness of city streets. His heart and mind are opening up to see more. Now, as he looks around, he sees a daddy and his little girl—family. Though his family may be far away, may have been changed by death or worse, yet suddenly family is real and love is real. The experience of family pulls him in and he experiences the laughter and the love as a dad and daughter enjoy the swings. Family, loving, smiling, laughing family brings hope, and as he watches, the Singer feels that hope, that joy. It touches something inside of him, something else he thought he had lost and he realizes it is still there. He is not as cynical and jaded as he thought. He does still have a heart—it's beating, it's warm, it's alive, and the life circulates through his being and inspires his spirit. He can feel. It is good.

After this, who knows what else could happen? Now he is looking, actively engaged in seeing what else he might experience on this lonely Sunday morning. He is beginning to believe there are all kinds of possibilities if he but takes notice, and notice he takes. It's music that catches his ears and he is drawn to the window of a Sunday school room where children are singing. It's not someone's iPod cranked up. It's not a radio blaring from a passing car. It's a Sunday school class where children are singing about Jesus. God is entering his life. In the quiet, he could finally hear it. God no longer has to shout above the noise of the Singer's own songs, the noise of the band behind him, the noise of all that encircled his life. With the streets empty and the air quiet, the Singer finally hears the whisperings of a God who had been whispering for a long time, but whose whispers had been drowned out. There is a God. "Over my head I hear music in the air. There must be a God somewhere."[21] This world, even the singer's world, is not empty. It's just empty of all those empty things that create a sense of feeling full, but leave you emptier than ever. In such an empty world, that which the world is full of—God—can finally be heard, and it brings the Singer to a stop. He hears God's voice as if for the first time because God's voice has been drowned out by other voices for so long. "Over my head, I hear music in the air. There must be a God somewhere."

21. "Over my head." In Nafziger, et al., *Sing the Journey*, #18. This is a song sung occasionally at Emmaus Mennonite Church and it was sung the morning this sermon was preached.

The Singer's life has been changed. Hope that started with the first faint whiff of frying chicken, hope that grew as the sound of a child's and her daddy's laughter reached his ears, and the sight of a happy family swinging focused his eyes, this hope is now grown big, as big as a Sunday school song and the God it's about. Now he's no longer wandering aimlessly, puffing desperately, and wondering longingly where he might deaden the feelings he has. His feelings are now hopeful. He wants to feel them for life is not just empty, not just to be escaped. Life is to be lived. It is possible to live life. Life is good. There is much good in the world. There is much good in his life. There is much good and there is God.

And so he turns toward home, back toward life, toward, well, whatever the future will have for him. But the emptiness of the Sunday morning and the loneliness of quiet streets have one more gift for him, a bell ringing and its echoes keeping the "music" going. The bell and its echo, the ringing back and forth, louder and fainter, reminds him of his dreams, dreams forgotten, dreams given up on, dreams lost, but now, maybe not. If a bell can keep ringing in echoes even when its original ring is gone, then maybe dreams too can keep going even as the original dream seems lost. The echo is not identical to the original, but it recalls the original and receives its life from the original. The dream can go on. Dreaming is still possible.

And so, filled with hope and sensing that dreaming may still be possible, the Singer's stride becomes more purposeful. No, he does not begin walking to get somewhere. He's not walking home to get things done. The moment is too precious for that. But he now walks with a lightness of step. He's no longer shuffling, dragging his feet. He is walking, walking in the emptiness of a morning that is no longer empty. It's full, filled with memories, filled with love and hope, filled with God, filled with dreams.

It is a morning that, as Eleanor Farjeon wrote six decades ago, has sprung from the Chaos as a Word was whispered on the wind, not unlike that first morning that was "In the Beginning."[22]

Such is the possibility in the empty loneliness of a Sunday morning. Such is the possibility in the empty loneliness of any morning or any other time for that matter. The empty loneliness can become a God-filled solitude. That is what happened to Elijah in the story we heard earlier.[23] He too, had a "cleanest dirty shirt" kind of day, a day when a couple of

---

22. Farjeon, "Morning," In Slough, ed., *Hymnal*, #648.
23. 1 Kgs 19:1–13.

beer for breakfast and bag of weed for the day would have seemed welcome. The night before, his evening had been filled with excitement, with people, with challenge, with meaning, with victory, and now, emptiness, sheer, utter, haunting loneliness, not in a city on a Sunday morning, but out in the wilderness where there was no chance of seeing anyone or hearing anything but the wildness of the place.

"I've had enough, Lord," Elijah said, "take away my life. I want to die!" Then he lay down and fell asleep. Death did not come as quickly as he had hoped. He was in for a long, lonely walk, not a morning's walk, but a month's journey on foot, every step of it alone, every step taking him deeper into the emptiness of wilderness, the emptiness of loneliness. At the end of it, on the side of a mountain, once all the noise and wildness died away and it was perfectly still, when he was completely alone—no people, no iPod, no radio, no cell phone, no TV, no shopping, no lawn to rake or garden to put in—when there was nothing, absolutely nothing to do or hear, sheer silence, there in the silence, in the emptiness, in the loneliness, Elijah heard God. The silence, though silent, was full and the moment, though empty, was overflowing and the place, though wild, was sacred. Loneliness turned to solitude, and Elijah found new life.

Such a transformation is possible for us too, in our loneliness. Loneliness can turn to solitude if we will pay attention and see and hear all that is in the emptiness of the moment and the loneliness of the place. I found it so that morning on the railway overpass in Winnipeg. In the loneliness with no distractions, I could contemplate hopping a freight to Banff, but I could also take time to contemplate why and what might be if I did so. I realized some things about myself, some important things about myself I needed to face. Had I not been lonely on a sidewalk in a city asleep, I might never have learned something important, something crucial to life.

The Singer's song, God's story about Elijah, and the example of Jesus who got up early to go to a deserted place[24] are invitations to us not to run from the loneliness, but to welcome the loneliness. Embrace the opportunity to be alone. Notice. Listen. Look. See. Hear. Let the loneliness take everything away so that nothing distracts. Feel your heart beating. Notice your breathing—in and out, in and out. Let the tension slide from your body. Then begin to notice all that is around you—a world filled with many things that wish to speak to you of love and life and hope and

---

24. Mark 1:35.

God and you. Listen, and the music will begin in the distance. You won't be sure at first where it comes from, but you will realize there must be a God somewhere. Memories will speak. What you see will speak to you. What you hear will sing.

The Spirit will whisper, "There is a God somewhere." The moment will transform and you will be a changed person. Your loneliness will not be less alone, but it will no longer be empty. Your loneliness will be filled with hope, with music, with God, with love, with warmth, with life. The curse of loneliness will become the gift of solitude. The terror of loneliness will become the welcome embrace of solitude. The emptiness will be full, full of life.

Such can happen on a "Sunday morning comin' down."

Chapter 8

MOVIES AND THE WORD

AT OUR LAST CONGREGATION, I was known as a bit of a movie buff. I probably watch more movies than anyone else, maybe more than any two other people put together, especially if you add the offerings of Netflix to the list. No, I am not a student of film. I cannot comment on their artistic value nor, by and large, how good the actors, directors, and cinematographers are. Occasionally I may comment on a script. Yeah, I watch the Oscars occasionally, but ultimately I watch movies that interest and entertain me and occasionally those that take me to another level and make me think.

Sometime after having done the music series, I thought it might be interesting to do the same thing with movies. Doing so is a little more complicated since there is not enough time on a Sunday morning to show the movie and do the other things, including preach, that we normally do on a Sunday. The series also ended up being shorter than I would have really liked. However, it was also difficult to get nominations. One more factor that played into this series is that we have parishioners with very sensitive ears. One movie that was nominated—*The Book of Eli*—would have made for a great sermon starter, but the language and some of the scenes were such that people would have been offended if we showed it Saturday night.

Here's what we did. We had four Sundays so I picked four movies, two that were nominated and two that I picked. The four were: *Horton Hears a Who, Get Low, My Sister's Keeper,* and *Ice Age*. With these four, we showed the movie at church on Saturday night[1] for anyone interested and then Sunday, as part of the sermon, I showed a short clip.

I have used other movies at times. Usually I simply tell part of the story. The year I preached this series, I showed clips a few more times since we had paid for the license and it was good for a year. Other movies I have used include *Pay it Forward*, *Dangerous Minds* (I had to be quick on the pause button so no one heard the f-word), and *The Making of an American Quilt*. I used the last one on a Sunday when we dedicated fifty or so quilts that had been made in our church basement that winter to be taken to Mennonite Central Committee.[2] An important line in the movie and for the sermon was: "I don't want to end up with some damn ugly quilt." I had to improvise so that everyone would know what the woman said, even while I could not say "damn" in church.

I had difficulty choosing which sermon to include as an example, so I included two, the one built around *Horton Hears a Who* and the other inspired by *My Sister's Keeper*. If you have not seen the movie, *My Sister's Keeper*, nor read the book by Judi Picoult, you should do one or the other. If you do both, a word of warning: The endings are significantly different. For the rest, I think the movie captures the book well.

DARE TO HEAR A WHO

Informed by the movie, Horton Hears a Who!

> I meant what I said
> And I said what I meant,
> An elephant's faithful,
> One hundred percent![3]

With these words as his motto, in the movie version of *Horton Hears A Who*, Horton the elephant commits himself to a task, guided by a philosophy, opposed by all clear-minded folks who will stop at nothing to

---

1. We bought a license that allowed us to show movies and movie clips in our church for one year.

2. Mennonite Central Committee (MCC) is a relief, development, and peace and justice advocacy organization owned by several Mennonite denominations. Receiving and distributing quilts is part of its Material Aid Division.

3. Quoted from the movie. The quotation does not show up in the book the movie is based on. It comes from the book on Horton's first adventure, *Horton Hatches the Egg*.

keep their way of thinking from being changed, motivated by a sense of calling and mission:

> I meant what I said
> And I said what I meant,
> An elephant's faithful,
> One hundred percent!

In the story, Horton the elephant hears a sound that piques his curiosity. He discovers that it comes from a small speck that, as he soon finds out much to his amazement, is a world all to itself, inhabited by Whos, surely the tiniest creatures of all. But, in Horton's mind, it doesn't matter the size of a person. The people on the speck deserve to be saved and protected "Because, after all, a person's a person, no matter how small."[4]

However, it's not so simple. The children who are friends of Horton at first go along with Horton, their imaginations engaged, and soon there are a bunch of tiny worlds riding along, gently cushioned on soft clovers. Mother Kangaroo, however, knows better and will have none of this weirdness. Tiny specks inhabited with tiny people, indeed. We cannot allow our children to be misled and their minds poisoned by such frivolity, such misleading and harmful frivolity. We all know specks are not inhabited. And the sooner Horton stops his foolishness and the children are saved from their imaginations, the better.

Horton refuses to bend. He insists that he has talked to and with the people on the speck. They are in fact real and he has promised to save them. He insists:

> I meant what I said
> And I said what I meant,
> An elephant's faithful,
> One hundred percent!

When Mother Kangaroo is unable to dissuade Horton from his foolishness, a foolishness that will forever poison all the children of the Jungle of Nool, she engages the services of Vlad—not Vlad, the cookie-baking bunny, but Vlad, the evil vulture who promises to destroy the clover and its speck forever and Nool will be rid of the foolishness and the children of the Jungle of Nool will be saved.

---

4. Dr. Seuss, *Horton Hears A Who.*

Vlad steals the clover with the speck from Horton and sets out to destroy the speck, or, at a very minimum, hide it so Horton will never find it. Horton follows, determined not to give up, determined to do whatever he has to do to save the Whos of Whoville living on the speck. After all, as Horton said:

> I meant what I said
> And I said what I meant,
> An elephant's faithful,
> One hundred percent!

According to the book the movie is based on:

> All that late afternoon and far into the night
> That black-bottomed bird flapped his wings in fast flight,
> While Horton chased after, with groans, over stones
> That tattered his toenails and battered his bones,
> And begged, "Please don't harm all my little folks, who
> Have as much right to live as us bigger folks do!"
> . . .
> And at 6:56 the next morning [Vlad] did it.
> It sure was a terrible place that he hid it.
> He let the small clover drop somewhere inside
> Of a great patch of clovers a hundred miles! [5]

As Vlad flies off, laughing, Horton begins looking for the clover with the speck that has Whoville on it. Horton picks one clover after another after another after another. More careful, more intent, and more committed than a *CSI* tech, Horton keeps going. All day Horton picked clovers for, as he had said:

> I meant what I said
> And I said what I meant,
> An elephant's faithful,
> One hundred percent!

And he was not going to quit. Finally, on the three millionth flower, Horton finds his speck and takes off for Mount Nool where the speck will be safe.

---

5. Seuss, *Horton Hears A Who*.

Mother Kangaroo hears that the speck has not been destroyed and Horton is continuing his foolish journey. She gathers the animals of the Jungle of Nool and inspires them with a speech to join up with her in stopping the foolishness that threatens the way of life in the Jungle of Nool, where it used to be that people were people and specks were specks. That time of peace and normality must be brought back and can only be done if Horton is stopped. Listen to her speech:

(1:05 to 1:07)

In the end, because Horton refuses to give up, Whoville and the speck are saved, and the animals of the Jungle of Nool come to realize that "after all, a person's a person, no matter how small."[6]

For centuries, millennia in fact, since before people began telling stories—if there ever was such a time—there have been Hortons who have dared to hear Whos, who have stood up to the evil designs of Vlads, refused to be dissuaded by the reasonable logic of Kangaroos, and have given themselves to a dream and a cause as silly in our world as the idea of a speck with a city of Whos on it in the Jungle of Nool. These Hortons refused to give up in the face of incredible opposition and even hostility because they too believed "a person's a person, no matter how small," and therefore worthy of love, of help, of acceptance, of respect, of compassion, and of our best care.

Joseph, the eleventh son of Jacob, heard a Who and followed the dream when Dad and his brothers wrote him off as a silly boy with an overactive imagination. Sticking to what he heard, Joseph saved his family and the dream and plan of God from starvation. Moses heard a Who and was able to lead the Hebrew slaves from slavery in Egypt to freedom in Canaan when all sane thinking people knew it could not be done. Daniel heard a Who and though he ended up in a den full of lions and his friends in a fiery furnace, they would not be persuaded to give up their belief that they had been called for a purpose and they and their God could not be stopped. They kept the faith alive.

Mary, the teenage girl in Nazareth, heard a Who and though everyone knew her story was ludicrous and they all knew what she had done to be pregnant, she stayed with the mission and history has never been the same since. Paul heard a Who and became convinced, just like Horton, "a person's a person, no matter how small" or how strange or how different. Like few others before him, other than Jesus, Paul realized that God is not

---

6. Seuss, *Horton Hears A Who*.

a racist and there are no people specially favored by God. All are equally loved and equally God's children.

And so the stories continue to pile up throughout history. In the last couple of hundred years, Wilber Wilberforce heard a Who and took a stand against slavery. "A person's a person, no matter how small" or what color his or her skin. Mother Teresa heard a Who and decided that the most despised in India were as important and loved by God as anyone else because "after all, a person's a person, no matter how small." She gave her life for the poor and despised of Calcutta.

Our world continues to need people who hear Whos, people who know the world is more than what we normally see and hear, who realize that the norms of society and culture are not what is best for us and will not give us the dream God has for us, a dream in which each person is valued, each person is cared for, violence is rejected, everyone has enough and no one has too much.

When you hear a Who and take on the saving of the world on a speck that no one else sees, hears, or believes exists, you may well initially be filled with a sense of enthusiasm and excitement, a sense of adventure and fun. Just like Horton, heading for Mount Nool, believing all is well with the world. Don't be fooled. There are Mother Kangaroos in our world just like there were in Nool. People who will mock what you believe, laugh at what you have heard, despise what you are trying to do, and rally others to help stop the foolishness that threatens their world, their sense of comfort, their normal, their rights, and sense of entitlement.

There are Vlads in our world, not with foreign accents, but with messages as slippery as the Vlad that Horton faced and hearts as intent on evil. There are many in our world who do not believe in Whos, who do not want Whos to be real, who do not want anything to change, whose lives and desires are best served by keeping things the same. They will try to stop you and many times you will feel you are alone, as if it's you against the world.

Don't give up—and here I want to digress from *Horton Hears A Who*. This is where the movie's message is incomplete. Horton was alone. Morton tried to be supportive, even rally some support for Horton, but in the face of Kangaroo's determined glare, he's "out of there." Not so in our world.

In the Biblical story, Elijah of old also hears a Who and stands up to the king, Ahab, and his scheming queen, Jezebel.[7] Jezebel threatens to kill him and Elijah "heads for the hills," hides in the wilderness, and begs God to let him die. (Not sure why he ran from Jezebel if he wanted to die, but so goes the story, and God letting him die could be a lot less painful than Jezebel's torture and execution.) God, however, won't give up on the cause and isn't done with Elijah. Among other things, God tells Elijah: "You are not alone. There are seven thousand people who, like you, have heard a Who, and are in on the Whoville project." When you hear a Who, realize you are not the only person who has heard a Who. There are many others and they are all keen on joining with you in saving the speck and saving the Whos for "a person's a person, no matter how small."

So, unplug your ears, tune in to what can be heard. It may mean pulling out the earphones connected to your iPod. Listen above the din of the world in which we live, and dare to hear a Who. Maybe it's something at school that needs doing and/or changing, a person who needs you to be their friend, bullies who need someone to stand in their way. Dare to hear a Who and commit yourself to doing something about it.

Maybe it's something in the community. A family that needs help. Racist jokes, attitudes, and emails that need someone to say, "Enough." An alternate reality and vision that need someone to speak for it and live it. A community project that could make a difference. Dare to hear a Who and commit yourself to doing something about it.

Maybe it's something in our world. Politicians who need to be held accountable. A government that needs a conscience. Violence that must be stopped. A playground that needs building.[8] Dare to hear a Who and commit yourself to doing something about it.

Maybe it's a story that needs telling, a picture that needs painting, a message that needs spreading. The message that peace is possible if only we will dare to believe it and imagine it.[9] The story of Palestinians whose land is being stolen, whose homes are being demolished, whose

---

7. To read Elijah's story, see 1 Kgs 19:1–18.

8. During Advent 2012, our church, where this sermon was preached, collected money to help Lajee Center, a children's drop-in center outside Aida Refugee camp in Bethlehem, buy land and build a playground.

9. Emmaus Mennonite Church, where this sermon was preached, had a billboard along Highway 4 south of Swift Current that read: "Imagine peace. It is possible." This example and the playground example were included to affirm the congregation in what it was already doing.

children are being imprisoned and even killed, whose rights are being denied, whose way of life is being destroyed.[10] The picture of life in many First Nations communities, people demoralized, children sniffing gasoline, teenagers doing drugs, adults giving up. The reports of poverty and hunger in Haiti and Somalia and many other parts of the world. Dare to hear a Who and commit yourself to telling the story and spreading the message.

There will be those who will laugh at you, oppose what you are trying to do, mock your idea and your message, and try to stop the cause. They haven't heard a Who, they don't want to hear a Who, they refuse to believe there could be Whos, and they will not put up with the possibility of Whos. Don't give up. Remember you are not alone and commit yourself to the cause:

> Mean what you say
> And say what you mean.
> Let this world know
> This person is faithful
> 100 percent.

Dare to hear a Who.

IS GOD A RACIST?

Informed by the movie: My Sister's Keeper

Isaiah 49:14–16; Ephesians 3:14–19

On December 26, 2004, the third strongest earthquake ever recorded shook the planet off the coast of Indonesia and resulted in a massive tsunami that hit fourteen countries and killed in excess of two hundred thirty thousand people in south Asia. There were people and preachers (as if preachers aren't people), people, including preachers, who suggested that the tsunami was God's punishment for sin and God's call to the West, especially the people of the United States and Canada, to repent, to change their lives, to turn back to God and be saved. Really? God would kill two hundred thirty thousand people in Asia so that Americans and

---

10. Rachelle Friesen, a member of Emmaus and our daughter, worked with MCC in Palestine, as a peace development worker. Hence, there is a special connection between the Palestinian cause and my heart, as well as the heart of our congregation.

Canadians might repent and be saved? Why wouldn't God have killed two hundred thirty thousand Americans and Canadians so Asians could repent and be saved? There's a fault line running past Vancouver and San Francisco. God could have given that fault line a good shaking, caused parts of Vancouver and San Francisco and parts in between to slide into the ocean and killed at least two hundred thirty thousand. Then all those Asians who were killed could have repented and been saved and all the rest of the Americans and Canadians. It might have had an even stronger impact on us surviving Westerners and we would have gone running for church, like many did early on after 9/11. We would have to conclude that the reason God did not do this is because God loved Westerners more than Asians and sacrificing Asians for the benefit of Westerners was no problem, or at least the negative press God would get from it and the pain endured by Asians was outweighed by the benefits—Westerners getting saved.

I have heard the same kind of thinking played out in smaller ways in communities in which I grew up. A person would die a sudden death—a twenty-year-old felled by an aneurysm, a couple of teenagers killed in a car accident—and it was concluded that this person or these persons had died and died so suddenly so that other young adults in the community might come, or come back, to God and change their lives. Sometimes the person who died was someone perceived to be a fine, committed young Christian and sacrificing him or her was okay because they were now in heaven. Sometimes the persons killed were clearly, in the minds of community members, rebellious and therefore unsaved, compounding the tragedy but also the impact: see what could happen to you if you don't get right with God? Now God had not only cut short the life of a young adult, but also ensured that the young adult would suffer the pains of damnation forever, all for the sake of those who might be saved as a result. Really? One would again have to conclude that God loved some more than others, for God had been willing to sacrifice some for the sake and welfare of others, when God could just as easily have killed the ones who survived so those who were killed could get saved. The purpose of the life and death of those killed was so that those who survived might benefit.

If God is a loving parent—the Biblical story makes that comparison again and again—then God is like the mother in the movie, *My Sister's Keeper*. In that story, based on Jodie Picoult's book by the same title—the book has a very different ending, raising even more questions—in the story, the Fitzgeralds have two children, a son, Jesse, and a daughter, Kate. When Kate is still a young child, the doctors diagnose her with leukemia. Her form of leukemia would be best treated, and her chances of both quality of life and longer life greatly enhanced, if there was someone who was a genetic match who could donate whatever it is that Kate needs, starting with stem cells that can grow into and replace the diseased cells in Kate's system. Stem cells come from umbilical cord blood. The best genetic match for donations is a perfectly matched sibling. So the best solution for Kate and her parents would be if Sara & Brian—the parents—were to have another baby, genetically engineered to be that perfect match. They do precisely that, through in vitro fertilization, and Anna is born, the perfect donor baby and child for Kate. Thus begins a long odyssey for Anna as she has to donate whatever Kate needs whenever Kate needs it—blood, cells, bone marrow, and ultimately, a kidney. It is when the kidney is needed that Anna engages a lawyer to sue her parents for medical emancipation.

The story raises a variety of ethical issues that we may want to pursue in Sunday school. For now, let's focus on Sara, the mom, and her love for her children. Does she love her daughters equally? Kate is a person in her own right, worthy of saving, worthy of whatever it takes to keep her alive. Anna is conceived for one purpose—to serve as a donor for Kate. Anna is raised for one purpose—to provide for Kate what Kate needs to overcome the devastations of leukemia. Anna is asked to potentially put her life on the line for one purpose—to save Kate's.

Let's watch a clip of a scene in the courtroom. Anna, as I said, hires a lawyer and sues her parents for medical emancipation. In the courtroom, Anna's lawyer has asked her mom a series of questions about all that Anna has endured since birth, all without her consent, sometimes with her held down as she screams—blood donations, bone marrow donations, and so on, sometimes involving several days of hospitalization. All of this to possibly save Kate's life.

Listen to the exchange between Sara, Anna's mom, and the lawyer:
(Movie clip: 1:15:27 to 1:17:30, 1:18:18 to 1:19:35)

Is this a true mother's love for her children? Is this the kind of love that God has for us if God's love for us is like the love of a mother for her child?

When we hear the Biblical story, watch the Biblical movie, as it were—probably two-thirds of that movie portrays this kind of God, a God who loves some of God's children more than others. Genesis 1 and

Ephesians 3 both tell us that all people—all people who have ever lived, live now wherever they might be living, and will ever live—all people are God's children. However, the Old Testament story is, from Genesis 12 to Malachi, the last of the twelve little guys, the last book in the Old Testament, the story of people who understand that God loves them more than others. God chose them—the story of Abraham—because God loved them more than others. God worked with Abraham, Isaac and Jacob because God loved them more than others. God saved them from starvation in Egypt and then wiped out the Egyptian army because God loved them more than the Egyptians. God helped them kill armies and nations in their way on the way to the Promised Land because God loved them more that the people getting killed. God directed them in and helped them with an ethnic cleansing of the land of Canaan, insisting on massacre time and again, because God loved these people and not the others. God centered all of history around these people, guided the ebb and flow of the nations because God loved these people and not the others, or if God loved the others, not as much as these chosen people and God was quite prepared to have others suffer, lose their land, even die, for the sake of these chosen, loved ones.

The movie sequel, not to *My Sister's Keeper*, but to the Old Testament movie which could aptly be titled, *My People's Keeper*—the sequel known as the New Testament—opens with the same understanding of God and God's love. God loves some of God's children more than others. Jesus grows up with this understanding of love and it shapes the beginnings of Jesus's ministry. Jesus thinks himself to have been sent to and for the Jews only. Though Jesus might not have been as crass as were the Jews of his day, thinking that Gentiles—all non-Jews—were created by God simply to fuel the fires of hell, Jesus did think himself to have been sent for the Jews.

But then something changed. There is a collection of stories in both Matthew's and Mark's versions of the Good News that tell of this transformation in Jesus's thinking, in slightly different ways, but with the three main stories assembled in the same way to make the point. Follow me in Matthew's version of Jesus's conversion.

In Matthew 10, the good News Storyteller tells us the story of Jesus's twelve disciples being sent out in ministry, in spreading the good news by proclaiming its core message: "The kingdom of heaven has come near,"[11]

---

11. Matt 10:7. NRSV.

and demonstrating its reality by curing the sick and raising the dead. As Jesus sends them out, he is clear: "Go nowhere among the Gentiles, and enter no town of the Samaritans, but go rather to the lost sheep of the house of Israel."[12] Jews only are loved by God.

In chapter 14, Matthew tells us the story of the feeding of the five thousand. All the people fed are Jews and the symbols in the story—five loaves, two fish, twelve baskets—are all Jewish symbols. Jesus has come to give life to the Jews.

The pivotal story follows in chapter 15. A Canaanite woman, a non-Jew, a descendant of the people who were the enemies of the Jews in the Old Testament story, a descendant of those who were to be ethnically cleansed, comes to Jesus and begs for help. Jesus first ignores her and then, when she won't leave, tells her, "I was sent only to the lost sheep of the house of Israel."[13] Jews only are loved by God. However, the woman refuses to accept Jesus's answer as the final word and has a rebuttal for Jesus's proverb that Jesus thought would shut her up. Jesus's response: "Woman, great is your faith! Let it be done for you as you wish."[14]

That experience seems to have been transformative for Jesus. Certainly Matthew believed it had been, and tells the story in that way. Soon after that experience in Matthew's (and Mark's) version, in chapter 16, there is another feeding story, this time of the four thousand. This feeding happens in Gentile territory and involves Jesus feeding Gentiles. All the symbols—seven loaves, seven baskets, and four thousand instead of five thousand—are Gentile, Greek, and Roman, pagan symbols. Jesus is now feeding Gentiles, non-Jews, for Jesus realizes that he was not sent only to and for the house of Israel—Jews—but to and for all people, for as one of our favorite hymns says and we love to sing, God loves everyone in the world.[15] Jesus's final words in Matthew direct the disciples to go to "all nations."[16]

It's the conclusion, I think, that Sarah also comes to in the movie. She loves both daughters equally. She also realizes that letting Kate die may be as much an act of love as her commitment to give her the best medical care possible. She realizes, I think, that love is larger than life

12. Matt 10:5–6. NRSV.
13. Matt 15:24. NRSV.
14. Matt 15:28. NRSV.
15. Mukungu, "God loves." In Slough, ed., *Hymnal*, #397. One of our congregation's favourite hymns.
16. Matt 28:19. NRSV.

and death, sickness and health. Love is embracing all that happens in life and living the life that is and dying the death that comes, in the context of love, love of all children equally.

The early church struggled with the same issue for turning back two thousand years of tradition and changing a faith that had developed over twenty centuries is not easily done. But they did it. They did it following the example of Peter, who had a vision that brought him to the profound realization that "[w]hat God has made clean, you must not call profane."[17] In obedience to that vision, he visited Cornelius, the Gentile, non-Jew centurion. During that visit, Peter saw Cornelius, his family and his servants gifted with the same gift of the Holy Spirit that the Jewish Christians had received. Peter's response was: "I truly understand that God shows no partiality."[18] And later, in reporting to the church, Peter says, "Who was I that I could hinder God?"[19] Who indeed? God is not a racist. God loves all equally.

Under the leadership of Paul—whose missionary activity started with the Jews but then, like Jesus's, spread to non-Jews—the church continued the struggle, conversion, and transformation, until it could say with Paul, in Ephesians 2: "[Jesus Christ] reconcile[d] two groups to God in one body."[20] And then add, in chapter 3, in the piece that Sabrina read for us: "[God], the Father, from whom every family in heaven and earth takes its name."[21] All people are God's children. And when the Good News Storyteller, John, then tells us that "God so loved the world," we have three of the early church's foremost leaders conclude that God is not a racist, that God loves everyone in the entire diversity of humanity, and loves them all equally.

God loves all people equally:

- The Asians who died in the tsunami as much as the Canadians who survived, so I suspect the tsunami was not God's doing.
- The teenager who died in a fiery car crash after driving drunk as much as the teenager who was at a prayer meeting that night. So I suspect God had nothing to do with the accident.

17. Acts 10:15. NRSV.
18. Acts 10:34. NRSV.
19. Acts 11:17. NRSV.
20. Eph 2:16. NRSV. This snippet must be read in the larger context of Eph 2:11–22.
21. Eph 3:14–15. NRSV.

- The Taliban fighter as much as the Canadian soldier, so I am not convinced God fought on the side of NATO in Afghanistan.
- The Muslim Imam as much as the Christian evangelist.
- Your son or daughter as much as mine, you as much as me, Hindus as much as Christians, First Nations people as much as people of European descent.

So, what might we conclude from all this? A few things:

1. God is not a racist, never has been—no matter what the Old Testament Hebrews thought, and never will be.
2. God did not give Palestine to the Israelis in 1947. The UN did—some of it—and the Israelis took more in 1948 and even more in 1967. None of it was God's will, nor does God have any higher commitment to an Israeli state than a Palestinian state. God's will, on every piece of land that is on this globe, is for a multiethnic, multiracial community that lives in peace, where all respect each other equally and all equally experience God's love.
3. God does not wish for some to have too much while others do not have enough. God has given us what we have and blessed us materially so that we might share, not so that we might build a better life for ourselves. God wishes the material blessings of this earth to be experienced by all equally.
4. All people, by whatever path they get there, are welcomed into a relationship with God.

God loves everyone, no matter who they are. Amen.

Chapter 9

Advent

It seems to me that there is no season that offers as much possibility and opportunity for creative preaching as does Advent and Christmas. I used to tell myself that on Christmas Eve and Christmas Day, the bottom line was that we dare not bore the people, that they have some nugget or inspiration or meaning of Christmas to take home with them, though I hoped for it, was always secondary to "Do not bore the people!" When it came to creative preaching the rest of the year, there were times I might not make it to first base, but Christmas I had to hit at least a triple. More on that in the next chapter.

Though I did not apply as much pressure during Advent, in terms of creative preaching, it still seemed to me to be important for it was the season of creativity and imagination. And, like a few other worship times—Good Friday, Easter, and Pentecost—the story was always the same one. During Advent at least, if one followed the lectionary—the set of texts was the same not every year, but every third year.

I try every year to set up the four Advent sermons as a series, each sermon some further unfolding of the theme for that year. I try to make the themes different every year, even though the underlying theme is always Advent and the texts repeat every three years. I am also more inclined than some of my colleagues might be, especially my Lutheran friends, to preach the Old Testament texts rather than the Gospel text. That does not mean that the Gospel and even the Epistle don't make a cameo appearance, but all of those texts are post-Christmas stories and texts. Advent, as we know, is pre-Christmas.

I recall that while I was at Zion Mennonite Church, we would sometimes have some pretty elaborate displays, inspired by materials in *Leader Magazine*, published by MennoMedia. The suggestions for both displays and worship materials each year were developed by a different Area Church in the larger Mennonite Church USA and Mennonite Church Canada denominations. I recall a mountain with an actual spring bubbling up. (One complaint—those who could hear the bubbling spring had a hard time making it through worship without a bathroom break.) Another year we had an old fashioned window through which we could see the scene on the other side. Each Sunday we filled one pane until the entire scene was visible. During that time I also had more help to make these kinds of displays possible. One year, for whatever reason, we chose not to follow the lectionary and, instead, worked on symbols of Christmas—angels and stars for sure. One may have been Santa Claus. Not sure about the fourth one—maybe snowflakes. Whatever the four, people were invited to bring Christmas tree ornaments for that symbol each week and the sermon used that symbol as the center point with which to preach Advent and Christmas. The ornaments became the congregation's collection and we used them every year.

Rather than give you one or two sermons as examples, I decided to share with you some of the themes I followed and what I might have done to add to the creativity.

Year A: In 2013, I focused on the theme of waiting, waiting for something in a world that is a real mess.

Sunday 1: I set up a comfortable chair on stage and had piles and boxes of books all around. Musing on the state of the world, I recalled an ancient book that might speak to our situation. I also played a piece of music on a CD player (some of us still remember what those are) with the Singer singing a song about praying for the peace of Jerusalem.[1]

Sunday 2: It was the same scene. Further musings on the state of the world. And then: "Not sure my praying changed anything. And yet that ancient book keeps insisting it can be and will be different—after finding it last week, I thought I should maybe keep the dust off it by reading it a little more often. I read some amazing stuff."

Sunday 3: I wrote a script for three people and we sat around a game board—Clue—and talked about finding clues that suggested a new world was breaking in.

---

1. Hewitt, "Ten Measures of Beauty" *Journeys*, track 1.

Year B: In 2014 I decided to use two things to carry the theme. One was the song, "It's beginning to look a lot like Christmas." We played a version of it each Sunday, just before the sermon. The other was the opening of the story in C.S. Lewis's *The Lion, the Witch, and the Wardrobe*. It lends itself easily to progression, so that you can tell a little more of it each Sunday:

- always winter and never Christmas
- sons of Adam and daughters of Eve show up
- snow starts melting and in the distance, the sound of bells and what might be
- Father Christmas and his sleigh

I also talked about the Old Testament prophets as folk singers and their poetry as folk songs, to help the people think about them in a different way. This is something I increasingly do when I talk about Ancient Poetry (Psalms) and the Ancient Folk Singers and Protest Singers (prophets).

Year C: In 2009, I began each sermon in the same way. The headlines and news reports can sometimes be overwhelming:

- WHO upgrades situation to pandemic
- 2 more H1N1 deaths reported
- 6.8 magnitude earthquake hits Samoa
- Philippine massacre death toll reaches 57
- 23 people killed in Kandahar suicide attack
- Latest jobless figures hit double digits
- Famine threatens millions in Horn of Africa
- One billion have inadequate nutrition
- By 2025 AIDS toll could hit 18 million in China, 31 million in India & 100 million in Africa
- Global warming may wipe out entire nations
- Ozone depletion means increase in skin cancer rates

Need I go on? The bad news in our world seems inevitable and relentless, at home across North America and around the world. The details may change from year to year and the specifics from country to country, but the badness remains. We live in a world where hope can sometimes be in short supply, unless you stick to football, *Dancing with the Stars*, and *Canadian Idol*. In football, there's always one more game on the horizon, and if there isn't, there's next year. In *Dancing with the Stars*, the glitz and glamour suggest nothing is wrong with our world. On *Canadian Idol*, hope springs eternal and who knows where they might discover another Susan Boyle. But in real life, well, real life is real life, and only fairy tales have guaranteed happy endings.

From there, each Sunday in a different way, I worked on how our Advent texts spoke hope to us in this kind of world.

And also: In 2012, I used a few things—at least four—to carry the theme. Each Sunday, just before the sermon, we played a little more of Jim Bryant's song, *Something's Coming*. My nephew's wife had just posted some pieces on Facebook about being pregnant, how much she liked it, and how much she anticipated the birth. So I used the theme of pregnancy, quoting some of her stuff. At Emmaus we normally celebrated Communion about four times a year. This year, we had the bread and wine each Sunday after the sermon, as a symbol of God feeding us in our world as we journey and anticipate. During Communion, we played Steve Bell singing *Keening for the Dawn*. With his permission, we printed the words to the song in the bulletin each Sunday.

I am hoping that the above ideas will get your imagination going or help it go further than it's gone before. If you want more details about some of the sermons, I would be happy to share them. (jumpintothestory@sasktel.net) However, as I have said other places, this is not about you preaching my sermons but about you being inspired to be ever more creative and imaginative in your preaching.

Chapter 10

CHRISTMAS #1

CHRISTMAS COMES AROUND ONCE a year (duh!). When I was a kid, it couldn't come fast enough. Now I'm often surprised how quickly it's here again. The opening of the CFL[1] season seems to drag its feet a lot more. Don't get me wrong, I LOVE Christmas. You may recall the Tim Allen movie, *The Santa Clause* (and its sequels). In it, Scott Calvin, played by Tim Allen, begins undergoing rapid change in late fall so that by Christmas Eve he has the girth and beard needed to be Santa Claus. Well, that's me, except I don't turn into Santa Claus. Around the first of December, I start undergoing changes so that by Christmas morning I am a ten-year-old boy. Woohoo. Let me at those gifts!

But this is about preaching, not Ray and the Christmas tree. After a number of years, you may find yourself wondering what to preach. As I said in my introduction, it's never okay to be boring, and doubly not okay in summer. It is simply completely unacceptable to be boring at Christmas. It seems to me that where other times you may have to work hard not to be boring, Christmas works the other way round. There is no season, liturgical or otherwise, that creates more opportunity for imagination and creativity. We may have only two versions of the story and the two may seem almost incompatible. But hey, that has never stopped us from merging them into one wonderful story and everybody shows up

---

1. Canadian Football League, Canada's premier professional football league. The season runs from late June to late November. I am a committed and passionate (my wife might add "crazy") fan of the league and the Saskatchewan Roughriders in particular.

in the nativity scene the same night. That already takes imagination and things just get better from there.

When Sylvia and I were pastors at Zion Mennonite Church in Swift Current, we had a candlelight service every Christmas Eve. Occasionally, the worship committee struggled to find appropriate material for the evening. As a result, I offered to write a readers theater each year. It had to have five parts each year—the script (okay, obviously), places for the Christmas choir to sing, a grandparent reading the Luke 2 Christmas story, a nativity scene around which the children could gather each year, and people in the congregation holding lit candles while singing Christmas carols. (This did not necessarily cheer the heart of our local fire chief.)

What follows is one of those scripts. (I have four others.) This one was later offered online and twelve to fifteen worshiping communities around the United States and Canada adapted it for use at their Christmas Eve or Christmas Day service. As it is here, it is my adaptation for a Christmas Day service at Emmaus Mennonite Church, without choir, nativity scene, or candlelight carol singing at the end. The grandparent is Reader 5.

When we included a nativity scene, the manger was in place throughout the service. After Reader 2 says, "Watch, and listen," the lights dimmed and the nativity scene characters took their places. Then, while a soloist coming in from the back sang "O Come, All Ye Children",[2] the children were invited to follow him/her to the nativity scene and gather around it. Once in place, the congregation sang and the grandparent read the story.

IS IT REALLY POSSIBLE?

(That there is a story so powerful it can stop war?)

(A table with a stool is nice to have somewhere on stage, for Isaiah [see below]. The table should have an open scroll and a quill with an ink pot.)
Congregation: "O come all ye faithful"[3]
Welcome
Congregation: "Veiled in darkness Judah lay"[4]

---

2. Von Schmid, "O Come." In Oyer et al, ed., *Mennonite Hymnal*, #470.

3. Wade, "O come." In Slough, ed., *Hymnal*, #212.

4. Rights, "Veiled." In Oyer et al, ed., *Mennonite Hymnal*, #114. This is a less commonly known Advent hymn, but it was well-liked in our congregation.

Solo: "Christmas in the Trenches"[5]

READER 1: Do you think that's really possible?

READER 2: Is what really possible?

READER 1: Do you think it is possible that there is a story so powerful that it could stop war?

READER 3: Probably not.

READER 2: Why not?

READER 3: Then people would be telling it and war would be no more.

READER 1: Think of the difference it would make, if there was really such a story, and if we could tell it!

READER 2: The difference it would make for the children of Iraq.

READER 1: The difference it would make for the mothers of Baghdad.

READER 2: For the people of Darfur and Congo and Afghanistan.

READER 1: The children of Gaza and Ramallah and Jerusalem.

READER 2: For the people and churches and pastors of Columbia.

READER 1: If there was really such a story, so powerful, that it could stop war.

READER 2: There used to be someone who believed in such a story, or at least that such a story could be.

READER 1: There did? Who?

READER 2: He lived in Jerusalem.

READER 3: Jerusalem could use such a story.

READER 2: He was a prophet.

READER 3: What's a prophet?

READER 2: A prophet is someone who sees all that is, but sees more.

READER 3: How can you see more than what is? To paraphrase our former prime minister, what is is and if it is it is, and that is it.[6] There is only what is.

READER 2: Are you sure? Maybe you can just see only what is. Maybe there is more than what is, if you only had the right eyes.

READER 1: Could you two stop all this "is" stuff and get back to this story that might be?

---

5. McCutcheon, "Christmas," *Winter Solstice*. My favorite singer who does a cover of this song, and whose concert first planted the seed for this script in my imagination, is John McDermott.

6. During the lead up to the war in Iraq, former Canadian Prime Minister Jean Chretien was asked what would constitute proof of the existence of weapons of mass destruction. His reply was: "A proof is a proof. What kind of a proof? It's a proof. A proof is a proof. And when you have a good proof, it's because it's proven." (You can't make this stuff up!)

READER 2: Prophets saw all that is. This prophet's name was Isaiah.

READER 3: Do you mean Is-aiah?

READER 2: The prophet's name was Isaiah, and he had seen war. He wrote about war.

ISAIAH: *(enters in costume with a staff from either left or right depending on your setup and moves to center stage)* "The city writhes in chaos; every home is locked to keep out looters. Mobs gather in the streets; crying out for wine. Joy has reached its lowest ebb. Gladness has been banished from the land. The city is left in ruins, with its gates battered down. Throughout the earth the story is the same."[7] *(falls to his knees, or at least one knee with hand on his staff, bows head and is praying.)*

READER 1: Sounds like Baghdad. The news reports I saw just last night.

READER 2: Or Jerusalem, or Gaza, or Congo, or . . .

READER 3: Okay, okay, we know war. You don't have to tell us. But that doesn't mean there is a story so powerful it could stop this war. Maybe it means there isn't such a story.

READER 2: War isn't all Isaiah saw. Isaiah looked at the war, saw the war, felt the war, and then he listened to something deep inside him, and heard another story, a story of "not war."

ISAIAH: *(rises, a look of hope on his face)* "In days to come the mountain of the LORD's house shall be established as the highest of the mountains, and shall be raised above the hills; all the nations shall stream to it. Many peoples shall come and say, 'Come, let us go up to the mountain of the Lord, to the house of the God of Jacob; that [God] may teach us [the Lord's] ways and that we may walk in [the Lord's] paths.' For out of Zion shall go forth instruction, and the word of the Lord from Jerusalem. [The Almighty] shall judge between the nations, and shall arbitrate for many peoples; they shall beat their swords into plowshares, and their spears into pruning hooks; nation shall not lift up sword against nation, neither shall they learn war anymore."[8]

READER 1: Now that's "not war!" That's powerful!

READER 3: Yeah, right. Anyone can dream.

READER 1: And he really believed this?

READER 2: He believed that, and more.

---

7. Isa 24:10–13, NLT.

8. Isa 2:2–4, NRSV.

ISAIAH:
"A shoot shall come out from the stump of Jesse,
And a branch shall grow out of his roots.
The spirit of the Lord shall rest on him . . .
Righteousness shall be the belt around his waist,
And faithfulness the belt around his loins.
The wolf shall live with the lamb,
The leopard shall lie down with the kid,
The calf and the lion and the fatling together,
And a little child shall lead them.
The cow and the bear shall graze,
Their young shall lie down together;
And the lion shall eat straw like the ox.
The nursing child shall play over the hole of the asp,
And the weaned child shall put its hand on the adder's den.
They will not hurt or destroy on all my holy mountain;
For the earth will be full of the knowledge of the Lord as the waters cover the sea."[9]

(moves to sit at table and alternates between writing, being in deep thought and praying)
READER 1: If that could really be true? Imagine!
READER 3: Yeah, and if pigs could fly.
READER 1: Did the people believe the dream, that it was more than a dream, that the prophet was seeing things that could be, that *would* be?
READER 2: They hoped because they were tired of war. They longed for peace.
Congregation: "O come, O come Emmanuel"[10]
READER 1: How was this going to happen? What kind of story would it take?
READER 2: The prophet Isaiah kept listening and looking and writing. Then it came to him.
ISAIAH: *(gets up and moves to center stage)*

---

9. Isa 11:1–9 (excerpts), NRSV.
10. Neale, trans., "O come," In Slough, ed., *Hymnal*, #172.

"Look, the young woman is with child and shall bear a son, and shall name him Immanuel."[11]

"For a child has been born for us, A son given to us; Authority rests upon his shoulders, and he is named Wonderful Counselor, Mighty God, Everlasting Father, Prince of Peace. His authority shall grow continually, and there shall be endless peace."[12] *(Exits)*

READER 1: Endless peace! Sounds wonderful, too good to be true.

READER 3: If it sounds too good to be true, it probably is.

READER 1: Endless peace! Amazing! And all this from the story of a baby.

Congregation: "To us a Child of hope is born"[13]

READER 1: But when and where can we find such a story?

READER 2: A lot of people wondered when and people wondered where.

READER 3: Yada, yada, yada. That's all fine and good, some old guy dreaming dreams and writing them down and people wondering when and where. I've had dreams of a better life. I've done lots of wondering. That does not make me some special prophet and it sure as shootin' doesn't mean there is a story anywhere that could stop war. Dreaming and wondering isn't going to help the people of Iraq, and the United States, and Afghanistan, and Northern Ireland, and Columbia. If there is such a story, we need to find the story. But before I go looking for it, you better convince me that I am looking for something real, something that is. I don't have time for some wild goose chase.

READER 2: Do you think we should tell him?

READER 1: Maybe we should.

READER 3: Tell me what?

READER 2: I'm not sure.

READER 3: Tell me what?

READER 1: It might change his mind.

READER 3: Tell me what?

READER 2: Okay, you tell him.

READER 3: Finally.

READER 1: There are people who already know the story, and the story made a difference.

11. Isa 7:14, NRSV.
12. Isa 9:6 & 7, NRSV.
13. Morison, "To us a Child." In Slough, ed., *Hymnal*, #189.

READER 3: There are? Yeah, I'm sure! Some more of your dreamers, no doubt.

READER 2: They did dream, but they were able to dream because they knew the story, they knew the story to be true, and they felt the power in the story.

READER 1: In 1963, a man, a black man who had been beaten up, attacked by dogs, and thrown in prison simply because of the color of his skin, stood before thousands and made a speech:

READER 4:

> I have a dream that one day on the red hills of Georgia the sons of former slaves and the sons of former slave owners will be able to sit down together at a table of brotherhood ... I have a dream that my four children will one day live in a nation where they will not be judged by the color of their skin but by the content of their character. I have a *dream* today ... I have a dream that one day every valley shall be exalted, and every hill and mountain shall be made low, the rough places will be made plain, and the crooked places will be made straight, "and the glory of the Lord shall be revealed, and all flesh shall see it together." This is our hope ... [14]

READER 1: Martin Luther King Jr. believed the story and today much of what he dreamed for is true.

READER 2: Five-year-old Larissa Friesen[15] of Winnipeg, Manitoba knew the story.

READER 4: When her friends in the neighborhood played war with the help of toy G.I. Joes and tanks, she decided that because of the story she could not participate in killing, even play-killing. So she decided she would cook the meals for the soldiers. It was a form of alternative service that made sense to her in her setting, allowing her to play with her friends and stay true to the story.

READER 1: Andrea Kraybill, a Grade 8 student in Elkhart, Indiana, knew the story.

READER 4: Andrea was asked to be the narrator in her school's reenactment of the Battle of Lexington and Concord, complete with Minuteman costume and wooden rifle. She took the role but negotiated a different costume—a lady of the era. During the battle itself, she played the part of a woman crying because her

---

14. King Jr., "I Have a Dream," para. 18, 20–21, 24–25.

15. Larissa gave me permission to use this story.

husband died in battle. Andrea knew the story and witnessed by her actions to the difference the story can make.[16]

READER 2: People in Columbia believe the story.

READER 4: On October 23, 2003, Pedro and Juan met for the first time at the Iglesia Menonita Villas de Granada. This was Juan's first Sunday in church. Six weeks earlier, had Pedro and Juan met, they would have killed each other on the spot. Pedro and Juan were sworn enemies in the civil war in Columbia. Pedro had been a commander in the paramilitary, Juan a commander for the guerillas fighting to overthrow the government. Now, this Sunday, they were here, together, brothers. Together their voices rang out in song:

> Christ breaks the chains
> You have freed me from sin and death
> I don't know how I shall live without my Jesus.[17]

READER 3: And all because they heard this story you say exists?

READER 1: Because of that story, enemies were now men who loved each other.

READER 3: I want to hear that story. Please tell me the story, a story so powerful that it stops war, overcomes racism, and brings peace.

READER 2: Watch, and listen.

Songs: "O Beautiful Star of Bethlehem"[18]
"O little town of Bethlehem"[19]

READER 5: Luke 2:1–20

Congregation: "Joy to the world"[20]

Silence

READER 1: Well, aren't you going to say something?

---

16. Thanks to Nelson Kraybill, one-time president of Anabaptist Mennonite Biblical Seminary and more recently president of Mennonite World Conference, for this story about his daughter. I have his permission to use this story.

17. Thanks to Ferdinand Funk, then-pastor at Springfield Heights Mennonite Church, Winnipeg, MB, for the use of this story. He was a member of a delegation that was in that church that morning and met with Pedro and Juan. Names of the Colombians have been changed to protect the two men and their families. I am using it with Ferdinand's permission.

18. Pace et al., "Beautiful Star." At Hymnary.org.

19. Brooks, "Little town." In Slough, ed., *Hymnal*, #191.

20. Watts, "Joy." In Slough, ed., *Hymnal*, #318.

READER 3: What can I say? What a story! There really is such a story. There really is a story so powerful that it can stop war.

READER 2: Because of this story, during World War 1, war stopped for a day on the battle fields of France and the Germans and the English sang Christmas carols, first by turn, then they sang one together, each side singing in its own language.

Duet: (*one in English, one in German*) "Silent Night"[21] (vs. 1)

Congregation: (*vs. 2 and 3*)

READER 2: Because of this story, war turned into a soccer game and the killing fields of France hosted a wonderful Christmas party.

READER 1: Because of this story, sons and daughters of former slaves and sons and daughters of former slave owners do now sit together at the same table and hold hands in joyful worship.

READER 2: Because of this story, Pedro and Juan in Columbia have put down their guns, live with their families, and worship together as brothers. Because of the story, the war in Columbia is smaller.

READER 1: Because of this story, a story so powerful that it can stop war.

READER 3: If it has done it once, twice, three times, it can do it again, this story of a baby born. What can we do to help this story stop war today?

READER 2: We can tell the story.

READER 3: Tell the story?

READER 2: We can tell the story to everyone we meet, wherever we go, whenever we have the chance.

READER 1: We can tell the story to our children and grandchildren, to our friends and neighbors, to everyone we meet.

READER 3: We can tell the story, and every time the story is told, the chance of peace, an end to war and violence, grows brighter and bigger.

READER 1, READER 2 & READER 3: We can tell the story.

Congregation: "Go tell it on the mountain"[22]

READER 1, READER 2 & 3: And live the story!

READER 1: At home.

READER 2: At school.

READER 3: At work.

READER 1 & 2: Tell the story and live the story!

---

21. Mohr, "Silent Night." In Slough, ed., *Hymnal*, #193.
22. Work Jr., "Go Tell It." In *African American*, #202.

READER 3: And watch peace come to our world, one storytelling at a time.
Congregation: "It came upon a midnight clear"[23]
Benediction

---

23. Sears, "It came." In Slough, ed., *Hymnal*, #195.

Chapter 11

Christmas #2

In some ways, this piece could be part of "Chapter 12: Christmas in the Community." I originally began writing it in 2016 in case I needed something somewhat less "religious" for use in the community. The goal was, as in chapter 12, to take the Christian Christmas story and make it relevant to all people, without expecting them to be or become Christian. I started in 2016 because the idea came to me in 2016. I did not need the piece that year. The next year I decided to finish it.

Like stories have a tendency to do, this one pulled me along and by the time it was done, it was more than three thousand eight hundred words. That is too long for a sermon or community presentation. I prefer my sermons to run two thousand two hundred to two thousand four hundred words, with occasional ones going to two thousand seven hundred. However, it seemed too good a story not to use. So I decided to break up the presentation with congregational songs so people would not have to listen to a storyteller for quite such a long stretch of time without a break. I used it at the Emmaus Mennonite Church Christmas Day worship time that year.

A SWIFT CURRENT CHRISTMAS

(No matter what your faith or no faith at all)
(But you will need imagination, the foundation of all faith)

Inspired by our three most famous storytellers:
Matthew, Luke, and Charles[1]

The moment Jose (his friends all called him Joe) walked in the door that Friday night, Maria knew something was wrong. What now? Hadn't they had enough? The raging fire that burnt through Fort McMurray that had them all fleeing last summer?[2] Sure, their house had been spared, but Joe missed days of work, and some of their friends had not been so lucky. Then the uncertainty of start up after the fire and the uncertainty caused by dropping oil prices and what it was doing to the equity in their home. She had lost her job a month ago, but given the nature of Joe's work, his job would be secure. But now something else had gone wrong! What could it be?

"I got my two-week notice today," Joe said. "Two weeks of work and I'm done, along with a bunch of other guys."

"Oh, no!" was all Maria could manage as she fell into Joe's hug and started to cry.

Both toyed with their food at supper. They tried talking, but what could they say? Two weeks and they would be out of work and without a paycheck. A mortgage on the house. Payments on the truck. They had to eat and pay utility bills. What would they do?

As supper finished, Joe's cellphone dinged. Joe checked his text messages and read the newest one.

"It's from Zack," he said. "He and Liz want to have breakfast tomorrow." When Maria raised her eyebrows in question, he added, "Yeah, Zack also lost his job."

Zack and Liz were their closest friends. The fact that Zack and Liz were Muslim (they had changed their names when they moved to Ft. Mac so no one would guess they were Muslim and they trusted in the forgiveness of Allah the Merciful when it came to head scarves), the fact

---

1. Matt 2, Luke 2, and Charles Dickens, *A Christmas Carol*.

2. Fort McMurray (Ft. Mac) is the city of close to ninety thousand people that services the extraction operations in the Alberta tar sands. In May 2016, a wildfire necessitated the evacuation of the entire city and the shutdown of the tar sands plants. Approximately two thousand four hundred structures were destroyed.

that they were Muslim and that Joe and Maria were Mennonite did not matter. Friendship, a deep friendship by now, overcame any barriers religion might raise.

The next morning, the four of them sat over breakfast at their favorite diner and talked. What would they do? Where could they go? Suddenly all four cellphones dinged, indicating a text message. They checked and realized they had all received the same message: "Go to Swift Current. There is work in Swift Current."

No one recognized the source of the texts. They looked at each other, perplexed. Where had this come from? Who was texting them?

Zack was the first to speak. "I have heard the rumor and I know a bunch of guys are thinking of going. Maybe, if we hurry, we can get there and get work quickly. Apparently they are building a new gas-fired electric plant and there is work in construction and in the service industries. Maybe we can all land jobs."

"Sure," said Maria. "What do we have to lose?"

For a moment, all four looked at each other, and then started making plans. Zack, who had a company truck, would have to give it up. Maria's car was an old beater and they would just leave it with neighbors who were looking for a second car. They owed as much on their houses as they were worth. They would simply turn in the keys. With Joe's truck, they would have a way to Swift Current and a little bit of cash until they got jobs. Wolf Energy had said they would be happy to give them pay in lieu of notice. On Monday, Zack and Joe would pick up their checks. Hopefully it would be enough to tide them over until they got work in Swift Current.

Late Wednesday, they pulled into Swift Current. They were all hungry, but decided they should first get motel rooms. They stayed on the highway and the other three watched the motel/hotel signs as Joe drove. Maria felt a tightening in her chest as sign after sign read "No Vacancy." From the K Motel on the western edge to the Comfort Inn on the eastern edge, all signs said "No Vacancy."

"Let's try in town," Zack suggested. "Those ones will probably have lots of room."

They tried. Best Western's sign had the same news, so they headed further downtown. Seeing the Shamrock Hotel (the Irish? In Swift Current?), they decided to try it. There was no sign out front, so Zack offered to go inside and check. He came out and his face said it all. The Shamrock was full as well. What with travelers and job hunters in town, there wasn't a room available anywhere.

"Let's try the Rockin' J," Liz suggested. "The worst that can happen is that they are also full." No one wanted to think about what that would mean—sleeping in the truck in the minus twenty cold. Zack walked into the bar and asked if there were any rooms available.

"Sorry," the manager/bar tender said. "We haven't rented rooms in years."

"Look," replied Zack. "We are desperate. We need someplace warm for the night. Forget the dust and mold, or sheets. We have our own sleeping bags. Just let us sleep in one of your rooms. We'll even buy a case of beer and we promise not to tell anyone."

About to say "No," the manager changed his mind. It was cold outside. He knew there would be no rooms anywhere. This guy did look desperate. What could it hurt to sell them a case of beer and let them sleep in one of the upstairs rooms? They would be gone before any inspector of any kind would hear about this. He could always tell the inspector the four had snuck in when he wasn't looking and he had told them to leave when he found them the next morning. Sometimes helping desperate people was more important than rules.

"Okay," the manager said. "You have a deal."

Doing the best they could with the dust and garbage, they chose adjoining rooms, threw down their sleeping bags, and then, finding four chairs that weren't broken, they gathered in Joe's and Maria's room to sip beer and talk. No one felt like sleeping and why should they? There wasn't a whole lot waiting for them the next morning, except job hunting, and right now even that seemed too much to imagine.

Inevitably, their conversation circled around to what they had been talking about a lot lately. Given their current experience, the topic was all the more real and pressing—the pain and unfairness that seemed to control the world. Was this—they looked around the room—and what was happening in Syria and inequities in economic wellbeing or lack thereof, and refugees and genocide in south Sudan, and even worse poverty in Yemen, and racism, and religious bigotry, and . . . The list never seemed to end. Was all that and more really all there was in the world? Was there no other way? Would things simply continue to spiral out of control until Iran or North Korea or Russia, or the United States, for that matter, dropped the first bomb in arrogant self-righteousness and the whole world turned to nuclear waste?

Tired! Discouraged! In the dumps, for sure! Despairing! Hope but a distant memory! Good thing they didn't have any kids! No one should bring kids into this kind of world!

And then suddenly, all four cellphones turned on at once and bright Light came from each until the entire room was filled with it.

"What you see is not all there is. What has been is not all there will be." It was a Voice unlike any they had ever heard before. They weren't sure whether to be afraid, run and hide, laugh it off, or take it seriously. "The dream of the universe," it continued, "the dream of the universe is for peace, justice, enough for all and nobody with too much."

Yeah, right! Joe thought, but he did not dare say it for by now he had realized that this Light and Voice was coming through on FaceTime and where there was a Voice, there might also be an Ear.

"What was does not have to be. What really is may be stronger than what seems to be. Tonight is the beginning of something that has not happened in a long, long time. Okay, some in bits and pieces, but starting tonight, here in Swift Current, in this room with the four of you, something will start, if you agree to join up, that will not stop until it has entered every corner of the world, circled the globe, east, west, and north, south. Peace. Justice. Love, with enough for all and no one with too much. Are you in?"

"Are we in?" they stammered, almost in unison. "Are we in?"

"Is there an echo in this room? Yes, are you in? Is that so hard? You know, in and out? With the program or not with the program? Are you in?"

Joe found his voice first. "Can we have some time to think about this?" he asked. "Consult with my wife? With my friends here? Talk about it?"

"You've talked about this for months," the Voice said. "But, I suppose. Talk some more. You've got two hours."

"Two hours?" This time it was Zack and Jose together. "Two hours? With no more info? We don't even know if you are real or what you are or anything. What will we be expected to do?"

"It won't be rocket science. You can do it, or I wouldn't be asking you. I'll give you the details once you tell me if you're in. No sense wasting my breath if you are going to say no. Two hours."

"Okay," all four said. "Two hours." And with that, the Light was gone and the room was back to its dreary, dusty, musty, smelly, dark self. The two couples looked at each other, no one sure what to say next.

Song: "Lo, a gleam from yonder heaven"[3] (vs. 1 and 2)

Meanwhile, two blocks away at the local Tim Hortons, the night staff stood around, talking. All the cleaning had been done, coffee was fresh, and there were more than enough donuts in case a customer wandered in. With the boss gone and no customers, the women who worked the counter and drive-through night after night slipped into their native language, what they had first spoken in the Philippines and what still came most naturally. And, like many other nights—and without knowing the conversation at the Rockin J—they soon were discussing life in the Philippines—drug cartels, dictatorships, violence, poverty, minimum wages, and working conditions.

Suddenly—seems things tended to happen suddenly all over the place—suddenly music filled the air, the best, liveliest, foot-stompingest, hip-swingingest, heart-grabbing music they had ever heard. Without conscious thought, their feet were dancing already. The light on the customer side of the counter turned brighter, brighter than they had ever seen. It seemed to come from the screens advertising donuts and muffins and coffee and specials. One of the waitresses ran to check.

"Come guys, quick!" she yelled to the others. "Hurry!"

The others joined her and looked at the screens. Their mouths dropped open. Now their feet were no longer dancing with joy; their knees were shaking with fright. Given their Catholic tradition, they dropped to their knees, crossed themselves, and began praying "Hail Marys," as fast and furiously as they could.

Then a Voice—we would have recognized it as the one from the Rockin' J—a Voice spoke, the kindest, safest Voice ever, yet it spoke with an authority that could not be denied.

"Don't be afraid," it said.

"Yeah, right. Don't be afraid. Whom are you kidding?"

"Don't be afraid," the Voice repeated. "Seriously. I'm not here to scare you. I have some good news of great joy, for all people. I heard your conversation earlier."

(They weren't supposed to be afraid what with the Light and a Voice eavesdropping on them?)

"I am with you. It's time to change the world and I have a plan. I need your help to make it work. Show up in room 212 in the Rockin' J in fifteen minutes and I will tell you all about it." And then, with one last

---

3. Beery, "Lo, a gleam." In Slough, ed., *Hymnal,* #591.

clash of cymbals and blast of trumpets, the Light was gone and the Voice silent. The screens were advertising donuts and coffee again.

The four women looked at each other, speechless, which was unusual for them. Then one said, "I'm going to check this out. You guys coming?"

"What about the coffee shop?"

"Who cares?" the first woman said. "This is bigger than donuts. Who needs donuts at 2 in the morning? Besides, Pete Fehr will never know. Let's go."

One more moment of the four looking at each other, and then they turned and headed for the door. Coffee and donuts at Timmy's would be self-serve for the next while.

Song: "While shepherds watched"[4]

Meanwhile, out east, in Toronto actually, earlier that day four friends were having drinks in a pub on the York University campus. There was Mary, professor of Political Science, Nathan from the Department of Economics, Susie, head of the School of Social Work, and Bernie, president of Unifor, the largest union in Canada. All four were discreet about these meetings because their social justice concerns could be taken by some as suggesting Marxist leanings. It wasn't particular political leanings that mattered to them. They cared about people. They met every month to discuss the situation in Canada and the world. It seemed like the world was getting messier and messier all the time—more violent, more racism and bigotry, more opioid overdoses, more poverty and oppression, and climate change, but one industrial chimney and five SUVs away from catastrophe. Something had to be done, but what?

Suddenly—that word again—suddenly, just as Nathan finished making a point that he thought particularly poignant and brilliant, the GPS on each of their phones lit up. As they looked, a map of Canada appeared with a blue line from Toronto, through Chicago, to southern Saskatchewan. They each hit the "Home" button on their phones, and the map disappeared.

Freaky, they thought, as they returned to their conversation. Then it happened again. And then three more times as they tried to ignore what was happening and get back to their conversation.

Finally Mary said, "To hell with classes. I'm going to Regina to check this out."

---

4. Tate, "While shepherds watched." In Slough, ed., *Hymnal*, #196.

Bernie was quick to reply, "Me too. A union can run without a president for a week or two."

The other two did not need convincing. "I'll check with Expedia," said Susie.

"And I'll get a cab," Nathan added.

An hour and a half later, they were in the air, on their way to Saskatchewan. When they landed in Regina, the four rented a car and headed to the Legislative Building. It seemed as good a place as any to start. Maybe they could catch the Premier, Premier Door,[5] at the end of the evening sitting of the Legislature. When they got there, they asked for a meeting with Premier Door. He agreed to give them a few minutes and invited the four guests into his office. The visitors from Toronto introduced themselves.

Oh great! thought Door. *A commie, the de facto leader of the federal NDP, a left-leaning Trudeau Liberal, and a namby-pamby social worker. This should be good. Not!*[6]

"Wow. There's a lot of wisdom in this room," Door said. Looking at Nathan, the Premier continued, "Can you help me balance my budget?"

"I probably could," Nathan replied, ever confident in his own abilities.

"And we could do it without cutting wages for union members," Bernie chimed in. Mary and Susie smirked at each other and rolled their eyes. These two guys never lacked for self-confidence.

Mary jumped in, afraid they were getting side-tracked from the mission. "We have reason to believe that something special is about to happen and it's going to start in Saskatchewan."

Door was all ears. This could pump up his already high ratings across Canada.

"We think the world is about to change and justice, fairness and peace will actually have a chance. We are wondering if you might know where we should look. Is this the direction your government is going?"

---

5. At the time I wrote this and presented it, the premier of Saskatchewan was Brad Wall.

6. Unlike the United States, Canada has several political parties. Federally, the main parties are the Conservative Party (significantly right-of-center and supported by Premier Door's Saskatchewan Party), the Liberals currently led by Justin Trudeau and forming government (slightly left of center), and the New Democratic Party, (significantly left of center) often thought of as being funded and controlled by unions, surely a tool of the communists.

"We do have the best government Saskatchewan has ever had," Door replied. "However, this sounds new to me. Let me check with my cabinet. They are gathering in the next room for a meeting."

Thirty minutes later, the Premier was back. "This could be something we might consider, but we think this is more grassroots than government. We think you should check Swift Current. It is, after all, where Medicare started in Canada, the best system of universal health care in the world. Seems the place for good things to start."

He almost blurted out "It is after all where I was born and my constituency," but he stopped himself, just in time.

"Oh, and when you find out, let me know." He did not say the rest of what he was thinking. This sounded bigger than Sask. Party or NDP and could jeopardize both their parties, the very system of government in Saskatchewan, even Canada. He and Fadingfork[7] of the NDP would have to get together to put a stop to whatever was getting started, in his constituency no less.

Speaking a collective thanks, the four Easterners left the office and building and got into their car. Nobody needed to say, "Let's head to Swift Current." It was understood. It did not matter how late it was. As they turned on to the highway, their GPS's lit up again and the blue line appeared, connecting Regina to Swift Current.

Song: "From the eastern mountains" (*see end of story*)

Two hours later, as they approached the city, they saw the sign on the eastern outskirts: "Swift Current, where life makes sense." This had to be the right place. No one in Toronto had ever heard that such a place existed, let alone in southwestern Saskatchewan. However, as they thought about it some more, it just made sense that whatever was about to happen would start where life makes sense.

Their GPS did not let them down. It guided them off the Central Avenue exit, left at the lights, left again at the end of the street, and right to the Rockin' J Hotel. They looked at the hotel and then at each other. It seemed rather dubious. This is where something big was going to start, something worthy of their trip from Toronto.

"This was your idea," Susie said to Mary. "We should have stopped you. What foolishness to come out here. Stupid, thoughtless, caught-up-in-the-moment decision."

---

7. At the time I wrote this, the leader of the New Democratic Party, forming Her Majesty's Loyal Opposition, was Trent Wotherspoon.

Bernie spoke up. As a union leader, he had seen a lot worse. "Come on. We are here already. We may as well check it out."

As they got out of their car, their phones lit up again, and from four phones, Siri spoke. "Go to room 212." As they turned toward the hotel, four young Filipino women came running around the corner and down the street. They got to the hotel door first and entered, with the four Torontonians right behind them. Up the stairs all eight ran, turned at the top, and stopped in from of room 212. Now what? Should they knock? Just go in? This was the moment of truth, and for a split second, they all felt kind of foolish. Then one of the waitresses opened the door and all eight pushed their way in. Jose, Mary, Zack, and Liz looked up in surprise, shock actually. What the hell was going on?

And then eight cellphones—the four from Fort Mac and the four from out east—lit up and the Voice spoke. "Well, have you decided?"

"Decided what?" Bernie asked. "And whom are you asking?"

"Actually, I'm asking all twelve of you. Have you decided to join me in changing the world? Bringing an end to violence, bigotry, racism, sexism, and some people having too much and some not enough? Creating a world of justice and peace, of safety and love? I have a plan, but I need twelve people to help me get started. Are the twelve of you in? I need to know."

The four from Fort Mac had had two hours to think about this. "We're in," they said in unison.

The four from Timmy's felt like they had nothing to lose. "By all means, we're in too," they said in one voice.

That left the Easterners. They stared at each other, then at the others in the room, and then at each other again. "Are we in?" It was what they had talked about for two years. It was what they wanted. It seemed miraculous that all twelve of them would be gathered together here in this room at the same time.

"I'm in," said Susie.

"Me too," offered Mary.

And then the two guys, almost in unison, "Yep, me too."

And so it began, in the most unlikely of places, in a little western city where life makes sense, in a hotel room that had seen neither visitors nor vacuum and cleaning rag in years. So it began with twelve very unlikely partners. But it began and who knows where it will end?

"From the Eastern Mountains"

(Inspired by lyrics to a song by that same title)[8]
(Tune: "Onward Christian soldiers")

1. From the eastern mountains
Pressing on they come
Wise ones in their wisdom,
Seeking God's new world;
Stirred by deep devotion
Hasting from afar
Ever journeying onward,
Guided by a star.

Refrain:
Onward came the wise ones
Traveling through the night
Ever searching humbly
Looking for the Light.

2. There the hope of ages
Shone like yonder star
Wondrous Light for nations
Shining near and far.
Ever now to lighten
Nations from afar
As they make decisions
By the guiding star.

Refrain

3. Thou who dreamt a vision
Showed us what to do
Who now calls your people
To dream that vision too
May we find the star light
May we catch the dream
And with all our effort
Help that light to stream.

8. Thring, "From the eastern." In Oyer et al, ed., *Mennonite Hymnal,* 140.

Refrain

4. Justice for the nations,
Hope with no despair
Peace to stop all killing
Love we all can share
Light of Light eternal
Shining through the night
Always there for searchers
Longing for the Light.
Refrain

Chapter 12

Christmas in the Community

Around 2008, I decided to join our local Kiwanis Club, the most active service club in Swift Current and the largest Kiwanis club in Western Canada. We meet every Friday at noon. Each year, at the meeting immediately before Christmas, someone delivers a Christmas message. Before every meal, someone leads us in a table grace, always someone who comes with a Christian perspective. This has caused some controversy since not all members are Christian. Our club includes agnostics and atheists and we have at least one Sikh member. Our practice has not changed, though when I am asked to give the blessing, I try to be creative, not use phrases like "Father God" and "In the name of Jesus," and occasionally give a "blessing" that is not specific to one God or any God.

In 2010 when I was asked to give the Christmas "message," I decided to attempt to give one that would be rooted in the Christian Christmas story, but might have wider appeal. I did not tell anyone what I was trying to do, nor did I ask anyone if I had succeeded. "Imagine!" below was the result. A version of it was subsequently published in the *Canadian Mennonite*[1] and the *Southwest Booster*.[2]

In 2012, I threw out a challenge. I would put $100 on the table saying I could deliver a Christmas message based on the Christian Christmas story that would be acceptable to all people in the club. That is, though based on the Christian story, it could speak to anyone. If I did so, all

---

1. *Canadian Mennonite* (November 25, 2013. Vol. 17, #23).

2. *The Southwest Booster* is Swift Current's community newspaper that is distributed throughout southwest Saskatchewan.

money put on the table would go to Lajee Center just outside Aida Refugee Camp in Bethlehem, West Bank, Palestine. It is a children's drop-in center operated by Muslim refugees with the support of Christian NGOs. If I didn't fulfill my promise, the money would go to a local charity. We had three judges—a pastor, an agnostic, and someone who might self-identify as Christian, but is not active in any faith group.

A local pastor who is also part of our club, when told about my challenge, insisted what I was attempting to do could not be done. After my presentation, he conceded I had done what I said I would do. We raised $1,300 for Lajee Center. My presentation is below, entitled "There's a New Song in the Air."

IMAGINE!

A Christmas Message

In Charles Dickens's well-known story, *A Christmas Carol*, anyone who dares enter the inner sanctum of Ebenezer Scrooge's office with so much as a suggestion of Christmas is greeted with the by-now famous words "Bah! Humbug!"[3] His nephew is told: "If I could work my will every idiot who goes about with 'Merry Christmas' on his lips, should be boiled with his own pudding, and buried with a stake of holly through his heart. He should!"[4]

Many are tempted to suggest that Scrooge's famous response to Christmas was motivated by his greed and his self-centeredness. Maybe, but I am inclined to believe it was not so much greed as it was lack of imagination that caused Ebenezer Scrooge to have no heart for Christmas, no heart for those who did business with him, and no heart for those who needed his help at "this festive season of the year."[5] It was the loss of his imagination that had caused the loss of heart.

This loss of imagination is a malady that afflicts not only those who count money three hundred and sixty-four days of the year and then are tempted to count presents under the tree on the three hundred and sixty-fifth. It is a disease of epidemic proportions in our world, with, it would seem at times, very few escaping its deadening impact. I am convinced it

---

3. Dickens, *A Christmas Carol*, 9.
4. Dickens, *A Christmas Carol*, 11.
5. Dickens, *A Christmas Carol*, 15.

is lack of imagination that has us believing war will solve the problems in Iraq and Afghanistan and more and larger prisons will deal with crime. It is lack of imagination that causes millions to go to bed hungry and teenagers in our own city to drift from couch to couch because they have no safe place to call home. It is lack of imagination that builds walls in Palestine and pits religion against religion around the world.

What may in fact be the saddest truth of all is that religion may suffer from the most severe case of lack of imagination. As a result, we are quick to divide ourselves and others into insiders and outsiders, damn one group to hell while the other basks in heaven's glory, and sends us out convinced that we must convert all to our way of life, using the threat of God's wrath at a minimum and suicide bombers and holy war at its worst.

Unfortunately, Christianity is not free of this loss of imagination that creates an inability to sense God's presence, understand God's truth, experience God's power, or channel God's love. It is this loss of imagination that has turned the Biblical story into a document primarily for polemic and rule making, thereby weakening almost to the point of death the power inherent in the Story. Take, for example, Genesis 1. Read it without imagination, as a science textbook, and insist on seven literal, twenty-four-hour days and you really have nothing, except something to argue over. Set your imaginations free and you have a powerful story, a movie that rivals anything Steven Spielberg may give us, an experience that has the power to change life and history. As you imagine, the scene will draw you into itself and you will be there as lights explode in the swirling darkness and galaxies form. You will be there as trees and flowers grow and the desert is transformed into a garden. You'll see the deer leaping over shrubs, feel the bears nuzzling your hand, be entranced by the magic of butterflies and humming birds, dance to the music of the birds. No science text can do that. No argument over creation and evolution can do that. It's as you imagine that the power of the story will grab you.

The same is true of our reading of the rest of the Biblical material—its stories, its poetry, its sermons, its letters, and its fantasy literature. It is particularly true of the Christmas story. That story begs us to engage our imagination, to set it free. Without imagination, Christmas trees would be simply branches covered in junk, gifts but tools, books, and toys wrapped in gaudy paper, a favorite drink but milk mixed with raw eggs, Christmas music just mushy, sentimental repetition, and a baby is born on a manure pile. Without imagination, we read about the song of the angels but we fail to hear the music. We forget the wonder of where and to whom they sang, and lose the message in the chorus.

"Glory to God in highest heaven, and peace on earth to those with whom God is pleased,"[6] they sang. We hear that last phrase—"to those with whom God is pleased"—and believe it to be an exclusionary phrase. We are convinced that God favors some and not others, and proudly see ourselves as the favored ones. What if those words were not meant as an exclusionary clause but rather as a descriptive phrase, a phrase describing all people, all people who not only are favored by God, but who will now experience peace? What then? Without imagination, we can't go there. With imagination, the horizons begin to widen and the possibilities grow.

With imagination, the song of the angels is a "Hallelujah"[7] chorus for all people, as wonderful as the one sung in some food court and making its rounds on YouTube.[8] With imagination, Christmas carols engage our emotions as they lift our hearts and spirits until they burst. When we begin to imagine, decorated trees transform rooms and space until the warm glow of twinkling lights seems like they were sent from heaven itself. With imagination, gifts raise anticipation to a fever pitch. With imagination, love breaks out everywhere. You need imagination to do Christmas and Christmas invites you to start imagining and never stop. Christmas invites us to see more than meets the eye, to see what really is and what surely will be, a planet visited by God, life and history infused with Christmas, a world transformed by what happened that first Christmas.

A barn is just a barn—smelly, maybe old and rickety, dirty, perhaps cold and drafty, dark, walkway slippery with manure, the air tight with the smell of urine. But bring in Christmas and it is transformed into a nativity scene—peaceful, gentle, warm, filled with a soft glow, doves cooing, rough men and polished intellectuals equally awed by the possibilities, homeless, pregnant-before-marriage teenagers no longer the source of angst but the means of hope for our world, and in the distance, the faint sound of angel choirs.

Have you ever considered who it was that gathered in that first manger scene around a newborn baby boy, around God present in the world, a concept that all by itself requires imagination? Who was there?

6. Luke 2:14. NLT.

7. Handel, "Hallelujah," 171.

8. A video of a mob singing Handel's "Hallelujah" chorus in a mall food court was making its rounds the Christmas season this was written.

Follow your imagination. Joseph, the betrayed lover. Mary, the pregnant teen. Shepherds known for their tough language, hard ways, and always a jug at the handy. Skeptical intellectuals, pagans actually, who believed all kinds of things that would drive most self-respecting Jews of their day, or Christians of our day, to distraction. This is who we will see around the manger if we use our imaginations.

Starting with that story and setting our imaginations free, we can bring that same Christmas into our world and change a barn-like existence into a nativity scene of hope, light, and life. If we imagine Christmas in our world, we will be amazed who shows up in the nativity scene. We will be breathless at the love that will flow and engulf all those who gather. We will be left speechless—truly a gift in a world made unbearably noisy by too many words too stridently spoken—at the possibilities we can imagine. And if we can imagine them, we and God can see them happen, for the same story that brought us Christmas also insists that God is able to do even more than we imagine.[9]

Think of the possibilities if we imagine the nativity scene. Imagine it not only in a story "once upon a time," but imagine it today. Imagine it in Bethlehem, where it first happened, and the wall separating Israelis and Palestinians begins to shake, pieces of concrete begin to crumble, and then with a crash, all seven hundred twenty kilometers of it falls down, clearing the way for those whom God favors to shake hands with each other. Imagine a nativity scene five miles away in the city of Jerusalem, held to be holy by three of the world's best known religions, and notice that, haltingly at first, but soon more courageously and boldly, until it swells into a chorus with Muslims, Christians, and Jews together joining the angels in their song: "Glory to God in highest heaven, and peace on earth to those with whom God is pleased."[10]

And then, as if on cue, all those who believe in God, however they articulate and practice their faith, join in, for what could be better than peace on earth among all people, for God loves and is pleased with all people—not with everything they do, no matter what their faith, but with them as people, God's much-loved children. If we've imagined this far, why stop there? Imagine now what we can imagine for the whole world? Taliban and Canadians, equally favored by God, recognizing they are

---

9. "Now to [God] who by the power at work within us is able to accomplish abundantly far more than all we can ask or imagine, to [God] be glory in the church and in Christ Jesus to all generations, for ever and ever. Amen." Eph 3:20–21. NRSV.

10. Luke 2:14. NLT.

brothers and sisters intent on the same thing—God's blessing for all—and joining hands to plant gardens, build roads, and erect schools. If we can imagine that, we can imagine enough food in the Sudan, in Somalia, in Ethiopia, in Haiti, and in our own inner cities.

In Canada, imagine the possibilities! First Nations, French, English, and all others now convinced that our country is not for one group or the other, nor only for those who have lived here "x" number of years. Imagine us joining hands to create a truly diverse society respectful of all, generous to all, and joining arms to welcome more people from around the world who need the safety and economic benefits of life in Canada. Imagine treating our planet with the respect God intended and with the spirit of generosity that makes each of the earth's seven billion residents an equal partner in what the earth can produce. Imagine an end to homelessness, drug use, broken families, violent fathers, despairing mothers, frightened children. Imagine a personal transformation as profound as that experienced by Ebenezer Scrooge. Imagine the Leafs making the playoffs. Okay, there may be a limit.[11]

All of this and more is wildly improbable only if we decide the Christmas story is limited to one way of reading, serves one purpose, is restricted to one version as it appears in "dried ink marks on the page."[12] Set the story free to be what God intended. Engage your imaginations in the way God designed them. Dream your dreams in the way God gave them to you, dreams of the world that is possible, and a world already being dreamt by God. Imagine the possibilities, and there may be no limit to what can happen.

This Christmas, as you gather around a nativity scene at Christmas Eve worship, join hands and hearts with family around the Christmas tree, admire the beauty of trees and decorations, enjoy the appetizing sights and smells of a table laden with turkey and trimmings, imagine what is possible because of what was, imagine what will be because of what is, and be prepared to be amazed at the transformation of life and world that you will see.

11. The Toronto Maple Leafs are a Canadian team in the National Hockey League. They used to be a powerhouse, but have not won a Stanley Cup since the 1960s. A few years ago, they did actually make the first round of the playoffs, were leading in game 7 by two goals with less than two minutes to play, and lost in overtime. At least one member of the Kiwanis club is a die-hard Leafs fan, and takes a lot of ribbing for it.

12. I first encountered the phrase, or one like it, in Barbara Brown Taylor's *An Altar in the World* when I read it several years ago. Taylor uses the phrase in various pieces she has published and/or posted on Facebook, including *Leaving Church*, 106.

And if your faith tradition, family history, and/or personal journey does not include the Christian Christmas story, that's okay. You have your own stories that plead for imagination and contain the promise of peace. From those stories, join those of us who gather around the nativity scene this time of the year, and dream with us and imagine with us what can be possible in every home, on every street corner, in each downtown, on every farm, and in each country. This Christmas "Imagine!" and see what happens.

THERE'S A NEW SONG IN THE AIR

Kiwanis Christmas, 2012

In one of his less known but possibly more profound songs, Stompin' Tom Connors (some of you probably did not realize that Stompin' Tom could be profound) sings about the importance of singers and songs to the collective character of a people, a clan, or a nation.[13] For centuries, songwriters and singers have written and sung the songs that gave life to, and shaped the character of, the community. They were convinced, with Stompin' Tom, that in song people give voice to the values and dreams that beat in the heart of a nation. With a fervor that knew that life, community and peoplehood depended on it, they taught the songs to the next generation. Symbols might inspire loyalty. Stories fire the imagination. But it was songs that stirred the soul and captured the spirit and defined a people.

When I was a teenager, we had a portable record player on which you could load five LPs and start playing them, knowing the player would shut off when the last record had been played. I used to load the turn table with achy-breaky country songs—Tammy Wynette singing about her "D-I-V-O-R-C-E"[14] and Johnny Cash singing "Born to lose/I've lived my life in vain,"[15] and fall asleep to the music. Then I would wake up at two in the morning and have no idea why I felt this overwhelming sense of sadness and despair. Such is the power of song.

The Sunday school teachers, in the tradition I grew up in, knew about the power of song and taught us to sing. One song was "One door

---

13. Connors, "The Singer," *A Proud Canadian*, track 20.
14. Wynette, "D-I-V-O-R-C-E," track 7.
15. Cash, vocalist, "Born to Lose." On Cash, *The Original*, track 8.

and only one, and yet it sides are two. Inside and outside, on which side are you? One door and only one, and yet its sides are two. I'm on the inside on which side are you?"[16] And another generation of good little Evangelical Mennonite boys and girls knew themselves to be specially chosen by God and many of the rest of you in grave danger of being outside the embrace of God's love and grace. Such is the power of song.

The same was true in public school. Every morning we would stand at attention and sing to the great country in which we live and vowed to "stand on guard for [it]."[17] We knew there was no better country anywhere. Even today, at the beginning of each Kiwanis luncheon and each Bronco[18] game, I feel the stirring within as I sing to "the true north strong and free."[19] And then, I must confess, when the Broncos play the Spokane Chiefs and our soloist sings "Oh say can you see,"[20] I have to resist the urge to salute the American flag. Such is the power of song.

This is not a recent phenomenon. I wonder if the Holocaust would have happened if it hadn't been for the power of *Deutschland, Deutschland über Alles*—"Germany, Germany above everything, above everything in the world."[21] Written by Joseph Haydn in the eighteenth century and rooted in German musical, religious, and theological superiority, it was a short distance to biological and genetic superiority and the Holocaust. Three hundred years earlier, the Scottish Independence fighters marched into war against the English. Their kilts might have inspired loyalty, but it was their bagpipes that convinced them they were invincible, and struck fear into the hearts of their enemies. Such is the power of song.

Such was the power of song one thousand three hundred years earlier when the mid-eastern air was filled with the ear-drum shattering music of patriotism, revolution, and religious superiority—drum beats and trumpet blasts of a world-conquering Roman army, the revolutionary songs of the Zealot guerrilla fighters, and the rousing "pipe-organ music" of Jewish people who knew God cared more for them than anyone else.

16. Leslie, "One Door." In *Salvation Songs*, # 22.
17. A line in Canada's national anthem. Lavallée, "O Canada." *O Canada*.
18. The Swift Current Broncos are members of the Western Hockey League, which is part of the Canadian Hockey League, playing Canada's and northwest USA's top junior players.
19. Another line in Canada's national anthem.
20. Key, "The Star-Spangled Banner." In *The Star*.
21. Haydn, "Deutschland, Deutschland über Alles." In *Deutschland*, track 12.

With all that music to fill the hearts, move the feet, thrill the soul, and capture the spirit, few heard another song that was whispered on the breeze and sung in the quiet of the night, an alternative song to songs of war, political elitism, and religious grandeur. On a Bethlehem hillside, a group of shepherds sat around the fire, watching their sheep. Here, away from home, they could tell whatever stories they wanted, and say and do whatever it is men do around the fire, away from the civilizing influence of wives and girlfriends, while they passed around a little brown jug to drive back the chill of the night. These men were not worth the attention of the Roman generals, did not have time for Zealot revolutionaries, and were despised by the Jewish organists. It was these men who heard, above the echo of war and superiority and revolution, that other song, first faintly as if the rustle of the wind in the grass, and then in a rising crescendo of sound until they knew it was being sung by an angel chorus. It scared the %$#&*% out of them. At the same time, it was a song so beautiful, so radical, so powerful it nigh blew their circuits as it filled their ears, expanded their hearts, caught their imagination, and convinced their minds that they were hearing a new song, surely a song from another world that had the power to reshape this world:

> Peace and goodwill to all on earth,
> Peace and goodwill to all who hear.
> Peace and goodwill, oh take up the song,
> Peace and goodwill both far and near.[22]

Here was the promise of something new! Here was the promise of a world they had not thought even possible to imagine. Here was the promise of a song quieter than those of war and religion, patriotism, and revolution, empire and judgment, elitism and guilt, quieter, but more powerful and more life-giving.

Through the centuries since, that song has often been drowned out by the cannon's roar, the trumpet's blast, and the pipe organ's crescendo. And still, through those same centuries, there have been those who heard the song, those whose souls were reawakened to life by that song, those whose spirits were inspired by the possibilities, those whose feet sensed the beat and joined the dance.

---

22. This is my own composition.

In 1863, this new song of the angels, the song of peace and goodwill, was almost drowned out by the roar of cannons, the scream of the wounded, and the terror of all, Confederates and Unionists alike:

> Then from each black, accursed mouth
> The cannon thundered in the South,
> (*wrote Henry Wadsworth Longfellow*)
> And with the sound the carols drowned
> Of peace on earth, good will to men.
> It was as if an earthquake rent
> The hearth-stones of a continent,
> And made forlorn, the households born
> Of peace on earth, good will to men.
> And in despair I bowed my head
> "There is no peace on earth," I said,
> "For hate is strong and mocks the song
> Of peace on earth, good will to men."
> Then pealed the bells more loud and deep:
> "[The Song's] not dead, nor doth [it] sleep;
> The wrong shall fail, the right prevail
> With peace on earth, good will to men."[23]

Barely two generations later, the roll of war drums, blasts of angry trumpets, boom of death-dealing cannons, and roar of newly developed tanks threatened to drown out the new song forever. And then, on Christmas Day, 1914, in a pause in the hell-bent intent to kill each other, the soldiers in the trenches in France heard the angels singing as clearly as did the shepherds so many centuries earlier. The story is told in movie and song. The song—"Christmas in the Trenches"[24]—was written by John McCutcheon and has been covered by a variety of artists. I first heard John McDermott sing it in concert here in Swift Current. The movie is *Joyeux Noel* and was released in 2005. The soldiers, first German, then English, and then both sides together singing "Silent Night", each in their own language, joined that angelic chorus and brought a stop to war, at least for a day.

Song: Duet (*singing one verse of "Silent Night", one voice in English, one in German*):

23. Longfellow, "I heard."
24. McCutcheon, "Christmas," *Winter Solstice*.

Silent night, holy night	*Stille nacht, heilege nacht*
All is calm, all is bright	*Alles schlaeft, einsam wacht*
Round yon virgin mother and child	*nur das traute, hochheilige Paar,*
Holy infant so tender and mild,	*das im Stalle zu Bethlehem war*
Sleep in heavenly peace,	*bei dem himmlischen Kind,*
Sleep in heavenly peace.	*bei dem himlischen Kind.*[25]

A few years later, in 1921, just seven years after their community became a city, a group of people in Swift Current heard, above the din of development and prosperity, the ring of cash registers and the pounding of hammers, the whoosh of steam engines, and the screech of train whistles, above all that—or maybe sneaking in and amongst all that noise—a few people in Swift Current heard the song of the angels and decided to form a club that would work for the welfare of all children, whatever their race or religion, and build a community for the benefit of all who came. The Kiwanis Club of Swift Current was born and now all we need is for Dave Cyca[26] to write our song, the song of the angels for twenty-first-century Swift Current Kiwanians.

More recently still, Bob Dylan heard the angels sing and wrote and sang "Blowin' in the wind"[27] to remind us all of this alternative song. In 1969, with the song of the angels echoing in his ears, John Lennon wrote "Give peace a chance"[28] and a whole generation was helped to hear and then feel, imagine and believe in the song of the angels. The hope for our world did not rest with war in Vietnam, the stockpiling of nuclear weapons, and the development of the largest, most expensive army the world has ever known. The world's true hope could be seen reflected in the twinkle of stars and heard in the night breeze, so beautiful it had to come from the lips of angels, a song that could grow in the imaginations of people and be realized in the new ways of the human race:

> Peace and goodwill to all on earth,
> Peace and goodwill to all who hear.
> Peace and goodwill, oh take up the song,

---

25. Mohr, "Silent Night." In Slough, ed., *Hymnal*, #193.

26. Dave Cyca is a member of our club, a singer and composer, and the leader of group known as "Creek City."

27. Dylan, "Blowin' in the Wind." On Dylan, *The Freewheelin'*, track 1.

28. Lennon, "Give Peace," *Give Peace a Chance*, track 1.

> Peace and goodwill both far and near.

Today we hear the echo of the angels' song in the poetry and music of people of various faith and worldview perspectives, people sometimes separated by differences that can run deep but drawn together by a yearning and dream that runs even deeper:

> Peace and goodwill to all on earth,
> Peace and goodwill to all who hear.
> Peace and goodwill, oh take up the song,
> Peace and goodwill both far and near.

You hear echoes of the angel chorus as Western Christians sing at this time of year: "To us a child of hope is born."[29] You hear it in the songs of Arab Christians who join their voices in the chorus:

> On the night of Christmas . . . Hatred will vanish
> On the night of Christmas . . . The earth blooms
> On the night of Christmas . . . War is buried
> On the night of Christmas . . . Love is born[30]

You hear the song of the angels in the ancient song of the Jews, who dream of the time when:

> they shall beat their swords into ploughshares,
> and their spears into pruning-hooks;
> nation shall not lift up sword against nation,
> neither shall they learn war any more.[31]

You hear that same echo in the poetry of the Muslim Poet, Mahmoud Darwish. He heard the song of the angels and reminded all those who would conduct war not to forget those working for peace.[32]

You hear a version of the song of the angels in the Buddhist blessing translated by Thich Nhat Hahn:

> May everyone be happy and safe, and may their hearts be filled with joy.

---

29. Morison, "To us a Child" In Slough, ed., *Hymnal*, #189.

30. Thanks to my daughter, Rachelle, for giving me this piece and the one from Mahmoud Darwish, the Muslim poet, below.

31. Isa 2:4. NRSV.

32. Darwish, "a candle in the dark." (sic)

> May all living beings live in security and in peace... May all of them dwell in perfect tranquility.
>
> Let no one do harm to anyone. Let no one put the life of anyone in danger. Let no one, out of anger or ill will, wish anyone any harm.[33]

And of course there are those who stand in other spiritual traditions or no identifiable tradition, but dream and sing with John Lennon and Yoko Ono: "Give peace a chance."

This afternoon, I invite you to sing another version of this song. This is one that is found in most Christian Christmas carol collections, but was written by a man who did not share the traditional, orthodox Christian belief in Jesus. He too heard the new song of the angels and discovered it captured his spirit, fired his imagination, set his feet a dancin', and his tongue a singin'. If you believe in angels with your mind, sing this song and find yourself strategizing new ways of peace. If you believe in angels with your heart, sing this song and allow your heart to swell with love until it overflows to all those around you. If you believe in angels with your imagination, sing this song and realize that if you can imagine the angels singing the song of peace on earth, you can imagine peace itself, and who knows what will come of such imagining. Sing, and be assured wherever the echoes of our singing are heard, peace will grow.

Song: "It came upon a midnight clear"[34]

Amen. *Salam a lay kuhm.* *Shalom.* Give peace a chance.

---

33. Hanh, "Hanh's Translation," para. 4
34. Sears, "It came upon" In Slough, ed., *Hymnal*, #195.

Chapter 13

COMMUNITY PREACHING

As an active member in the local ministerial, and a few periods of times serving on the Executive, including as President, I have had a variety of opportunities to speak, pray, and preach in our larger community. When that happens, there are certain responsibilities and limitations that must be taken seriously. You do not have a congregation that hears you week after week so you can put one sermon in the context of a longer series and in the context of five or ten years of preaching. You know you will be speaking to people from different denominations whose pastors have different perspectives on some things and whose faith and spirituality have been nurtured differently than yours and that of the people in your congregation. It's not the time to step on toes even when, if all you serve is Pablum, you may be wasting everyone's time.

I have preached at Advent services and Lent services, usually able to use the sermon I preached at Zion or Emmaus the previous Sunday and adapting it to the mid-week community service. In 2014, I was asked to preach at the annual "Week of Prayer for Christian Unity" service. I had said "no" to the same request from the same person (a good Catholic friend of ours) a few times—begging off because of a busy schedule as preacher and mediator. In 2014, I decided I could not say "no" again and so, when the request came, I said "yes." (And I did my best to explain to my wife later why I had taken on one more assignment.)

I think I was fortunate in the assigned text for that year. It was Paul's comments on a theme very important to me—unity in the Christian community in one city. Paul wrote to the people in first-century-Corinth;

I was being called to preach to the people of twenty-first-century Swift Current, a Christian community even more divided than Corinth. Here it is not only "I belong to Paul, Apollos, Cephas or Christ."[1] We had Menno Simons (with at least five different brands), Luther (two kinds), Wesley, Calvin, Booth, Azusa Street and who knows who started the Associated Gospel Churches and the Churches of God and the Baptists (at least two kinds in this town). So I wanted to make a bold call for unity even while respecting the differences. What follows is what I came up with.

"HAS CHRIST BEEN DIVIDED?"

1 Corinthians 1:1–17
Week of Prayer for Christian Unity Joint Service

I don't know how many of you noticed in this morning's edition of the *Leader Post* that Corey Chamblin[2] has decided to make some major changes to the Saskatchewan Roughriders. "I know we won the Grey Cup in 2013," Corey is quoted as saying, "but, you know, I was a defensive back when I played football and a coach of the defense for most of my coaching career. Thinking about that, I realized that all you need to win football games is the defense. The defense can stop the other team from scoring and it can score points itself, so there is no need for the offense. So in 2014, the Riders will have only a defense. That way, we don't have to pay a high-priced quarterback, and we have more backups at each position in case someone gets hurt."

When asked about the dramatic changes happening in Saskatchewan, Wally Buono,[3] general manager of the BC Lions who had two Grey Cup appearances as a coach, said, "That's the kind of misguided thinking going on in our league. Everyone knows it is offense that wins football games, and it's offense that gets butts into the seats and pays the bills. The Lions are also making changes for this coming year. We will be an all-offense team. The offense scores far more points than a defense ever

---

1. 1 Cor 1:12. NRSV.

2. At the time this was written, Corey Chamblin was head coach of the Saskatchewan Roughriders, Saskatchewan's team in the Canadian Football League (CFL), Canada's professional league.

3. The CFL's winningest coach who is known for his teams with a strong offense and the quarterbacks he kept developing.

will, and besides, if the offense doesn't give up the ball, the other team can't score."

One reporter dared ask what the Lions would do after scoring a touchdown, since they have to kick the ball to the other team. Buono replied, "That's the kind of negativity and football heresy that detracts from football. Questions like that only send you in the wrong direction. Offense wins games."

Wanting to check with players, the *LP* talked to Chris Milo[4], who is one of many players being released by the Riders. "Being cut from the Riders?" Milo said. "No problem. I was going to leave anyway. We all know the game of football is called *foot*ball. That means it's a kicking game. Luca Congi and I have already talked and we are going to form a team of kickers. It's time to get back to the basics and what football is all about—football, kicking the ball. We will have a team of all kickers. And if they don't let us into the league, we will form our own and finally play the game the way it was meant to be played." No one told Milo there is already a game and league like that around. It's called soccer in Canada and the United States, but football in the rest of the world.

Okay. Those of you who read the *Leader Post* know there is no Sunday morning edition and therefore no sports article like the one I just quoted from. Those of you who know football know how ludicrous the scenario that I just sketched is. No coaches of Chamblin's and Buono's stature, or any football coach for that matter, would ever say or even think the things attributed to them by me. And yet the amazing thing is that what we know to be fanciful and unworkable and impossible in football, we accept as normal in the church and the body of Christ. Not only do we accept it as normal, but Christians and their coaches—pastors, bishops, and popes—all too often actively support and encourage this kind of thinking for the Kingdom of God and God's game of life.

Mennonites will tell you that unless you follow Jesus in your personal life, living out his teachings and values, and see Christ's cross as a way of life for all Christians, you are far from the Kingdom of God. Full Gospels, Pentecostals and other charismatics boldly proclaim that all that matters is that you have the Holy Spirit and only those who speak in tongues have it. Our United Church friends are quick to point out that it is obvious Christianity is all about the social gospel and transforming society and politics, working for social justice, human rights, and real

---

4. Chris Milo and Luca Congi were kickers in the CFL.

change in our world. And Lutherans will, of course, tell all of the rest of us that it is all about grace, the wonderful, unconditional grace of God. Everything else is but a shadow of the truth. Only Catholics are able to trace their history back to Peter, the first pope, and therefore know they stand the best chance of being the true church. All the rest of us have probably deviated from the truth.

Okay, I will make another concession. I have caricatured each group I mentioned, painted less than a complete picture, and been a little unfair to each—that's why I started with Mennonites, my own denomination. At the same time, if you are part of one of the groups I mentioned, you recognize yourself and know there is more truth in what I said than we care to admit. And I could continue the list. Baptists know that what matters is that we believe the right things about Jesus and get completely wet when we are baptized. The Alliance Church knows that if it is not about prayer and missions, we are wasting our time—I actually had an Alliance pastor tell me that. I know, some of you will feel left out because I didn't include you and your claim to being the true church in my list. Sorry. Time prevents me.

Having said what I have said, let me hasten to add that I am not opposed to the variety we have in the church. I believe the variety reflects the beauty and wonder God worked into the Creation. What I do find seriously troubling and a betrayal of our claim to be the body of Christ is how we got here—by self-righteousness and quarrelling—and the claims we make about being closer to the truth than our brothers and sisters in another denomination. Do you know there are congregations in some areas who will not join in ministerial groups, like the one we have in Swift Current and area, because they do not want to associate with certain denominations and their obviously heretical and misguided views? That, I believe, is a tragedy.

We need each other, friends, each one of us within the Christian family of churches. There is no one we can do without.

Let me give some examples of what I mean, and again, some of you will get left out. To name everyone would have us here longer than we have patience for in church.

Mennonites, focused as we are on personally following Jesus and often content on letting the rest of society go "to hell in a handbasket," need the United Church to help us understand we are called to live in the world, partnering with God to bring transformation to that world. The United Church needs Mennonites and Baptists to give them a center in the historical reality of Jesus and his resurrection, without which no social gospel is sustainable. The United Church and Mennonites try to do all this wonderful ethics and social justice stuff but need, often desperately, the Holy Spirit folk to show us where to find the power to be effective and to keep going. You Holy Spirit folk have all this tremendous power, but you darn near explode with it because you don't know where to use it. That's why you need the Mennonites and the United Church to show you what it's for. We all need the Lutherans and grace, or the guilt in the face of so much failure would overwhelm. The Lutherans need the rest of us to realize that we've been given God's grace, not just for ourselves but so that, as God told Abraham, we might be a blessing to others. Conservatives need Liberals to expand their horizons, help them imagine what can be, and give them wings. Liberals need Conservatives to keep them centered on Jesus and God's Kingdom and to give them roots. Protestants need Catholics to teach us to pray and give us a history and tradition that inspires and guides. Catholics need Protestants so that history and tradition can be a steadying guide and not a deadening weight. And so the list goes on. There is not a single denomination that is not needed to do what God is doing in our world. There is not a single congregation in Swift Current and area that you and your church can do without.

All of this comes together, I believe, and grows from God's table of welcome, grace, and forgiveness known to us by various names—Communion, Eucharist, Lord's Supper, the Mass, among others. Gathering around God's table of grace to eat and drink is the symbol and experience, the metaphor and reality *par excellence* of the togetherness that Christ came to bring and the unity that is absolutely foundational to God's dream for our world and its people. Joining in the bread and wine without judgment or barrier is not the end goal of unity. It is the beginning and foundation stone of togetherness.

Jesus celebrated it with five thousand Jews in Galilee and with four thousand Gentiles in the Decapolis. He celebrated it with twelve or 120 in the Upper Room, with a group of disciples including Judas, who had already made a deal to betray Jesus, and Peter who Jesus knew was going to deny him. Jesus celebrated it with Mr. and Mrs. Cleopas in Emmaus on Easter Sunday. Nowhere in the Gospels is there any evidence that anyone for whatever reason was excluded, that only certain people were allowed to participate. But Friesen, you say, in 1 Corinthians 11, Paul warns us not to participate "unworthily." So he does. And the thing that in 1 Corinthians makes people unworthy is creating divisions at this table of grace, forgiveness and acceptance.

If we truly believe in Christian unity, that we are all brothers and sisters in Christ, the unity must begin at God's Table, in the bread and wine. If any one of us would bar another person from the table of grace, we have turned the Table into a table of judgment and betrayed whatever claims we make to be believers in, and followers of, Jesus. Until we can all take Communion together without regard for who leads and serves, men or women, clergy or lay, Catholic or Protestant, Evangelical or Mainline, Mennonite or Reformed, and who comes to be served, until then, this service today is but a pretty veneer covering an ugly reality. We were not made guardians of the bread and wine, the blood and body of Christ. We were called to be dispensers and servers of it to all God would welcome. Since the New Testament teaches that God loves the world and wishes for all to experience grace, we have been called on behalf of God to welcome anyone and everyone at the table. When we refuse to serve anyone, no matter who they are, what they have done, or what denomination, if any, they come from, we cease to be Preachers of Good News and have become Peddlers of Religion. It is time we ask ourselves: Do we believe in a God who loves the world, a Jesus who came for all, and a Gospel meant for the world? Or are we peddlers of a Christian religion with a specific label meant for a few?

I dream of the day when we, all of Swift Current and area, will gather on the soccer pitch at Southside Park for a Communion Service where every person will be invited and encouraged to receive the bread and wine, feast on the food of God, participate in grace and togetherness, and experience the body of Christ. I dream of all of us holding hands—Liberals with Conservatives, Catholics with Protestants, Evangelicals with Mainline folk, and Holy Spirit people with workers for social justice. I dream of the day when we will come, hand in hand, and be served by Joell Haugan and Linda Hall, Paul Israelson and Zoria Shumay, Kevin Snyder and Ruth MacArthur, Mike Smart and Sylvia Friesen, Jonathan Hoskins and Jonathan Kwon, Father Jasiak and Captain Ramsay.[5] Yes, Michael, I know you don't celebrate Communion in the Salvation Army, but I believe we can teach you to serve bread and wine even as you show us how to feed the five thousand.

5. Captain Michael Ramsay was pastor of the Salvation Army in Swift Current at the time, as well as heading up all their social programs. The Salvation Army practices neither baptism nor Communion.

When that day comes, Swift Current will finally have the evidence they need to believe that Jesus is real, the Spirit is powerful, God is at work, and the Gospel makes a difference. Then we will have reason to ask people to believe the good news, follow Jesus, and work for a transformed world, a new society, and a healed community. Let us pray that the day will come in our lifetime. Amen.

Chapter 14

EASTER AND THE COMMUNITY

As a member of the Kiwanis program committee, I would occasionally have conversations with the committee chair, a practicing Catholic, about how it was possible to make the Christmas message less specifically Christian,[1] but how that would be more difficult with Easter. In 2015 I decided to give it a try. When I asked for a volunteer from Kiwanis to help me with the presentation, an agnostic friend, without seeing the script first, volunteered to help. He had been convinced by my Christmas message in 2013 that I could be trusted. Below is what came from my attempt.

WHY DID JESUS AND THE EASTER BUNNY CROSS THE ROAD?[2]

Why did Jesus and the Easter Bunny cross the road? To visit the Goat & Camel, a traditional pub, for a conversation over a pint or two of Black Bridge Brewery's finest.[3] That, it seems to me, is the least important question and the easiest answer. What I am really curious about is what

---

1. See chapter 12: "Christmas in the Community."
2. I got the idea for the title from Brian McLaren's book, *Why Did Jesus?*
3. Black Bridge Brewery (BBB) is a micro-brewery in Swift Current. A partner in the business and father of the man who operates it is a member of Swift Current Kiwanis.

Jesus and the Easter Bunny might discuss as they sip their Milk Stout and Centennial Rye Ale.[4]

Well, through the marvels of twenty-second-century time travel, twenty-first-century technology, but mostly with the use of this century's and any century's imaginations, we have an opportunity this noon hour to listen in. You may well notice as you enter the Goat & Camel that the Easter Bunny has an uncanny resemblance to Lorne Uher and Jesus has a lot less hair and a much whiter beard than you are used to in his pictures. He also looks suspiciously more Mennonite than Jewish. So, turn your imaginations on full energy, give them free rein, and join us at the Goat & Camel for an experience of a lifetime—or just a way to kill the next twenty minutes or so. Unfortunately for all of you, all you get is tea, coffee, and water while they enjoy their pints (or cans).

EASTER BUNNY: So Jesus, have you been to Walmart recently and noticed how many chocolate Easter Bunnies they sell compared to how many chocolate Jesuses? I guess that tells you who is more popular.

JESUS: Okay, so you get the pre-Easter season, but how many Easter bunnies do you see in nativity scenes at Christmas?

EASTER BUNNY: So even you haven't noticed. At Christmas, I come disguised as Santa Claus. I still have you beat.

JESUS: Did you come here to engage in a pi—-, I mean, an egocentric argument over who is the most popular or what?

EASTER BUNNY: Good point. You invited me and I took over the conversation by laughing at you. I know, that's me. But you do have to admit I'm more popular than you in this world. And I think I know why. Two reasons.

JESUS: Why am I not surprised that you think you have the answer to everything?

EASTER BUNNY: No, but seriously, hear me out. I think I'm more popular because you have to admit your story is a little farfetched, actually, really farfetched. A guy is executed, put in a stone tomb, comes to life thirty-six hours later and is still alive two thousand years later? You actually expect people will believe that?

JESUS: This from a male rabbit sitting here, drinking a beer, having a conversation, and claiming to lay colored chocolate Easter eggs every spring?

4. Two of BBB's beers listed on their website in 2015.

EASTER BUNNY: Touché. But listen to my second reason. People don't like religion. That's why they don't like you.

JESUS: I don't like religion. I hate religion.

EASTER BUNNY: What? What's more religious than Jesus, crosses and all that sh—, I mean stuff? You are religion personified. Don't like religion? Give me a break.

JESUS: Pity Easter bunnies can't read. If you could, you could read one version of my story and discover that I took on religion head-on and let the religious types know what I thought of religion.

EASTER BUNNY: Yet you are the center of religion.

JESUS: Guilty as charged. Unfortunately I have no control over what people have done and are doing with my story. But before you feel too good about yourself, you are also the center of religion.

EASTER BUNNY: Me? Yeah right. Get real.

JESUS: No, hold on a minute. Think about it. You show up at a certain time of the year. There are rituals around your coming. You serve chocolate eggs and bunnies, not unlike my bread and wine, and you have stories that seem pretty far-fetched, more like a fantasy, something only believers believe.

EASTER BUNNY: Okay, I concede. We both hate religion, but we are both at the center of religion. What are we going to do about it?

JESUS: And even worse, people who created the Jesus religion and the people who created the Easter Bunny religion are, maybe not physically, but in many other ways, fighting each other. Your people think Jesus religion is stupid, legalistic, and confining and my people think Easter Bunny religion is superficial, hedonistic, and narcissistic, and takes away from the real meaning of Easter, which they insist can be found only in my story.

EASTER BUNNY: Not even sure I know what those words mean, but okay. So, what are we going to do about it?

JESUS: I have an idea. Let's see if there is anything on which we agree. Maybe, instead of fighting each other, we could get my people and your people to gather in more pubs over more pints of BBB beer (Stenson would like that) and discover they are partners, not enemies.

EASTER BUNNY: Good idea. Bunnies make lousy soldiers.

JESUS: And can you really see me hunting Easter Bunnies or wiping out people and villages with bombs?

EASTER BUNNY: What are you thinking? Where do we start?

JESUS: Let's start with spring, the season for both our stories. What is it about spring that people like and we might both agree on?
EASTER BUNNY: It's the time of year when a young woman's fancy turns to that on which a young man's has dwelt all year.
JESUS: You bet. And what is the result of such fantasies?
EASTER BUNNY: Life! You know how many bunnies there are in a litter?
JESUS: Quit bragging. So, spring is about life.
EASTER BUNNY: Pussy willows. Tulips. Daffodils.
JESUS: Green grass, planting gardens. Longer days.
EASTER BUNNY: Okay, and how does that relate to you and me?
JESUS: Why do you hide Easter eggs? Why eggs?
EASTER BUNNY: Oh, I get it. Eggs hold life. They carry life. They break open and life emerges.
JESUS: And in my story I come out of the tomb, break out of the tomb, and come to life, and bring life.
EASTER BUNNY: So both of us are about life. We favor people breaking free from whatever is keeping them locked in.
JESUS: I sure do, and you seem to agree. Egg shells and rocks that need rolling away come in many forms.
EASTER BUNNY: Addictions.
JESUS: Like chocolate.
EASTER BUNNY: Hey, remember, we are partners. Don't pick on my people overdoing the chocolate.
JESUS: Right. Sorry. Fear is another rock that needs rolling away.
EASTER BUNNY: Shame.
JESUS: Guilt.
EASTER BUNNY: Poverty.
JESUS: Injustice.
EASTER BUNNY: So, whether Jesus or the Easter Bunny, Easter is about life and freedom.
JESUS: And celebrating life and freedom.
EASTER BUNNY: Celebrate? You? I thought you were a party pooper, not a party guy.
JESUS: You know how that happened?
EASTER BUNNY: This could be interesting.
JESUS: In ancient times, manuscripts were copied and re-copied by hand. Eyes, brains, and hands sometimes got tired. This work was done in monasteries and the scrolls were kept in their basements. One monk, curious how it is that monks had to be celibate, decided

to do some research. Several hours later, he came back upstairs and his brothers noticed he was white as a sheet. They quickly gathered around and pestered him with questions. What had happened? "Guys," he said, "guys, there has been a terrible mistake. You know the word celibate? Well, I found out, it's not celibate. It's celebrate. Think of what we have missed."

EASTER BUNNY: So you are a party guy?

JESUS: Never heard about changing water into wine? When the wedding was almost done and people really had had enough to drink, I made another one hundred fifty gallons—eight hundred bottles—of the best merlot you've ever had.

EASTER BUNNY: That's a party!

JESUS: I bet Stenson and BBB didn't realize how much they are like me, though I think I still have the edge on quality.

EASTER BUNNY: Okay, the Easter Bunny and Jesus are both about Easter bringing life free of all that holds people back from partying. I think my people could go with that. Doesn't sound religious.

JESUS: Some of mine get a little uneasy with the party stuff, wished I had made a few gallons of Welch's grape juice instead. But I'll work on them.

EASTER BUNNY: Celebrating life. Set free to party. We do make good partners.

JESUS: There is one more thing.

EASTER BUNNY: Oh, oh. Here comes the religious pitch.

JESUS: Come on, trust me. Remember, we agreed we both dislike religion.

EASTER BUNNY: Okay, what's the other stuff?

JESUS: My story includes Good Friday.

EASTER BUNNY: I knew it. I knew it! You can't help being a downer. You have to bring in the sad stuff. Before you know it, this story will include rabbit stew.

JESUS: Help me out here before you get your ears all twisted in knots.

EASTER BUNNY: Okay.

JESUS: Let's start with you. You are warm and cuddly and fuzzy. You are all about bringing comfort and joy. Children especially like you. And when they are sad or lonely or hurting, holding and hugging a bunny touches their hearts and brings them comfort.

EASTER BUNNY: Yeah, but you know what wolves and dogs like to do with warm and cuddly. It's a dangerous world out there.

JESUS: Precisely. That's Good Friday. My whole life was about bringing comfort to hurting, lonely, sad people. Compassion, I call it. And the religious dogs and political wolves came after me like they come after you. Compassion is dangerous business. It's ended in many crosses, stonings, and rabbit stews. Yet would you want a world without compassion?

EASTER BUNNY: No, I wouldn't. So you and I are both willing to take the risk, bring compassion even if the wolves and dogs are nipping at our heals. So, we have three things where we can partner at Easter—life, parties, compassion. Though the third one—compassion—is sometimes a tough sell, I can sell that to my people.

JESUS: Yeah, my people have trouble with that third one as well, but I'm committed to keep trying to sell all three to mine.

EASTER BUNNY: We've got us a deal.

JESUS: Hold it. Not so fast. You know what I think this sounds like?

EASTER BUNNY: What?

JESUS: A Kiwanis Easter.

EASTER BUNNY: A Kiwanis Easter?

JESUS: Yeah. A Kiwanis Easter. Think of it. What is Kiwanis about? Life. Kiwanians want to set people free to live, especially kids, but all people. They are committed to helping people caught by things that take away life.

EASTER BUNNY: And it's true. I don't know of anyone who likes to party more than Kiwanis people.

JESUS: The Kiwanians I know would make short work of my eight hundred bottles of wine.

EASTER BUNNY: And Kiwanis is about compassion. That is the driving motivator of why they join and keep working at all the things Kiwanis does.

JESUS: They are even prepared to sacrifice so others can have life and can party.

EASTER BUNNY: That's the Swift Current Kiwanis Club. But, one problem.

JESUS: What's that?

EASTER BUNNY: When they do all this wonderful stuff, they don't talk about Jesus or the Easter Bunny. We don't get the credit.

JESUS: There's your ego again. Do you really care? Seriously? Let's forget about what they call it or who gets credit. I, for one, don't need my name attached to everything good in the world. The important thing is that it gets done. Life. Party. Compassion. They can call it anything they want, for all I care. I just like to see it happen.

EASTER BUNNY: True. I'm with you. And who knows, maybe I'll still sell a few chocolate Easter bunnies on the side.

JESUS: You mean the ones where you bite off the ears and find out the head is hollow—has absolutely nothing inside? You want to sell those and give yourself away? You go right ahead. But Easter Bunny, before you go, I hope you will join me in wishing everyone here:

JESUS & EASTER BUNNY: A Happy Kiwanis Easter. Life. Party. Compassion.

Chapter 15

Funerals

SEVERAL YEARS AGO, WHILE helping a family plan a parent's funeral, the son-in-law included the instruction that we had to make sure the gospel was preached. I had an inkling as to what he meant. I replied that I agreed with him and that I understood that God's love and care were at the very heart of the gospel. He conceded they were important, but we also had to let people know that death was waiting for them and they'd better get ready. What better place to do this than at a funeral where the reality of death stares you straight in the eye and friends and family members who normally avoid church (often for good reason) are a captive audience?

I have been to funerals like that. I recall one where the preacher pointed to the sign behind him that declared in large, bold letters: "Prepare to meet thy God." More recently, at a funeral the pastor compared us delaying to get ready to die to him forgetting to reply to a banquet invitation and now being shut out because all the seats were taken. The first preacher seemed to forget that we can never, ever, prepare ourselves to meet God. What is so wonderful is that God has prepared God's ownself to meet us. That's the good news. The second preacher did not have me convinced that there was a limited number of seats at God's wedding banquet.

I do agree with all three of these men that at funerals, we as preachers have a fantastic opportunity to talk to people who rarely show up in church (except for weddings and funerals). I also agree that we should make the most of that opportunity. Neither of the preachers mentioned above did, nor did the request of the son-in-law. The two preachers simply confirmed for the family and friends gathered that Christianity is a judgmental and irrelevant religion we are best rid of. Faith was old-fashioned, irrelevant, and boring.

So let's make the most of our opportunity at every funeral. Let's speak to people in ways that will connect with them and introduce them to the God revealed in Jesus, who is declared to be love. I recall one funeral, as we gathered at the graveside after the church service, one of the granddaughters of the deceased made a bee-line for me. She told me how her two young adult grandchildren had listened to every word I said at the funeral and could not stop talking about what I had said as they traveled to the cemetery. She was so excited. Hallelujah! Mission accomplished! I had the third generation down thinking about God and Great-Grandma's faith and spirituality and I had not told anyone God was keen to kick them into Hell's abyss unless they fell in line.

My goal when I write and preach a funeral sermon is:

- To preach in a way that will grab people's interest and imagination;
- To be true to the life and legacy of the person whom we are remembering;
- To exegete the life of the person we are celebrating for I believe there is that of God and what God wants to say in every person and his or her life;
- To pull in texts and/or stories from the Ancient Writings, what we call the Bible;
- To paint a true picture of God; and
- To be honest and not to make of the person someone they were not

I confess that meeting those goals is easier sometimes, more difficult at other times. I recall one family being very explicit that they did not want me to speak in glowing terms about their dad. Life with him had not always been easy. However, one thing that was true of him was he loved his music, including Old Tyme Gospel music. I decided to use the Ancient Poetry (collected and passed down as The Psalms) to speak God into the man's life and to the people gathered. The family assured me I had succeeded.

In another case, I was again aware that life with Mom had not always been easy for this family, particularly with regards to her judgmental nature and her attempts to "push religion down their throats." Still, they had loved their mother. My memory of her was that while I was her pastor, she would walk down the aisle after worship to shake my hand, wobbling on her two canes. It seemed to me an appropriate sermon title for her funeral was "Stumbling Heavenward."

Then there can be the really difficult ones. I've had a few of those. In one case, the funeral director came to me and asked me to do the funeral for a man who had died. I did not know the man. His only church connection was that long ago, his children had gone to our Sunday school. When no other minister who might have a connection to him in our town was available, I changed my schedule and agreed to take the funeral. The director proceeded to tell me about the man. He was estranged from his entire family, especially his daughter. The life the funeral director described seemed to have no redeeming values. Anyone from the community who would attend the funeral would see through any attempts on my part to paint him as anything other than who he was. With some relief, I heard the director say that one of the man's sons would be arriving in Swift Current from Florida the next day and would be able to fill in some details. Good. That would give me another picture of the deceased.

It turned out that the son simply told me more of the same. The text for that funeral included Romans 7:15–25.

Sharing a funeral sermon in a book is tricky because the sermons I preach are highly personal, not in the sense of revealing family secrets, but personal to the deceased and their family and friends gathered to celebrate a life and say goodbye. However, I decided I would give myself permission to share the sermon I preached at my mom's funeral.

There were a couple of things I kept in mind. One, again, was honesty. Mom's faith journey had taken her a long distance and her articulation at this stage was not necessarily shared by her children, nor was it, I think, always adequate even for her. At the same time, it was one strongly held to by her faith community and funerals are not a place to stir controversy. (A cousin and close friend of mine later called me "subversive." He understood. Those who would have found the sermon controversial did not catch some of the hidden meanings and understood what I said about Mom's faith journey in a way that fit for them.)

Secondly, all but one of Mom's adult grandchildren were going to be there. None of them are active participants in church. One would self-confess as an atheist. Two others camped in the neighborhood. I wanted to connect with them in such a way that they would actually listen to the sermon (even as my brother assured me they would not) and I wanted them to understand that though their worldview and/or faith and spirituality articulation were different from Grandma's, Grandma had still left them a legacy, firmly rooted in her faith, and one they could live out in their world.

Here is the result.

A MOTHER'S LEGACY

Luke 10:38–39

In thinking about what I might say this afternoon to bring together Mom's life, her faith, the faith of her community, and her legacy to her children and grandchildren, I recalled that recently, in working on a sermon on the story of Esther, I became keenly aware that in the Biblical story, when God wanted to speak God's presence into the world, God did so through humans. In fact, when God wanted to speak God's presence and love into people's lives and into the world in a most profound and powerful way to change both history and people, God could not do that as God. God did that as a human. This being the case, I realized that even though Esther lived in a cultural and religious context that limited her opportunities to speak God's presence into our world with words, Esther still spoke that presence of God into her world with her life in ways that continue to echo twenty-five centuries later. And so I asked myself, "Might the same be true of Mom, living in a context with some similar limits?"

I went looking for an answer to that question with the help of another Biblical story, this one a story of two other women, and discovered it to be true. There were things in Mom's life that profoundly spoke God's presence into our lives as her children and grandchildren and, I dare say, into the lives of many others she connected with. The story, from chapter 10 of Luke's Good News Story Book: "Now as Jesus and his disciples went on their way, Jesus entered a certain village, where a woman named Martha welcomed him into her home. She had a sister named Mary, who sat at the Lord's feet and listened to what he was saying."[1] Two sisters, who in their lives combined characteristics of Mom and Grandma who, I think, are an important legacy for us as children and particularly for those of you who knew this wonderful woman as Grandma.

1. Dora the Housekeeper

---

1. Luke 10:38–39. NRSV.

"*Jungess, doats teat tum Sinovent houlle.*"[2] ("Boys, it's time to keep Saturday.") Those words from my childhood still haunt my Saturday mornings. "*Jungess, doats teat tum Sinovent houlle.*" With those words, Mom set in motion another Saturday of addressing the accumulated messes, dirty floors, and general chaos that resulted from a week's worth of life in the Friesen household. There were floors to be washed and waxed, a basement to be tidied and swept, rooms to be made neat, chairs to be dusted—every rung and between all the spokes—and shoes to be polished, along with buns to be baked and *aitschoke mett shaell*[3] to be cooked, and, of course, a bath to be had at the end of the day. Sunday morning, we would wake up to a new world, neat and tidy, waiting for us and our guests, should some arrive.

I don't think Mom realized that in leading her crew through Saturday keeping, she was reenacting God's first and most foundational act—the Creation. When God walks onto the scene in the opening verses of Genesis, God is greeted by the primordial chaos, the mother of all chaoses and messes, the *tohu wa bohu*[4] of Genesis 1 that seemed at first so huge, so messy, and so chaotic as to resist all attempts at Saturday keeping.

However, God is not so easily stymied and in Genesis 1 and 2, we have the story of God's Saturday keeping and how God turned this chaos into the beautiful garden at the end of chapter 2, the new world that greeted people and animals alike as they got up Sunday morning of the second week. In Genesis 1, God achieved that Saturday keeping by speaking life and order into the universe, much like Mary Poppins does in her movie. What Bob and I earlier, and Lynette and Rosanna later (we're not sure Gerry ever learned Saturday keeping),[5] wouldn't have given those Saturday mornings to have had the ability to snap our fingers and sing a

---

2. I did not learn English until I entered Grade 6. I grew up with, spoke to Mom in, and still sometimes use with brothers and friends, Low German. It originated in the Netherlands (hence the "Low") and was shaped as the language traveled with the Mennonites to Prussia, Ukraine, and then the Canadian prairies. I would guess eighty to ninety percent of the people at the funeral understood Low German.

3. "Potatoes with peel." On Saturdays, Mom would cook these potatoes. Then they were ready for her to peel, shred, and fry on Sunday for the noon meal that would often include company.

4. The Hebrew phrase in Gen 1:2 that my NRSV translates as "formless and void." I like using the Hebrew even when preaching English because the sound seems to capture the spooky character of what was before God started "Saturday keeping."

5. Bob and Gerry are my two brothers, following me in the family in that order; Lynette and Rosanna are my two sisters, the youngest in the family.

tune like Mary Poppins or speak a word like God, and have the messes right themselves. Our experience, as was Mom's her whole life, was more like God in Genesis 2, where bringing Order out of Chaos and Life out of Death takes a good bit of digging, planting, shaping, and just downright hard work. That is the hard work Mom showed us and, as God did that first week, Mom, with our help, did every week of the year. With her Saturday keeping, she turned chaos into order and showed us who God is.

2. Dora the Hostess

Mom's life as God's hostess was a pilgrimage. It started in a fairly closed community in Blumenhof where she loved to welcome *Geschwista*[6] and *Freintshchaft*[7] for dinner and/or faspa—there were always lots of Plett and Reimer and Friesen cousins to visit with. She widened that circle to include friends and others from the church community, though with such large families as families of origin, it could be hard to find friends who weren't cousins, but Mom and Dad found them and enjoyed them.

In 1966, when we moved to Wawanesa, the community she and Dad were now part of suddenly was very different from the earlier Blumenhof, and offering hospitality changed. Neighbors were now people with different ways, different culture, a different first language, and, quite possibly a different belief system. Hospitality had to be reworked. At first, hospitality was a necessary part of ministry. Soon, however, that hospitality changed as Mom's life and belief system widened and, though these people might be different, these new neighbors were fellow travelers with God on life's pilgrimage.

Those horizons of hospitality were stretched even further as Dad began his prison ministry and Mom and Dad opened their home to those who were, by much of society including church society, labeled as outsiders and less desirable. It did not matter what others thought of these people—the "unwashed" of polite society. They were, Mom and Dad came to realize and showed us, their children, equally—that's right, equally—deserving of God's love. That truth would only be realized by these people if they were equally deserving of Mom and Dad's hospitality and so they spent time with, and invited to their home, people that others would have avoided and might have preferred Mom and Dad avoid.

---

6. Siblings and in-laws.

7. Relatives, particularly uncles, aunts, and cousins.

In Mom's actions, we and those around her came to see God's wide, gracious, and loving hospitality, or at least a good bit of it, and enough to point us in a direction. Mom's example encouraged us to see that the world is not so clearly divided into insiders and outsiders, the acceptable and the unacceptable. Rather, God's welcome is wide, as wide as the ocean, as the Sunday school song says, and is meant for all people, no matter who they are. Our homes, churches, and government have much to learn from Mom about God-like hospitality.

3. Dora at the feet of Jesus

Sitting at the feet of Jesus was, I think, for Mom, a more difficult journey than she would have expected or than how it is often described. Upon first thought, it would seem that surely there would be no better place for someone like Mom—committed Christian, baptized church member, fervent missionary—to sit than at the feet of Jesus. However, sitting there means listening to what Jesus has to say and what Jesus has to say can be very disconcerting and the exact opposite of comfortable. We need only read the Gospels to discover this—Matthew's push for the abolition of religion, Mark with a whole new vision for politics and society, Luke and his economic ideas that turn all our economic systems upside down, and John with his new take on faith and personal spirituality. But disconcerting though it may have been, Mom sat at those feet, listened to the Master's words, and then honestly and with commitment, struggled with their meaning in life.

There were three spiritual traditions that met in Mom's heart, mind, and life and they made for an uneasy journey. There was the *Kleinegemeinde*[8] tradition into which she was baptized, characterized by our paternal grandfather's lifelong question: "*Woat itt noch moll aula touriejche?*" (Will it ultimately be enough?) It was filled with humility, fear, and uncertainty. Heaven was not guaranteed. For this tradition, there

---

8. Literally "small church." It was the label somewhat derisively given to a group of Mennonites that broke away from the main church in Ukraine in 1812. They continued to be known by that label, one adopted by the adherents, until the 1950s when the Canadian members of the group changed their name to the Evangelical Mennonite Conference. There are still groups in Mexico and Belize who use the original label.

was no problem that her funeral happened at the same time as the Banjo Bowl[9]—we shouldn't even know about the Banjo Bowl.[10]

There was the Evangelical tradition learned from her Uncle Ben, full of certainty and new life, but with the threat of eternal punishment hovering in the background. Certainty, yet niggling fear. There was the tradition of her own parents she started with and one I sometimes wonder if she and Dad looked for all their lives without realizing it had been there all along—humility without fear, certainty without arrogance, and grace without condition. What I admire about Mom is that she struggled, I believe honestly, at times fearfully, sometimes desperately, to find within the wrestling match of these traditions that which would allow her finally to entrust the earthly lives and eternal destiny of her children, grandchildren, and great-grandchildren into the unconditional, unwavering, and fully-embracing grace of a God whose love knows no bounds, whose grace finds no limits, and whose forgiveness and acceptance are without end. I don't think she ever quite got there but she was on a journey, headed in that direction, and that is what matters to us. That is her example—sitting at the feet of Jesus means to never stop listening, searching, and rethinking. Thank you, Mom, for your faith struggle. There is much we can learn from it and from you.

And now what? Mom is gone (as is Dad). However, she has left us this legacy. What will we do with it? Is it one we, all of us as family but especially Mom's grandchildren, are ready to take on? You as grandchildren are really the next generation that can best take on this legacy and run with it. Will you take on the challenge? And then I look at your lives and as I think about each one of you, I realized the question has been answered. You have already started to take it on.

I believe you as Mom's grandchildren are, each in your own way, partnering with God—whatever it is you believe about God—in the ongoing work of Saturday keeping in our world:

---

9. The fiercest rivalry in the Canadian Football League is between the Saskatchewan Roughriders and the Winnipeg Blue Bombers. Each season they play each other in Regina on Labor Day Sunday. The following weekend they play each other again in Winnipeg. After a Winnipeg place kicker mocked the Rider fans, calling them "inbred banjo pickers," the rematch has become known as the Banjo Bowl. A majority of the people at the funeral would have been CFL fans, most cheering for the Bombers.

10. Mom's *Kleinegemeinde* tradition, one shared by most of her friends and relatives at the funeral, considered any participation in organized sports, and especially professional sports, as worldly and evil.

- Larissa, as you work with trouble students and their families[11]
- Rachelle, as you address the systemic issues of injustice and colonialism
- Ajay, as you bring your engineering skills to bear on two of the twenty-first century's major issues—climate change and energy
- Carley, as you design cities to be life-giving communities rather than storage places for humanity
- Cody, as you enter chaos, dangerous chaos, and brokenness, bringing rescue and healing
- Tony, as you take the most ordinary scenes of life, refocus them in your camera's lens, and show us that our world is in fact a world of tremendous beauty
- Roxie, as you go where certainly I, if not angels, fear to tread, and nurture dental health in people
- Jody as you feed, maybe not five thousand with five buns and a stick of forma *worsch*,[12] but feed people and make eating a pleasant experience
- Amber, as you help ensure people have a safe roof over their heads
- Jose Maria, at 3, as you potentially have the longest time to live this legacy

All of you, keep it up. You are living Grandma's legacy and God's dream for the world. Great stuff!

---

11. A note of explanation about the grandchildren may make this address to the grandchildren more understandable. Larissa is a social work clinician in the public school system. Rachelle, having worked in Palestine as a peace development worker for four years before being deported by Israel, had just started her Masters in Social and Political Thought at York University. Ajay is an engineer. Carley is trained as a city architect. Cody is a fireman in the City of Winnipeg. Tony is an increasingly recognized and sought-after wedding photographer. Roxie is a dental hygienist. Jody works in a restaurant. Amber worked in the office for a roofing company (and now is training as a chartered accountant). Those were, at the time, Mom's adult grandchildren. My one brother married a second time to a woman much younger than him, who had never had children. At the time of Mom's funeral, he and his second wife had one son, Jose Maria. Since, they have had a second, Juan Diego.

12. This is Low German for "farmer sausage," a standard Mennonite ethnic food. In fact, in my current community they call it "Mennonite sausage." It is something Jody's Grandma regularly served her family.

Take on the task of hospitality. God knows our world still has much to learn about welcoming people and overcoming the fear we have of those who are different. Show us how to build a world that includes and is welcoming of all, in our homes, in our churches, in our communities, and in our countries.

And "sit at the feet of Jesus"—that was Grandma's language; you may well have different words for it. Keep working at ways to make sense of spirituality, life, and the things we believe and the way we see the world. Learn from an earlier over confidence that humility is much better. Let's never be too convinced that the answers we rejected are wrong, the questions we ask are so much more enlightened, and the answers we find far superior to what Grandma and her generation had. Let's keep reworking what it means to live in our world as people filled with life, cognizant of so much that shapes us, aware that life and the universe are far more than we can see or fit into our cameras, test tubes, and engineering schemes. Keep asking questions. Keep giving new answers. Find new metaphors and paradigms. But always keep searching and changing.

Keep Grandma's legacy alive.

Chapter 16

Children's Stories

I believe children's stories are a crucial piece in the worship life of a congregation for both children and adults. We cheat our children if we ship them off to "Children's Church" to hear their stories, as if worship is really not for them. We cheat our adults if we tell children's stories in "Children's Church" and not in the family worship setting. We cheat them in two ways. One, the parents don't hear the stories their children hear, nor do they hear them told in the way the children hear them told. There is truth in the story and in the telling. If parents are to build on the story and the telling, they need to know what the story and the telling were. It's not enough to assume they know the story because they heard a similar story when they were children.

Secondly, the adults can learn as much from the story as do the children, and as much as they do from the sermon. In one congregation I was in, the adults suggested I tell a children's story even if there were no children that Sunday. And if I had taken the children into the basement to tell them a story while the adults did adult worship in the main sanctuary, they would have mutinied and followed me and the children into the basement.

In one congregation where Sylvia and I served, we did have a children's story each Sunday, but it was told by someone other than the pastor. I've noticed the same thing in other congregations at worship. That is both good and bad. The good is that all those who have the gift get to use it. The bad is that the children think the pastor and what s/he has to say is only for adults. I have found the children's story to be a great way to build rapport with the children. So if you have storytellers in your congregation, by all means, use their gifts. However, at a minimum, make sure the pastor takes a regular turn in the scheduling cycle. Depending on how many people are in the cycle, you may want to give the pastor a couple of turns each cycle.

In 2004, Sylvia and I started in a congregation that often had a few children at worship, but there was no children's story for them. So I made a promise to the children. If they would be at worship with the rest of us, I would have a story for them. And so it was that I was prepared every Sunday to tell a story. Sometimes I would write it out ahead of time, or at a minimum, sketch it out in notes. Sometimes I would think of the story I wanted to tell and simply tell it as it came to mind. I think my pre-planned and sketched stories were better. What you have in this chapter are three such stories. Often these stories were Bible stories, but not necessarily.

At another point, after friends told us about what their pastor did, I instituted a "story bag." I started with a paper bag, but then one of the women in the congregation sewed a cloth bag, complete with a label, for me. The children would take turns taking the bag home. The instruction was to put something into it the following Sunday morning and to bring it back to worship time with them. I would always introduce story time with "What time is it?" They would shout out "Story time!" and then come forward. When they came forward for story time, they would bring the bag with them and give it to me. I would open the bag, take out whatever was inside, and then include that item in the story. At the same time, my promise to myself was to somehow connect the story to the sermon I would preach a few minutes later.

Sometimes the story was easy. Sometimes I had to hum and haw for a while and the congregation would smile, snicker, and even laugh, in a good-natured way. They knew Friesen was struggling. One Sunday, I thought for a while and knew I had to start the story. I started it with no idea where we would end up nor how it would connect to the sermon. I no longer remember the story, but I do remember it ended so the possible lesson was similar to the one the sermon was meant to teach.

At some point in the congregation's history, children in worship became more of a rarity. Some grew up. Some decided to play sports on Sunday morning. We retired the story bag. However, any Sunday there were children, I tried to meet them before worship and suggested they think of something they would like to have as part of the children's story.

When they came forward, they would tell me what they had thought of and I would weave it into a story.

A word of warning: Be careful about having to end every story with "The moral of the story is . . . " Allow stories to speak in different ways to different people, including children. Stories manage to do that well, especially when you tell Bible stories. Rarely in the Bible do you find the Old Testament Storytellers, the Gospel Storytellers (except John), or Jesus himself saying, "And this is what you should learn." Jesus, in fact, seemed to resist doing that, though there are examples of him, with a note of exasperation in his voice, telling the disciples what a certain story meant because the disciples were so clued out.

Give your adults and children the benefit of the doubt. They'll figure out what the story means for them that day. Don't limit it. Especially, as I said, don't force Bible stories into a mold. Let the story go with them and it may speak different lessons to them at different times, as they need those lessons.

Here are three examples of stories from my pre-story bag days. Two of them are two different ways of telling a part of the Creation story. They are examples, I submit, of a few things:

1. The freedom we have with Bible stories, just like the original storytellers had freedom
2. What is possible when you set your imagination free
3. How the same story can teach similar and different lessons
4. How one can be more "lesson" focused and the other is set free to be whatever it needs to be.

"I'M NOT SCARED OF THE DARK"

Once upon a time, a long, long time ago, in land far, far away—and yet maybe not so long ago and not so far away—Mommy and Daddy and their two boys were sitting by the campfire, after supper. You see, in the land where this family lived and in the time they lived, they used their house (just a tiny cabin actually), mainly for sleeping and to get in out of the rain. They lived outdoors. Mom did all her cooking on the fire and in the evening, they would sit around the fire until it was time for bed.

The evening I am thinking about, supper was done and everyone had had a chance to say what they did all day. Mom turned to the boys and said, "Time for bed, boys."

"Can we have a story first, please, please, can we have a story first?" the boys begged together, as if they had practiced this.

"Please Dad, can you tell us a story?" Cain, the older brother continued. Dad looked at Mom who smiled and nodded, and Dad said, "Okay. Anything in particular?"

"The fireworks story, please, the fireworks story," Abel, the younger boy said, almost before Dad was done asking.

Dad looked at Cain, almost as if he was hoping for another suggestion.

"Yes," said Cain. "That's my favorite."

Dad resisted the desire to sigh in exasperation at having to tell the story for what seemed to be the one thousandth time, and this after a long day spent hoeing the corn. But Dad loved his boys and he knew it was a good story, an important story, and so he began.

"Once upon a time, before there was time, everywhere you looked it was dark, pitch dark, like there was nothing. You could see nothing! It was so dark you could feel the Dark, almost like it was choking you. It was a scary Dark!"

"Like when we wake up at night and the fire is out and the clouds cover the sky?" asked little Abel, as he did every time at this point in the story.

"Like that, and even darker, a spooooky Dark!" The boys shuddered, enjoying the feeling of fear and spooky. They could feel the Dark slithering down their necks, in behind their shirts. They shivered. It was a cold dark.

"All there was, other than the Dark, was a soft breeze, a warm breeze, softly touching your cheek. And then, from nowhere, yet sounding like it came from everywhere, loud but almost quiet, there was a Voice. It was a Voice so strong that nothing could shut it out, yet a Voice so soft you wanted to hear more. And the Voice said, (here the boys joined their dad in a big shout, for they knew the story) 'Let there be light!' and suddenly, Pow, Pow, Pow! Everywhere there were lights flashing—blue, green, white, red, yellow—all the colors of the rainbow, across the whole sky—Pow, Pow, Pow—lights so bright it hurt your eyes. It seemed like the fireworks went on for hours—Pow, Pow, Pow. They did, in fact, go on forever. They never went out. You looked up and there were stars, and a moon, and planets, and a sun, a sun so bright that it shut out all the other lights. Pow, Pow Pow.

"And the dark, the scary, spooooky Dark? It slithered into a hole in the ground because it was afraid of the lights and it knew that the Light was much stronger, than Dark. The Dark knew it was beat. It slithered away, deep into the ground. And God came and closed the door on Dark."

"Did God lock the door?" asked Cain.

"No," said his daddy. "God didn't lock the door. And so, every now and then, Dark peeks out of the ground, but always the light is so bright that it hurts Dark's eyes and Dark has to go back into the ground again. It can't stand the Light."

"Okay, boys," said Mommy, "now it's time for bed."

As she tucked her youngest son into the warm, furry blankets, Abel said, "You know something, Mommy? If I wake up tonight and it's dark and the clouds cover the moon, I won't be scared. I'll just feel the breeze on my cheek and I'll know God can send fireworks and the dark will have to hide. Dark can't scare me."

CREATION

In the introduction, I wrote about the use of pronouns for God and how it is important in our preaching to use language that clearly communicates that God is neither male nor female and at the same time God is both. In preaching, by and large, I find I can preach without using either pronoun. In storytelling that is more difficult and awkward. So you will have to decide how you are going to do that. In this case, since the male pronoun is generally used for God by those who use pronouns, including the Bible translations that I use, I have written this story using the female pronoun. I think it is really important, since children probably cannot think of God as not being either male or female, that they learn that God can as easily and appropriately be female as male.

God sat and wondered. She scratched her head. She was deep in thought. She got up, walked around and looked around. She looked at the far flung galaxies, the stars that twinkled, the planets that shone, the darkness that was a backdrop to it all. God was pretty impressed with herself. She had done good. And it had been fun, tossing those planets into outer space, setting the stars on fire. That had been kind of special as she lit each star in turn, blew on it gently to get it going and then watched it break into flame. Each time one more burst into flame, it helped light up the darkness until there was as much light as there was darkness. It was beautiful! Then, for good measure, God had added comets and black holes, just to make it interesting.

And now, it seemed done—stars twinkling, planets in their orbits, whole galaxies spinning. But God felt like she had just begun. What else could she do?

As God looked from galaxy to galaxy, she noticed something, in the far reaches of the Milky Way, one planet, somehow different from the others. She remembered making it and putting it there, thinking she might come back to it. Then, in the excitement of all the other stuff she had tossed into space, she forgot about it. Now she noticed it again. That planet had some possibilities. If she moved it a little closer to its sun—there, that was better, now it would be just the right temperature. Maybe if she tilted it just a bit, a little more, not too far. There, she liked that. Now what?

First, God would have to get smaller so God shrunk down in size, down in size even further, even more, for she had to fit on this tiny planet in the middle of a gigantic universe. A little smaller yet, and then God landed on the planet and looked around as she rolled up her sleeves. God had an idea, a plan, and she thought it was going to be good.

Second, God would need some help. God's plan was big and complex and it would take all the help she could get.

Plants, the first thing this planet needed was plants. Trees, a few trees would be nice. Shrubs for some variety. Flowers with big smiles that would cheer up the place. Soon the entire planet was covered with plants, plants of all kinds growing everywhere.

Then God realized she'd forgotten something. Plants would need water. No problem. She could always make it rain. But hold it. What if it rained too much? Then what would happen? No problem again. God and her helpers dug some rivers, this way and that way. Where they had to, they moved a tree this way and a shrub that way, until the rivers were ready to go. One big rain and they had water in them.

Plants were nice, but the problem with plants was they just stayed put. This planet needed things running around in it, crawling around on it, flying around above it. Creepy crawly things, animals and birds came next, and for good measure, God tossed a few fish into the river.

And then God stood back, dusted off her hands and jeans, and looked at all she had made. God's helpers joined her. For God, this might be easy. For them, it was hard work. They were tired. But they had to agree that what they had made was pretty darn good. God walked around and admired it all. She was quite proud of herself. And then a perplexed look came over God's face. There was still something missing. What was it? God looked here. God looked there. God scratched her head again. God consulted with her helpers. And then God's face brightened. God had another idea. She didn't tell anyone. She told her helpers to just stand back and watch. This was going to be good!

God hurried to a spot by the river. God remembered she had put a whole bunch of clay there. Clay stuck together nicely, not like sand that just ran through your fingers. With clay, you could make things, all kinds of things. And God was about to make something.

God took a lump of clay and started fiddling with it. God squeezed it here and there. She pulled it this way and that way. God looked at it, thought, looked some more. One of her helpers came and whispered in her ear. God's face brightened. God smiled. This was good.

So God tried some more. Squeezed here. Pulled there. Shaped another place. God started to like what she saw. God worked faster. Narrower here, wider there. God grabbed some more clay and rolled it into four rolls, sticking two at one end of what she had, two at the other. Then she took a look and changed her mind, taking the two at one end and made them stick out sideways, rather than out the end like the other two. God made a few more adjustments and then stood back. She liked what she saw. Her helpers began to cheer and clap. The animals gathered round. They had never seen anything like this before. Neither had God, but God liked trying new things.

The helpers looked at the "thing" on the ground and then at God. The animals looked at the "thing" and then at God. Back and forth, as if to say, "Nice, but what's it good for?" One of the helpers walked over and whispered in God's ear again. Sometimes it seemed God needed help with these things. God got so caught up in the big and the creative, God forgot the details.

God's smile faded. Right, now what? Suddenly the smile came back. God had it figured out. Now God had a look of excitement on her face. God walked over to the "thing" on the ground. God kneeled down, bent over, took a deep breath, and slowly breathed out, right into the "thing's" mouth. The helpers and animals watched. They all wondered what was going to happen.

Then they noticed, as God breathed another breath. The thing's chest moved up as God breathed in. Once more God breathed, and once more the chest moved up and down. Then it was breathing on its own. It began to move. It opened its eyes. It turned its head, back and forth.

God stepped back. Then, as God, the helpers, and the animals watched, the thing slowly got up, on its knees, then on its feet. The thing was a little wobbly at first, but then it got steadier. It took a few steps, then a few more, and then it jumped. The thing was starting to have fun, and it took a few more steps, and tried a dance step. This was fun! It danced some more, around and around the garden. God joined in. Then the helpers. And the animals. Soon everybody was dancing. The trees and shrubs and flowers couldn't dance, but they waved in the breeze.

God shouted out, "Clayton. I name you Clayton because I made you out of clay," and everyone cheered! This was awesome! What a wonderful world!

THE STORYTELLER[1]

Once upon a time in a land not so far away was a village, a happy village. In it, you could hear the sounds of laughter and singing. Dads whistled while they worked the fields. Moms hummed songs as they did the laundry. Children, when not helping Mom or Dad, ran and laughed and played. Teens dreamed dreams of futures filled with happiness and success and love, especially love because love was all around in this village.

In this village lived a Storyteller with white hair and a white beard. He had been telling stories for a long time. In the evenings, the people would gather in the village square and they would say to the Storyteller: "Tell us a story."

He would stroke his beard and the longer his beard, the longer and better his stories. No one ever wished that this Storyteller end his stories sooner because he told wonderful stories. His stories made people laugh. His stories made people cry, but it was a good cry. It helped them realized that when they cried for good reasons, crying was good because they were remembering good times and good people. His stories made the people want to be good, gentle, kind, caring, and forgiving.

---

1. If you want to have a Biblical text to go with the story, I suggest Psalm 78:1–4. While preparing this manuscript for publication, I happened to watch *Star Trek: Voyager*, season 6, episode 22 with my son-in-law. It makes the point about the power of storytelling, as I also try to do in the Christmas Reader's Theater in chapter 10.

The Storyteller told stories of men, brave in the hunt. He told stories of women who cooked wonderful meals and cared for and loved and nurtured their families. He told stories of dads who spent time with their children and moms who wrapped their families in love. He told lots of love stories, stories of young women who smiled, of young men whose hearts did somersaults. He told stories of forgiveness and hugs and celebrations. Because of these stories, the village was a wonderful village.

One day, some people arrived from a village that did not have a Storyteller, where the people did not gather in the village square to visit, sing, dance, and hear stories. These people were Angry People. There were no smiles on their faces. They were scary people, harsh and cruel. Their eyes looked old, even in the faces of young women and men. They carried weapons and spoke only in anger and with hatred.

These Angry People arrived in the evening, saw the people gathered in the square, and heard the Storyteller telling the story of a woman who had been brave and the man who loved her and helped her. The Angry People hated the story—such a story could not be true. They hated the Storyteller. They grabbed the Storyteller, beat him until he was barely alive, scattered the people, set a few houses on fire, and then left.

The Storyteller was very sick, very sick for months and months. He was so sick, he could no longer tell stories. The people began to forget the stories and they, and their village, changed. Instead of laughter, there was swearing. Instead of gentle crying, you heard angry yelling. Eyes that had sparkled with fun and joy and mischief grew cold and hard and seemed to hide evil thoughts. People spoke harsh words to each other when they met in the village square. They argued and were mean and cruel. Fights, terrible fights, would break out.

At home, moms and dads argued, seemed always to argue. Mom would yell at Dad. Dad would swear at mom. They both yelled at their children. The children grew afraid. Often they would hide when they saw Mom or Dad coming, especially if Dad had been drinking beer with the other men, and he drank a lot of beer. Then the children ran in terror for dads full of beer had become mean and cruel dads. At night, hiding under the covers, the blankets could not shut out the sounds of people being hit, women crying, and men stomping around in anger. In the morning, makeup did not hide the bruises.

Family gatherings where the aunts used to sing and laugh and the uncles told funny stories and the cousins played together, were no longer happy times. Uncles would swear, aunts told mean, gossipy stories, cousins would bully and tease in cruel ways.

One day at such a family gathering, Uncle Bill and Uncle Bob were arguing, and their argument was getting louder and louder and their words nastier and nastier. Cousins watched in fear. Would there be a fight?

Suddenly Angel, one of the cousins just about Alex's[2] age, got up, ran to Grandpa and said, "Grandpa, please tell us a story."

The room grew very quiet. Even Uncle Bob and Uncle Bill stopped for a moment. "What?" said Grandpa. "What did you say?"

"Please," repeated Angel, "please tell us a story."

"But I'm not a Storyteller," said Grandpa. "I have no beard to stroke. How can I tell a story? Only Storytellers tell stories."

Angel was like Alex. She did not give up easily. "So what if you have no beard? Surely you have heard enough stories that you can tell one story. Just a short one."

Everyone waited. The room was quiet. Grandpa reached for his chin. There was no beard, but he could still stroke his chin. He reached for his pipe and his tobacco. He could fill a pipe and light it. Everyone waited.

And then, as the first smoke from the pipe encircled his head, Grandpa began, slowly, stumbling at first, and then with more confidence, and he told a story. Grandma got a tear in her eye. A little smile showed on Aunt Jill's face. Uncle Bill and Uncle Bob forgot their argument. Angel and Sammy and Susie and Jimmy felt all warm inside.

After the story, Grandma said, "Let's eat." Everyone gathered round. Uncle Bill told a funny, kind story. Aunt Mary started a happy song. It was like happiness had returned to the family. All this from one story.

The next evening, Susie's Daddy was really grouchy, complaining about Mommy's cooking, yelling at Susie and Jimmy to be quiet or else he would give them something to yell about. Suddenly Susie said, "Mommy, tell us a story."

Mommy turned in shock—her tell a story? Daddy stopped in mid-sentence. "Please, Mommy," Susie said. "Grandpa told one without a beard. So can you."

Mommy was quiet for a while, and then she began slowly, stumbling over her words at first, but soon the story became a good story, a happy story, and a fun story. Daddy forgot his grouchiness. Susie and Jimmy

---

2. Alex was a young girl in our congregation when I wrote and told this story.

forgot they were afraid. Mommy forgot her sadness, and love for her family nigh burst her heart. Who cared that Jimmy's and Susie's room was always messy? Who cared that Daddy often came home from work late?

Down the street at Billy's and Sally's house, Mom was yelling at the dog, at Billy, at Daddy, and at Grandma on the phone. Suddenly Billy said, "Daddy, tell us a story."

Daddy, even though he didn't have a beard, remembered Grandpa and his story. If Grandpa could remember and tell a story, so could he, and he began, stumbling over his words at first, but soon the story came almost faster than he could tell it.

And then Bill and Susie heard Mommy say, "I'm sorry!" to Grandma on the phone. Then she walked over to Daddy and kissed him on the cheek, and Daddy smiled. Then she hugged Billy and Susie, and Billy and Susie smiled and felt warm all over.

And so it was, all over the village. Children asked for stories and moms and dads and grandpas and grandmas found their stories and told them. They told the Storyteller's stories, the ones they remembered. They told their own stories, and found they had many that needed telling. And in the village, laughter and singing of happy songs was heard again. When people cried, it was gentle crying, crying because the sadness reminded them of the love and the good they had enjoyed. People smiled and shook hands and hugged each other. In the evening, more and more gathered in the village square again to visit and discovered they had stories they wanted to tell each other and were able to tell and did tell.

Finally, the Storyteller got well again. Silently one evening he walked up to the outside of the crowd in the village square. He smiled as he heard the stories. This was good. Now the village had many Storytellers, as many as there were people in the village, not just one. And then on Saturday, the people invited the Storyteller back and asked him to tell a story. And so it was from then on, on Saturdays and on special days, the Storyteller would tell his stories, stories that had become even more wonderful. And the other days, why they hardly had enough days for everyone who had stories—for everyone had stories—to tell their stories.

And Angel and Jimmy, they would often go for walks and dream and talk about how one day they would be Storytellers, not just everyday Storytellers, but Storytellers for Saturdays and the special days.

Chapter 17

Scripture Reading

THERE IS ANOTHER AREA, other than preaching and storytelling, where I think that we as preachers and pastors can practice creativity in a way that will help those we serve. This is in our reading of Scripture and, in particular, rewriting pieces of text so that the jaded ears of those who listen may perk up and minds may reengage.

I will sometimes rewrite short pieces of texts as part of my sermon or other things I am writing. At other times, I will take a longer piece and work with it. Sometimes I make minor changes and give people parts so a long story can be read in worship without losing people. For example, John 4 and John 9. Still other times, I may rewrite in a significant way so that the reading of the text will help people, as I said, reengage with a text they may have heard many times before.

I know one person who is not particularly fond of such rewrites. He believes we should read the text as it comes to us. I respect that, but also respectfully disagree. Translation is already a rewrite, and translations can be quite different. Preaching is also rewriting of texts—helping the congregation catch the meaning of the text/story/poem. So my rewrites can be thought of both as expanded translations (though I do not work directly from the Hebrew and/or Greek, except with regards to occasional Greek words) and as condensed sermons.

I encourage you to do the same. All you really need is a fully engaged imagination. God has given you one. Never, ever shut it down.

I regularly consult the NRSV, along with the New Living Translation, and *The Message*, both when I work at sermons and when I want to rewrite a text. I find that in a variety of ways, all three help me get the flavor of the text and spark the imagination for what can be.

Here are some examples of what I have done. Hopefully they serve to spark your imagination until you can't keep up with it, and you write materials for your congregation.

A READING OF GENESIS 1

(Prepare the congregation ahead of time so that at a signal —a signal they will recognize—they will say with the readers: "And there was morning and there was evening—Day #.")

READER 1: In the Beginning . . .
READER 2: What beginning?
READER 1: The Beginning, the start, the first thing.
READER 2: Of what? The race? A novel? A TV show? A story? The beginning of what?
READER 1: Of everything, man. EVERYTHING! In the Beginning of everything, before there was anything else. That Beginning.
READER 2: Wow! That's a long time ago, that Beginning. So, in the Beginning, what was in the Beginning?
READER 1: Well, if you would just listen, I would tell you.
READER 2: I'm listening.
READER 1: Okay, then. In the Beginning, there was Nothing, so much Nothing it was actually Something.
READER 2: What? Nothing that was something? That makes no sense!
READER 1: Not even in Swift Current?[1]
READER 2: Ha, ha. Not even in Swift Current.
READER 1: It may not make sense to you, or anyone else for that matter, in Swift Current or anywhere else. But it was. In the Beginning, there was Nothing, so much Nothing it was Something.
READER 2: Okay, and so?
READER 1: In the Beginning, there was so much Nothing it was Something. And it was a mess. Dark, so dark you could feel it. So dark,

---

1. The City of Swift Current has as its motto—visible on the signs welcoming you to our community and wherever else mottos can be placed—"where life makes sense." Yeah, it's been the brunt of a lot of jokes. One village, not far from the city, in Swift Current's ranching country, decided, in response, to make its motto "where wife makes fence." Such is life in Saskatchewan's southwest.

you could see Nothing. Chaotic. Absolute chaos. So chaotic you could make sense of Nothing. Water. Water so deep and dark and cold that if you fell in, you would never stop falling and freezing and shivering and falling. Evil. It sent cold shivers up your spine. It was *tooohoooo waaaaa booooo whoooooooo*.[2] Like a black hole in space, it sucked everything into its dark, evil, cold chaos so that there was Nothing, except for one thing.

READER 2: Yeah?

READER 1: The wind of God blew gently over the waters. Like God breathing, in and out, life moving, gently rippling the surface of the dark, deep, cold waters. Had you been there, it would have caressed your cheek, the Spirit of God like a gentle, peaceful dove, hovering over top the chaotic deep. And yet, somehow you knew there was nothing that could stop this wind and the dove had the strength of an eagle.

READER 2: And then?

READER 1: And then a Voice.

READER 2: A voice? From where?

READER 1: A Voice, from everywhere and from nowhere. A Voice both loud and quiet, both strong and gentle, both commanding and inviting. A Voice that could never, would never, be silenced. It spoke, and its beauty, its melody, its strength, its assurance, its hopefulness, its authority sent more shivers up your spine, covered your skin in goosebumps, warmed your heart, and turned fear to hope.

READER 2: What did it say?

READER 1: It said and it sang, melodious, yet each word clearly spoken and articulated. It said, "Let there be light!"

READER 2: And?

READER 1: And there was light. Everywhere. All the colors of the rainbow, brighter and more alive than the fireworks on July 1st.[3] Everywhere explosions of light and color. You needed sunglasses, a welder's helmet even, yet you didn't want to miss any of its brightness and life. Light exploded and drove back the darkness. Even God was impressed with the light and its colors and its power to push back darkness.

---

2. The Hebrew phrase that the NRSV translates as "formless and void" is *tohu wa bohu*. It has that spooky feel to it when you say it.

3. Or July 4th if you are reading this in the United States.

READER 2: Did it destroy the darkness?

READER 1: No, God kept it around, giving it a kind of balance with light, though light would always be more powerful. However, with that balance, there could now be day and there could be night, time to sleep and time to be awake.

READER 2: And?

READER 1: (*with congregation*) And there was evening and there was morning—Day 1.

READER 2: That took care of the darkness. What about the waters? Now, half the time, you could see the chaotic, deep water. What became of that?

READER 1: That was next. So thanks for asking. God took the water and divided it in half. With half of it, God made the dome of the sky—blue sky, white clouds, dew, gentle rains, flashflood downpours, thunderstorms, hail, sleet, and snow.

READER 2: And the other half?

READER 1: Not so fast. By the time the dome and clouds and rain storms and snowfalls were all done and on track and in place and properly scheduled, well a day had gone by.

READER 2: And so, I bet—let me say it (*with signal to congregation*): And there was evening and there was morning—Day 2.

READER 1: There was. Then God got down to the other half of the water, and all the dirt that had been hidden by the chaotic, dark water. God dug ditches, built hills and mountains, made large ponds, drilled holes, and leveled out meadows. Well, God didn't actually do it. God's dream and God's Voice were so strong and authoritative, God just had to imagine it and speak it, and reality happened. Oceans, lakes, rivers, creeks, springs, and wells. All of the water now in its places, with dikes and shores keeping it in place. Lofty, snow-covered mountain peaks towered over deep, shaded valleys. Meadows waiting, waiting for something. Prairies, so flat and so vast you could see forever.

READER 2: And I bet God took a step back, looked at all that had been made, and was quite impressed, thought it pretty darn good. And the day must have been about done.

READER 1: God did and God was. And there was just enough day left to do some planting. And again, with a flash of powerful imagination and a proclamation of the Word, trees covered the lower slopes of the mountains and filled the valleys. Flowers grew in profusion in the meadows. And the prairies were covered with waving grass. River valleys had fruit trees—apple and peach, chokecherry, and saskatoon.[4] Fields that were especially fertile had potatoes and tomatoes, corn, and pumpkins in neat rows. Coral reefs were in the oceans, cattails in ditches. Moss and algae. By the time the sun set—wait, there was no sun—by the time the light went out and darkness moved in, it was all there. And just before God blew out the candle, God said, "Wow, this is good. I'm good. This world looks beautiful!"

READER 2: (*signal to congregation*) And there was evening and there was morning—Day 3.

READER 1: Half done.

READER 2: Half done? Already?

READER 1: What? You think God is slow and lazy? God gets stuff done. God's no slouch.

READER 2: But what about millions of years and dinosaurs and fossils and stuff?

READER 1: Can you imagine how long we would be here if I had to tell the story in "millions of years" sections? These people would all leave and go home for lunch and supper and work tomorrow and Thanksgiving next weekend, and you and I would still be here. Never mind millions of years. We have to get the story told. So three days—half done.

READER 2: Okay. Next day.

READER 1: The next day, God realized that candles would never do the job. This world needed lights to adjust the light. So God made a huge ball of fire—needed a good set of tongs for this job—and threw that ball of fire into space until it stopped at just the right distance, so it could provide bright light and lots of warmth, but not so it would burn things—well, except skin if you took off your shirt and forgot sunscreen. And God made it so that this ball of fire would shine on everything half the time and not shine the other half.

READER 2: You mean it had a switch or shut-off valve with a pilot light and timer?

---

4. Two fruit that grow wild on the Canadian prairies. They have also been domesticated and can be found in many gardens. If you use this reading somewhere else, use what plants make sense to your area.

READER 1: No, that's too complicated and could break down. The sun—that's what God called this ball of fire—the sun moved around the earth . . . Wait a minute. Or did the earth spin?

READER 2: The earth spin? You mean it was round, like a ball? Not flat like the prairies?

READER 1: Heck. Who cares? Round or flat? Earth spinning or sun moving? Does it matter? The important thing here is the sun was just the right distance from the earth, and it helped to keep track of day and night.

READER 2: And I bet God made a smaller light to shine at night, so it would never, ever again be so dark that Dark Nothing could take over, and then sprinkled more tiny lights—stars, God called them—across the entire dome. And when the sun hid behind the horizon, you could see them, in all their glory and awe-inspiring beauty.

READER 1: You could. And God nigh danced a jig. It was so beautiful and worked so well. (*Signal to congregation*) And there was evening and there was morning—Day 4.

READER 2: Only three days left to go.

READER 1: Three? Only two. God knew this creating business would have to make good time. Lots left, and only two days.

READER 2: Should have given God those millions of years.

READER 1: Yeah, and put this congregation to sleep. Two days. With God's hands being tired from making sun, moon, and stars, God went back to speaking.

So God said, "Fish in the sea, swim. Whales and sharks, get with it. Sea horses and starfish, all of you, come to life."

God looked up at the sky and imagined birds—robins and eagles, chickadees and meadowlarks, canaries and parrots. God spoke the dreams and imaginings and butterflies and bees filled the meadows. Birdsong filled the air. Fish splashed in the sea. Whales spouted. Wow. And to make sure there would always be enough of fish and sea monsters and birds and bees, God said, "Be fruitful and multiply. Make sure there is always enough of each of you."

READER 2: You mean God said to fish and whales and robins: "Have sex."

READER 1: What? No, don't say it again. Not in church. God said, "Be fruitful and multiply."

READER 2: Yeah, but to be fruitful and multiply you have to have . . .

READER 1: You just have to be fruitful and multiply. Now can we get back to the story?

READER 2: Wow, God said to have . . . Never mind, I won't say it. I bet that took all day. So, (*signal to congregation*) And there was evening and there was morning—Day 5.

READER 1: One day to go.

READER 2: And lots still to do.

READER 1: So let's continue the story. And don't get us sidetracked again with talk about, well, you know what. The last day. The sky was full of birds, the meadows had butterflies and birdsong, and the oceans and rivers teemed with fish and whales. But the land, the land needed something too, besides grass and trees and saskatoon and chokecherry bushes. So God kicked in that imagination one more time, and God spoke the dream that came to be. Cattle and horses, dogs and cats, lions and tigers, elephants and giraffes, bears and foxes, gophers and chipmunks. All of them. And in the dirt, beetles and worms, caterpillars and fleas.

READER 2: Wish God had skipped the mosquitoes.

READER 1: What? And starved the purple martins and dragonflies? All of the creatures were needed for the circle of life.

READER 2: And so God was done. And there was evening . . .

READER 1: Hold it, hold it. You forgot something. One last thing. Think about it. What is still missing?

READER 2: Hmmmm. (*counting on fingers*) Light. The dome of the sky. Oceans and prairies and plants. Sun and moon. The birds and the fishes. Animals. What else is there?

READER 1: Humans, you doofus. Humans. You and me.

READER 2: Oh, yeah. Humans.

READER 1: So God made humans, male and female.

READER 2: So they could have . . .

READER 1: Male and female, so they could be God's presence, God's representatives in the world. That would take both men and women.

READER 2: Yeah, but I bet God told them to be fruitful and multiply. And you know what that means.

READER 1: Oh, you. Yes, God told them to be fruitful and multiply. And God told them one more thing. God told them: "Take care of this beautiful creation. All of it. Keep its beauty bright. Keep its life alive.

Make sure it will always be there, and the healthier it is, the heathier you will be. Make good decisions. I trust you to take care of it. It's your mission in life. Take care of creation."

READER 2: And that's it?

READER 1: Well, almost. Then God had a good look around and just couldn't help but be proud, downright impressed. God had done good. By golly, God had done very well. Absolutely fantastic. And with humans in charge taking care of it, it would always be beautiful and fantastic and wonderful.

READER 2: (*signal to congregation*) And there was evening and there was morning—Day 6.

READER 1: And then God rested.

READER 2: God what?

READER 1: God rested. Six days of work was enough. And besides, tomorrow there would probably be more work. God already figured these humans might need some help, would probably mess up now and then and God would have to help them out. And so, God rested and set the example: six days of work and one day of rest. If that is good for God, surely it's good for everyone.

READER 1 & READER 2: (*with signal to congregation*) And there was evening and there was morning—Day 7.

Here is an example of what can be done with Genesis 12 and the Call of Abraham:

Hidden in other sermons, I have more extended versions of the retelling of the story, including Abraham's and God's conversation before Abraham informs Sarah.

Abraham's story is told in Genesis. Much of the pilgrimage is outlined in chapter 12, but actually begins in 11:31 where we are told Abraham's father, Terah, took his family (including Abraham and Sarah), pulled up tent stakes, and left Ur to go to Canaan. However, when they got to Haran, they decided to settle there. Some years later, Abraham, still known as Abram at the time, came to Sarah at the cooking fire one morning and said—after he poured a cup of coffee, helped himself to piece of BBQ goat, and grabbed a fresh pita—"Honey, I should probably tell you. We are moving."

"We are what?"

"We are moving." Oh boy, as if Ur to Haran hadn't been enough and just after they finally felt like they were part of the community. But

Abram was the man, and with Terah dead, the head of the family. So, if he said move, they would have to move.

"Where to?"

"I don't know."

"You don't what?"

"I don't know."

"What do you mean you don't know?"

"I don't know. You know, I. Don't. Know."

"You don't know?"

"That's what I said. I don't know. Here, sit down. Let me explain."

"This better be good."

"Last night, God came to me and said we are to move to a land God will show us. God did not say where this land is. God only said head west and then a little bit south and I'll get you there. So we are moving. End of discussion."

They pulled up tent stakes and headed west. As the Ancient Storyteller says: "Abraham said yes to God's call to travel to an unknown place that would become his home. When he left he had no idea where he was going."[5] Wilderness wanderers. Lost, but making good time.

I have done a lot of rewriting of Ancient Poetry:

It seems to me, given how ancient it is, originally written in another language, a country half a world away, and set in a distant time in history, it often needs some help so it can grab imaginations in the twenty-first-century West. I have done the rewriting to help my preaching and our worship. It also became something very important to me, as the Ancient Poems became an integral part of my journey with chemotherapy.

Psalm 8

> When I look up at the majestic sweep of the heavens,
> The Milky Way your star-studded bracelet,
> The moon's light cascading from the inky blackness of the sky,
> The stars like diamonds all around,
> I wonder, why are you remotely interested in us humans?
> Why give all your heart-love to us and commit to our welfare?
> Yet, you created us just shy of God,

---

5. Heb 11:8. *The Message*.

So close we can taste it,
Dazzling in our beauty, magnificent in our structure,
Unrivaled in our ability and creativity.
Wow!

Psalm 122

Yahoo! We're going to church!
I could hardly wait until we got there,
Until I could sing the songs, my feet could dance the rhythms.
Here, in worship, where God is and where God speaks,
Where people pray and poets grab the imagination,
Here it is safe to speak what needs speaking.
Here, I could begin to make sense
Of life, of me, of God,
Of all that has been, is, and might be.
Here God speaks, and things begin to fall into place.
Stories are told, memories recalled,
Perspective given, and things fit.
Here we can pray, and it seems possible.
Here we can pray, and dreaming of peace makes sense.
Here we can pray, and we no longer have to worry.
It's all in God's hands.
Friends, family, neighbors,
Believe it already.
God is God.
We are God's people.
This is God's world.
All is well.
Hallelujah.

The prophets have great things to say and can engage the imagination today as they did two thousand five hundred and more years ago.

Isaiah 49:14-17

In despair, filled with shame and in desperation, the people said, "Yahweh has left us, deserted. Forgotten that we exist."

"Come now," God replied. "Really? You think that could happen? Think of it, can a mother forget the child she is nursing, care nothing for the baby she has carried for nine months? Even if that were possible, I will never forget you. See, I have tattooed you on the palms of my hands, your names all up and down my arms, shoulders, chest and back. There is just no getting away from me and my love for you and my pride in you, even if you mess up sometimes."

Stories lend themselves to all kinds of rewriting: *Matthew 8:23-27*

Jesus and his disciples got into a boat and started across the Sea of Galilee. Suddenly, it was as if a huge earthquake[6] at the center of the sea floor shook the entire lake bottom and a huge tsunami swept across the waters, threatening to swamp the boat and drive it and its sailors to the bottom. The wind howled, the waves towered over the tiny vessel and crashed in on and over and into the boat. The disciples were terrified, convinced this was the end, while Jesus slept peacefully in the bow.

The men shouted at him to wake up. "Jesus, wake up! Help! Our boat's going down and we will all drown!"

They were in a dead panic and cried for help, even as they knew there was nothing Jesus could do, except maybe help with bailing, though what was one more ice cream pail against these monstrous waves.

Jesus rubbed his eyes into wakefulness and looked around. "What's with you guys? You've never been in a boat before? Seen a storm before? Where's your sailor courage? Your peasant bravery?"

Then, with a hand on the mast, Jesus looked out at the storm and said, "Stop! Silence! Peace!"

And, as suddenly as the roaring storm had hit, it stopped, and the water was perfectly calm, as if it had never known a wave, the boat motionless on a glass-like sea.

The disciples gawked at Jesus. "Who the heck is this?" they asked each other, "that even the wind and waves bow to his command?"

---

6. Check the Greek text. It actually says *seismos megas*. Matthew's love affair with earthquakes actually lends itself to some interesting creative preaching.

Sometimes, maybe the stories Jesus told meant something different than we always assumed:

LUKE 18:9-14

Jesus seemed to encounter the "genuine imitation"[7] folk on a regular basis, always hanging around, often in his face, mostly not pleased with him. They were full of themselves and looked down their noses at the more common, everyday folk who had no way of hiding (maybe didn't want to) who they really were. One day Jesus told this story to make the point about what God prefers: "genuine imitation" or "authentic vulnerability."

"Two men went to a chapel in the village to pray," Jesus said. "One was a successful businessman, conservative in his theology and politics, and fastidious in his piety. The other man was one of the local bookies. The businessman and pillar of the community stood off by himself, keeping a good distance between himself and the bookie, and prayed this prayer: 'God, thank you that I have accepted Jesus and live a good, moral life, a life that shows people my faith commitment and conscientious and strict discipline. I'm not even tempted by porn, I don't gamble, not even lottery tickets, and I give generously to missions and famine relief, run my business well, and attend worship regularly, always well-dressed in suit and tie. For the Lord, only the best. My wife volunteers for worthy causes. My kids are on the honor roll in college. Most definitely I'm not like that slimy bookie over there.'

"The other man had no grand illusions about himself. He knew who he was, how messed up his life was, the bad choices he had made, and how it was that he made his profits and enforced the payment of debts. 'God,' he said. 'You know me. The people in the community know me. This is me. There is no hiding. Find a place in your heart for me.'"

Another story told by Jesus:

In working on another writing project, I was using Theodore Roosevelt's quotation about "daring greatly." The point Roosevelt is making is win or lose, the important thing is that you tried, that you were in the

---

7. I used this telling of this story in a sermon that began with me telling of the time we received a flyer in the mail offering "genuine imitation diamonds" at a great price for any and all who might be interested.

arena. And if someone fails "at least [he] fails while daring greatly."[8] I wrote:

Over the course of the summer and into fall, I reflected on an experience I had had, Roosevelt's quotation, and Brown's book, *Daring Greatly*. It occurred to me that, though Jesus undoubtedly never heard Roosevelt speak nor read his quotation, Jesus meant the same thing as Roosevelt when the carpenter's son from Nazareth told the story of the first-century financier who entrusted his money to three of his fund managers and then left for an extended leave of absence from his business (to be president of his country perhaps or prime minister in his nation's government). Upon his return to retake control of his corporations, he asked for an update from each of his three managers. Two had doubled the investments they made and were highly commended. The third, fearing that the economy was unstable, the stock market might tank, and real estate prices fall, cashed in the securities, stocks, and bonds (the mutual funds) entrusted to him. He took the cash, put it into a secure, steel, waterproof safe, and buried it in his backyard. When the owner returned, the money would be safe and sound. He would not have guessed wrong and lost it in bad trades, invested wrong and gone bankrupt, or started a business and failed. The money would be safe and therefore he would be safe.[9]

When the third fund manager walked into the financier's office and returned the cash to his boss, safe and sound, the owner was livid. Rather than complimenting the manager for not having made mistakes in his business decisions and not losing the money in risky investments, the financier tore a strip off him, up one side and down the other.

"You wicked and lazy [fund manager]! You knew, did you that I reap where I did not sow, and gather where I did not scatter? Then you ought to have invested my money with the bankers, and on my return I would have received what was my own with interest."[10]

I think Eugene Peterson in *The Message* gets a little closer to giving us the emotions or the moment and connects us with Roosevelt's speech and the intent of this chapter with the words: "That's a terrible way to live! It's criminal to live cautiously like that! If you knew I was after the best, why did you do less than the least? The least you could have done would

---

8. As quoted in Brown, *Daring Greatly*, 1.
9. For one Good News Storyteller's version of Jesus's story, see Matt 25:14–30.
10. Matt 25:26–27. NRSV.

have been to invest the sum with the bankers, where at least I would have gotten a little interest."[11]

And, as a final example, Paul can often do with some help in making the jump from first-century Greek culture to twenty-first century Western society.

Romans 8:31–39

Bottom line: If God's on our side, who would dare be against us, judge us, or point the finger at us? I mean now, seriously! God demonstrated how much we are worth by giving everything, including life itself, for us in Jesus. It seems to me it can't get any clearer than that, the worth God thinks we have. And then who will accuse and prosecute us? God? Are you kidding me? God, who already has said our worth is infinite, our design perfect, our forgiveness unconditional, and our acceptance without qualification? No way! Jesus? The one who died for us? You've got to be joking! Clearly Jesus thought us worth dying for, so there is no way he will turn around now and shame us and point the finger at us and judge us. Why, he is our defense attorney in heaven, pleading our case for us, as if we needed that, given God's unconditional love and unqualified forgiveness. With judge, prosecutor, and defense on our side, and each with a heart bursting with love for us, well, it just doesn't get much better than that.

I would swear on a stack of Bibles (if I was the oath-swearing type) that there is absolutely nothing that will ever be able to make its way between us and God's love for us. Not how we live, no matter how we live. Not the Grim Reaper and all his gargoyles. Not angels who are with God all the time, nor demons who would like nothing better than to separate us from the love of God and destroy us. Not our regrets from the past, not what we are afraid of today, nor what makes us anxious about tomorrow. Not governments, organizations, institutions, culture, religion, or society. No matter how far into space we go or how deep into the earth we drill, or how often we circle the planet, or what science we use to explore the universe, big and small, we will not find anything, simply nothing, that can change how God feels about us, nothing that can take God's love away from us. Nothing. The simple yet profound truth is that God loves us, period, no questions asked. Why am I so convinced? Because we saw it so profoundly shown to us by and in Jesus.

11. Matt 25:26–27. *The Message.*

Chapter 18

LENT

At times I have kept Lent fairly simple, focusing on a confession, maybe blowing out a candle each Sunday, starting with six candles plus the Christ Candle and then blowing out the Christ Candle on Good Friday as we come to the part in the story where Jesus dies.

One year, inspired by Edward Hays's book, *A Lenten Hobo Honeymoon*, we used the hobo theme. The word "hobo" may well be a contraction of "**ho**meward **bo**und." We used pictures of hobos and set our Lenten worship times in a context that helped us think about ourselves as wandering and traveling homeward.

In 2018, we also used a journey theme. This time it was inspired by the Storyteller's comment about Jesus in Luke 9:51: "As the time drew near . . . Jesus resolutely set out for Jerusalem."[1] We imagined that on his journey to Jerusalem, he traveled through Swift Current. Each Sunday we walked with him and stopped at a different place in town and prayed. We stopped at the Credit Union, a gas bar, a housing development, an urban reserve, the court house, and City Hall.

Below is the script for the first Sunday. A copy was included in each bulletin. On subsequent Sundays, the first verse of the first song remained the same, as did the reading by the leader. Each Sunday, I had the appropriate picture. I wrote a new reading for Jesus each week, as well as a new second stanza for the song and a new prayer. The last song remained the same, one verse of "Spirit of God, descend."

1. NLT.

The 1st Sunday in Lent

"Walking with Jesus"

Luke 9:51: "As the time drew near . . . Jesus resolutely set out for Jerusalem."[2]

Song: "Jesus walked this earth for us" (vs. 1)

> *(Tune: "Go to dark Gethsemane"[3]):*
> Jesus walked this earth for us
> Traveled down life's dusty path
> Sat with all who felt his life
> Spoke with those who wished to learn
> Now he travels to the cross
> Bids us walk that way with him.

LEADER: As we walk through our city with Jesus,
> We come upon our Credit Union.
> Jesus raises his hand and bids us stop.
> Then he speaks:

Fig. 1. Pictured is the Swift Current Credit Union. Photo by Ray Friesen

---

2. NLT.
3. Montgomery, "Go to dark." In Slough, ed., *Hymnal*, #240.

JESUS: "You can't worship two gods at once.
>Loving one god, you'll end up hating the other.
>Adoration of one feeds contempt for the other.
>You can't worship God and Money both."[4]

Song: "Jesus walked this earth for us" (vs. 2):
>Bids us stop and pray with him
>At the banks we hold so dear
>Asks whom we do worship here
>God or Mammon, is it clear
>Turn now from life's privilege
>Share with all who need our help

PEOPLE: God, we confess our love for money.
>It is hard to tell the difference between need and want.
>Help us let go, and trust you.
>Help us share with those who need our money
>More than we do
>Set us free to live generously.

ALL: Amen.

Song: "Spirit of God, descend" (vs. 1):
>Spirit of God, descend upon my heart;
>Wean it from earth; through all its pulses move.
>Stoop to my weakness, mighty as Thou art,
>And make me love Thee as I ought to love.[5]

---

4. Matt 6:24. *The Message*.

5. Croly, "Spirit of God," In Slough, ed., *Hymnal*, #502.

Chapter 19

Songs

BOTH OF THE LAST two congregations that Sylvia and I were part of loved to sing. Singing has, within my own Mennonite tradition, been the one way that the congregation got involved in worship. Everything else was done from the front by the preachers.

At the same time, in our most recent congregation, we were significantly limited in what we could sing. We had two pianists. Although one was somewhat adventurous, the other preferred to stick with the "tried and true." We loved traditional hymns and old time Gospel music.

In that congregation, the pianists, with some exceptions, chose the first three hymns we sang. I chose the one after the Old Testament reading and the one after the sermon. I liked these to somehow connect with what had gone before. Finding those songs could be difficult given the above limits. We do not seem to have songs for some themes. Sometimes I find my own articulation of faith and spirituality so different from traditional hymnody and Gospel singing that I struggle with the songs we have.

So what recourse is there but to write songs for us to use? Okay, I do not know a lot about music. I neither read music nor write music. That means I am limited to tunes that exist and, of course, tunes that we know. However, there are lots of these around. Secondly, my ability to write rhyme comes and goes. We don't worry too much about that. So far, my sense is the congregation has been appreciative of what I have done. I use primarily Gospel song music.

Here are a few examples:

1. On the theme of Storytelling

How many songs do you know on the theme of storytelling? Yes, there is "I love to tell the story" and it has its good points, but also its limits. So, here is one I wrote.

"I love to tell the story"

(Sung to the tune by Catherine Hankey[1])

1. I love to tell the story drawn from God's holy word,
A story of God's justice, a story of God's love.
I love to tell the story of my own walk in life,
For when I tell it boldly, it fits in with the rest.

Refrain:
I love to tell the story! It shows us all God's glory!
It is God's great big story, of love and faithfulness.

2. I love to tell the story of God's creative Word,
Of Abraham and Moses, of David and his poems
And then there's all the prophets who sang and told the tales
Of how God loves the people and how God loves to save.

Refrain

3. I love to tell the story of Jesus and his birth,
Of Mary, shepherds, angels, of stars above the earth.
I love to tell the stories, the stories Jesus told
And of the resurrection, that story's surely gold.

Refrain

4. I love to tell my story, a tale both strange and good,
Of Mom and Dad who loved me, of friends I made on earth.
I love to tell of 'ventures, of crisis and good times,
For when I tell them boldly, they fit with all the rest.
Refrain

---

1. Hankey, "I love to tell the story." In Oyer et al., *Mennonite Hymnal*, #593.

2. Lent, 2017

I have never much cared for the theology of the song "This world is not my home."[2] (Okay, I struggle with much of the gospel song and southern gospel song theology even as I like the music). I believe there is a very real sense in which this world is our home. We have been created and called by God to live here and partner with God as a continuation of the incarnation. At the same time, we are citizens of the Kingdom of God. So, I took that first line and rewrote the rest of the song. During Lent that year, we sang the melody each Sunday. The first verse was the same each week. I wrote new verses for the other Sundays, theme specific.

"This world is not my home"

(Based on Psalm 32 and related to Lent #1, Year A texts)

1. This world is not my home, and yet God placed me here.
It's here that I was called; it's here that I may live,
To serve the Lord my God and all of those with me,
For this world is where grace is now working out in me.

Chorus:
Oh Lord, you know, you are my friend indeed.
With you here by my side, I live eternally.
The struggle can be fierce, the fight a bitter test,
But with you at my side, I will live victoriously.

2. The apple dangles near, and choices I oft blow.
I like to play at God, and my own way I go.
I often fail to choose the things that make for good.
Forgive me Lord I pray, may I do all that I should.

Chorus

3. Your love is very real in all my neighborhood.
You will not let me go, though surely that you could.
Forgiveness washes clean and takes me back to you.
While I live in this world, love can shine in all I do.

Chorus

2. Baxter, Jr., "This World." In Morris, et al., *Favorite*, #1.

3. SINGING SCRIPTURE

The Psalms, I think, were all meant to be sung. I try to remind our congregation that the Ancient Prophets were actually folk singers and protest singers. So, how can we sing those songs?

"ISAIAH 35"

(Sung to the tune for "Count your blessings" by Edwin O. Excell[3])

1. When your heart is fearful and your arms feel limp,
When your knees are wobbly and your spirit faint,
Think of all that's coming, God is sure to do,
And your hope will flourish and your faith grow strong.

Chorus:
See the garden
God is making here
Wadis running,
Desert now a'bloom.
God is working, dreams are coming true,
For the Lord is coming, glory to God's name.

2. God will do great wonders, turning life around.
Blind will soon be seeing, lame will dance for joy.
Vi'lence will be ended, fear have turned to hope.
Peace will rule the world and love will fill all hearts.

Chorus

---

3. Excell, "Count your blessings." In Armstrong, ed., Spiritual, #39.

"By the Rivers of Babylon"

(Based on Psalm 137)
(Sung to the tune for "Where the Roses Never Fade" by James C. Miller)

1. By the foreign Tigris River[4]
In a pagan land of fear,
There our voices choked to silence
And our eyes were filled with tears.

2. We had hoped God would defend us,
Thought our future was secure,
Now we have no hope to guide us,
No more faith to keep us strong.

3. O the cruel, cruel actions
Of the hated armies here,
Mocking they command our singers,
Tell us to perform for them.

4. "Where now is a god to save you?
Where the strength you thought you had?
Marduk[5] our own god is stronger.
Yours has turned his back on you."

5. God, how could this fate have caught us?
How are we to live again?
May we not forget our history,
Not forget where we have been.

6. Crush the ones who now torment us.
Kill their soldiers with your fire.
Show your strong right arm to save us.
Wipe out all the ones we hate.

---

4. The Tigris River was/is one of the two main rivers in Babylon [present day Iraq]. The other was/is the Euphrates.

5. Marduk was the chief god in the Babylonian pantheon. The Babylonians, the enemy in this song, had taken the people of Judah captive and were oppressing them both in Babylon (where they were told to sing songs of Yahweh, but could not) and in devastated Jerusalem and Judah.

4. From a sermon in a series on the book of Colossians

"Fill us with Light"

(Old Hundredth)

    1. Fill us with light, O God most high.
Give us a vision clear and true.
May we see clearly what you see.
May we find meaning here for sure.

    2. Fill us with resurrection pow'r.
Give us your hardest tasks to do.
Send us from here with love endued.
May we live lives of meaning true.

    3. Free us from guilt and awful shame.
Let us be free to live and love.
May we with boldness speak your name
And bring the peace that we can claim.

    4. Send us from here with faith renewed,
With hope that's bright and love that's sure.
Send us to change this world of hate
By blessing all and loving too.

5. For the Sunday after a sermon on the Wedding at Cana

"Shall we gather at the banquet?"

(Sung to the tune for "Shall we gather at the river" by Robert Lowry[6])

    1. Shall we gather at the banquet?
Round a table spread with food?
Wine is flowing here so freely,
In God's loving neighborhood.

---

6. Lowry, "Shall we gather." In Slough, ed., Hymnal, #615.

Chorus:
Yes, we'll gather round God's table.
A banquet here for us by God is spread.
Such a party filled with dancing
And the wine and living bread.

2. 'Tis a wedding feast we've come to,
Bride and lamb shall be as one.
God's own presence will not waiver,
For the vict'ry has been won.

Chorus

3. Let's go out and spread the good news,
God's great party has arrived.
All God's children here are welcome,
For the doors are opened wide.

Chorus

Chapter 20

Thanksgiving

Though I have often preached on Thanksgiving Sunday, on Thanksgiving and/or on generosity, in 2017 I thought we should give thanks another way. It seemed to me singing and Scripture would do just fine. What follows is the result.

Scripture texts used in this Thanksgiving worship are from one of the five sources used throughout this book. Small adjustments have been made to avoid the use of the male pronoun for God and to turn congregational readings into "we" instead of "I."

"God, we love you": A Thanksgiving Bazaar

Welcome
Call to Worship
Prayer
Song: "Praise the Lord, sing hallelujah"[1]
Introduction: *A Thanksgiving Bazaar*

Most Saturdays this summer, Sylvia and I went to Market Square.[2] As we wandered through what had been empty lots, we encountered various kinds of booths and tables, people offering their wares—handmade jewelry, baked goods, garden produce, meals, fruit, pottery, and

---

1. Kirkpatrick, "Praise the Lord." In Slough, ed., *Hymnal*, #50.

2. This is an outdoor market in downtown Swift Current that runs each summer from June to September.

books. We would wander from table to table and look at what was on offer, ask questions, allow ourselves to be tempted and always bought something—deep-fried dough covered in sugar and cinnamon,[3] pies, bread, herbs, cucumbers, tomatoes, jam, and, yes, as if I didn't have enough, books. Though in Swift Current we call it Market Square, it had a resemblance to the bazaars we visited several years ago in Bethlehem, Nazareth, and East Jerusalem. There was lots to offer.

This morning, I invite you to engage your imaginations—you know I have a love affair with imaginations—and join me at a Thanksgiving Bazaar. We will visit several booths and at each booth, you will be invited to reflect on something we have every reason to be thankful for. The hope is that our thankfulness will grow and we will leave this morning singing and dancing, our hearts filled with joy and gratitude for all that God has given us, and filled with a love for God who gave us so much. You are invited, at each booth before we enter the bazaar and then as we leave, to listen to Ancient Writings—especially poetry, read some of this poetry together, and sing, again and again. Two texts that carry the theme for us today are the Ancient Poem we know as Psalm 116 and a song called "God, we love you" set to the tune of "Count your many blessings."

So as we walk up to the bazaar and enter its canopy—whether of canvass or tree branches or sky—let's do so singing "God, we love you."

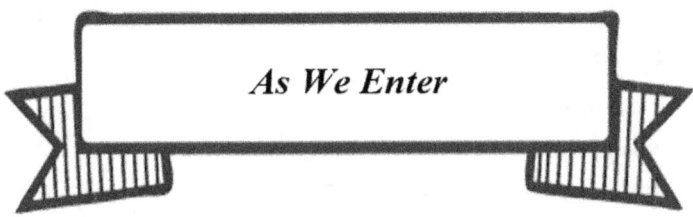

Song: "God, we love you" (vs. 1):

> (*Sung to the tune of "Count your blessings" by Edwin O. Excell.*)[4]
> When we think of all the good that God has done,
> Love just fills our heart, we're down on bended knee.
> God, we love you now.

---

3. A reasonable imitation of the treats sold by, and called, Beaver Tails, a Canadian company.

4. Excell, "Count Your Blessings." In Armstrong, ed., *Spiritual*, #39.

You are our friend indeed.
God, our love for you will never, ever end.
God, we love you
You are our best friend.
God, our love for you will never end.
God, we love you
You are our best friend.
God, our love for you will never, ever end.

Psalm 31:23–24:

23 Love the Lord, all you [people, God's children].
The Lord preserves the faithful . . .
24 Be strong, and let your heart take courage,
all you who wait for the Lord.[5]

Congregation: "We love [God], because [God] first loved us."[6]
Psalm 116:1–2:

I love the Lord because [God] hears my voice
and my prayer for mercy.
2 Because [the Lord] bends down to listen,
I will pray as long as I have breath![7]

Psalm 18:1–2:
Congregation:

1 [We] love you, Lord;
you are [our] strength.
2 The Lord is [our] rock, our fortress, and [our] savior;
[our] God is [our] rock, in whom [we] find protection.
God is [our] shield, the power that saves [us],
and [our] place of safety.[8]

---

5. NRSV.
6. 1 John 4:19, KJV.
7. NLT.
8. NLT

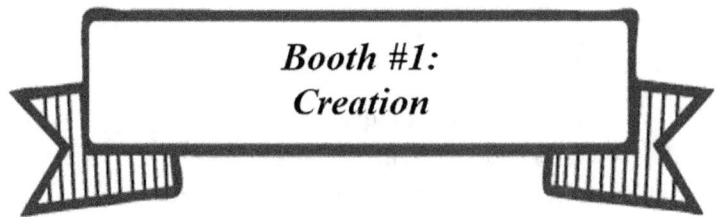

Booth #1: Creation

Song: "How great thou art"[9] (vs. 1 and 2)
Psalm 104:1–12:

> Let all that I am praise the Lord.
> O Lord my God, how great you are!
> You are robed with honor and majesty.
> 2 You are dressed in a robe of light.
> You stretch out the starry curtain of the heavens;
> 3 you lay out the rafters of your home in the rain clouds.
> You make the clouds your chariot;
> you ride upon the wings of the wind.
> 4 The winds are your messengers;
> flames of fire are your servants.
> 5 You placed the world on its foundation
> so it would never be moved.
> 6 You clothed the earth with floods of water,
> water that covered even the mountains.
> 7 At your command, the water fled;
> at the sound of your thunder, it hurried away.
> 8 Mountains rose and valleys sank
> to the levels you decreed.
> 9 Then you set a firm boundary for the seas,
> so they would never again cover the earth.
> 10 You make springs pour water into the ravines,
> so streams gush down from the mountains.
> 11 They provide water for all the animals,
> and the wild donkeys quench their thirst.

---

9. Boberg, "How great," In Oyer, et al. ed., *Mennonite Hymnal*, #535.

> 12 The birds nest beside the streams
> and sing among the branches of the trees.[10]

Psalm 104:31–35:
Congregation:

> May the glory of the Lord continue forever!
> The Lord takes pleasure in all [God] has made!
> 32 The earth trembles at [the Mighty One's] glance;
> the mountains smoke at [the Lord's] touch.
> 33 [We] will sing to the Lord as long as [we] live.
> [We] will praise [our] God to our last breath!
> 34 May all [our] thoughts be pleasing to [God],
> for [we] rejoice in the Lord.
> . . .
> Let all that [we are] praise the Lord.
> Praise the Lord![11]

Song: "God, we love you" (vs. 2):

> When we look at all the world that you have made,
> When we see the stars and sun and moon a-sail,
> We can't help but praise you.
> God, you are so great.
> And we know that love must surely conquer hate.
> God, we thank you for a world so great
> God, we thank you love will vanquish hate
> God, we love you, you are our best friend
> God, our love for you will never, ever end.

---

10. NLT.
11. NLT.

Booth #2: Harvest

Song: "We plow the fields and scatter"[12]
Deuteronomy 14:22–26:

> Make an offering of ten percent, a tithe, of all the produce which grows in your fields year after year. Bring this into the Presence of God, your God, at the place [the Lord] designates for worship and there eat the tithe from your grain, wine, and oil and the firstborn from your herds and flocks. In this way you will learn to live in deep reverence before God, your God, as long as you live. But if the place God, your God, designates for worship is too far away and you can't carry your tithe that far, God, your God, will still bless you: exchange your tithe for money and take the money to the place God, your God, has chosen to be worshiped. Use the money to buy anything you want: cattle, sheep, wine, or beer—anything that looks good to you. You and your family can then feast in the Presence of God, your God, and have a good time.[13]

Song: "God, we love you" (vs. 3):

> Food, we have a plenty and a bunch to spare.
> Corn and peas and tators, z'cchini to galore.
> Ham and chicken, sausage cooking,
> Steak that's rare,
> Lord, we'll have a banquet
> Where there's lots to share.
> God, your greatness surely can't compare.
> God, your grace has left us lots to share.
> God, we love you.
> You are our best friend.
> God, our love for you will never, ever end.

12. Claudius, "We plow," In Slough, ed., *Hymnal*, #96.
13. *The Message*.

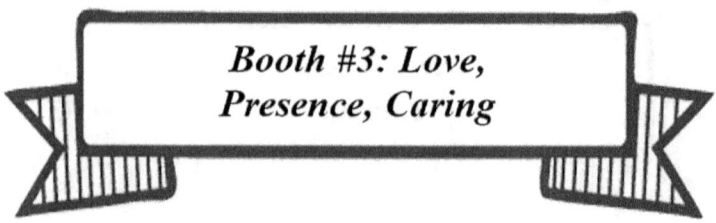

Booth #3: Love, Presence, Caring

Song: "When I'm lonely and defenseless"[14]
Psalm 116:7–9:

> I said to myself, "Relax and rest.
> God has showered you with blessings.
> Soul, you've been rescued from death;
> Eye, you've been rescued from tears;
> And you, Foot, were kept from stumbling."
> 9–11 I'm striding in the presence of God,
> alive in the land of the living![15]

Psalm 30:1–5:

> I give you all the credit, God—
> you got me out of that mess,
> you didn't let my foes gloat.
> 2–3 God, my God, I yelled for help
> and you put me together.
> God, you pulled me out of the grave,
> gave me another chance at life
> when I was down-and-out.
> 4–5 All you saints! Sing your hearts out to God!
> Thank [God] to [God's] face!
> [The Lord] gets angry once in a while, but across
> a lifetime there is only love.
> Weeping may last through the night,
> but joy comes with the morning.[16]

Psalm 16:7–10:

---

14. Rohl, "When I'm lonely." In Nafziger, et al., ed., *Sing*, #93.
15. *The Message.*
16. *The Message.*

Congregation:

[We] will bless the Lord who guides [us];
even at night [our] heart[s] instruct [us].
8 [We] know the Lord is always with [us].
[We] will not be shaken, for God is right beside [us].
9 No wonder [our] heart[s] are glad, and [we] rejoice.
[Our] bod[ies] rest in safety.[17]
For you do not give us up to Sheol,
or let your faithful ones see the Pit.[18]

Philippians 4:6:

Do not worry about anything, but in everything by prayer and supplication with thanksgiving let your requests be made known to God. And the peace of God, which surpasses all understanding, will guard your hearts and your minds in Christ Jesus.[19]

Song: "God, we love you" (vs. 4):

"When upon life's billow we are tempest tossed
"When we are discouraged, thinking all is lost"[20]
Then you hear us crying, count the tears we shed
And you tuck us safely in your warm soft bed.
God, we thank you.
You are always near.
God, we praise you for we shall not fear.
God, we love you.
You are our best friend.
God, our love for you will never, ever end.

---

17. NLT.
18. NRSV.
19. NRSV.
20. These two lines are borrowed from the original song, Excell, "Count Your Blessings." In Armstrong, ed., *Spiritual*, #39.

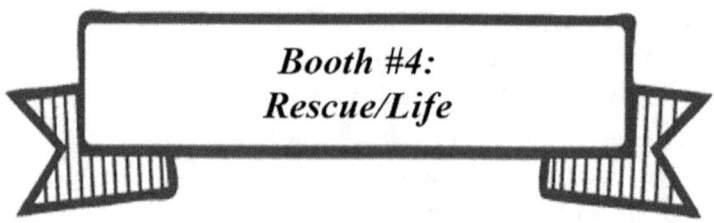

Booth #4: Rescue/Life

Song: "In the rifted Rock I'm resting"[21]
Psalm 116:3–4:

>Death wrapped its ropes around me;
>the terrors of the grave overtook me.
>I saw only trouble and sorrow.
>4 Then I called on the name of the Lord:
>"Please, Lord, save me!"[22]

Psalm 30:8–12:

>8–10 I called out to you, God;
>I laid my case before you:
>"Can you sell me for a profit when I'm dead?
>auction me off at a cemetery yard sale?
>When I'm 'dust to dust' my songs
>and stories of you won't sell.
>So listen! and be kind!
>Help me out of this!"
>11–12 You did it: you changed wild lament
>into whirling dance;
>You ripped off my black mourning band
>and decked me with wildflowers.
>I'm about to burst with song;
>I can't keep quiet about you.
>God, my God,

---

21. James, "In the rifted." In Slough, ed., *Hymnal*, #526.
22. NLT.

I can't thank you enough.[23]

Psalm 116:5–7:

> 5 How kind the Lord is! How good [God] is!
> So merciful, this God of ours!
> 6 The Lord protects those of childlike faith;
> I was facing death, and [the Lord] saved me.
> 7 Let my soul be at rest again,
> for the Lord has been good to me.[24]

Psalm 40:1–3:

> I waited patiently for the Lord to help me,
> and [God] turned to me and heard my cry.
> 2 [The Lord] lifted me out of the pit of despair,
> out of the mud and the mire.
> [God Almighty] set my feet on solid ground
> and steadied me as I walked along.
> 3 [The Lord] has given me a new song to sing,
> a hymn of praise to our God.
> Many will see what [God] has done and be amazed.
> They will put their trust in the Lord.[25]

John 10:7–10:

> Speaking another time, Jesus said to those around him, to those hanging on his every word: "There is no end of salespeople with their offers, their promises of life and excitement; snake oil salesmen offering patent medicine solutions to real life matters. Hucksters willing to sell you any baubles that catch your eye. There is no shortage of stories and storytellers with their re-written versions of what is good. However, if you buy in, you will wither and die. That's what they don't tell you. But I, I promise, I came but for one reason, that you, each of you, would have abundant life. What I offer is guaranteed to last—never out of date, never obsolete, rust-proof. My story so grand it will fill your imagination with adventure and awe and wonder. I offer life so real and so full and so enduring and so enriching, well, there are simply no words big enough or grand enough to

---

23. *The Message.*
24. NLT.
25. NLT.

describe it. All [God's] products are guaranteed to last—never out-of-date, never obsolete, rust-proof."[26]

Song: "God, we love you" (vs. 5):

> Jesus came to give us life that's truly real,
> Rescued us from death and fear and life's dark grave,
> Showed us that you loved us; took our guilt away,
> Filled our life with blessing every single day.
> God, we thank you
> For this life that's real.
> God, we love the way your Spirit feels
> God, we love you.
> You are our best friend.
> God, our love for you will never, ever end.

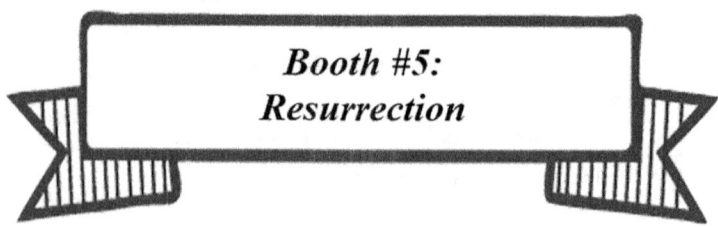

Booth #5: Resurrection

Song: "In the bulb there is a flower"[27]
1 Corinthians 15:1–6, 53–58:

> Let me now remind you, dear brothers and sisters, of the Good News I preached to you before. You welcomed it then, and you still stand firm in it. 2 It is this Good News that saves you if you continue to believe the message I told you—unless, of course, you believed something that was never true in the first place.
>
> 3 I passed on to you what was most important and what had also been passed on to me. Christ died for our sins, just as the Scriptures said. 4 He was buried, and he was raised from the dead on the third day, just as the Scriptures said. 5 He was seen by Peter and then by the Twelve. 6 After that, he was seen

---

26. My paraphrase of John 10:7–10. The last two lines of the paraphrase are from Psalm 111:7 in *The Message*.

27. Sleeth, "In the bulb." In Slough, ed., *Hymnal*, #614.

by more than five hundred of his followers at one time, most of whom are still alive, though some have died.[28]

In the resurrection scheme of things, this has to happen: everything perishable taken off the shelves and replaced by the imperishable, this mortal replaced by the immortal. Then the saying will come true:

Death swallowed by triumphant Life!
Who got the last word, oh, Death?
Oh, Death, who's afraid of you now?

It was sin that made death so frightening and law-code guilt that gave sin its leverage, its destructive power. But now in a single victorious stroke of Life, all three—sin, guilt, death—are gone, the gift of our Master, Jesus Christ. Thank God!

58 With all this going for us, my dear, dear friends, stand your ground. And don't hold back. Throw yourselves into the work of the Master, confident that nothing you do for him is a waste of time or effort.[29]

Song: "God, we love you" (vs. 6):

Resurrection shattered death's cold, dark domain,
Brought a change in history, nothing's now the same.
Life has burst upon us, changed our fear to hope
And [we] will be singing as the days go by[30]
God, we thank you for the life that came,
For the fact that death shall never, ever reign.
God, we love you.
You are our best friend.
God, our love for you will never, ever end.

---

28. NLT.

29. *The Message.*

30. This line is from Excell, "Count Your Blessings." In Armstrong, ed., *Spiritual*, #39.

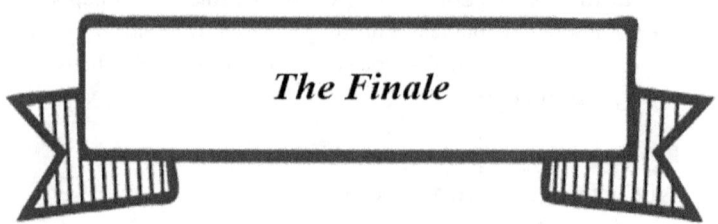

The Finale

Psalm 116:12-14, 17-19:
Congregation:

> What can [we] give back to God
> for the blessings [the Lord] has poured out on [us]?
> [We'll] lift high the cup of salvation—a toast to God!
> [We'll] pray in the name of God;
> [We'll] complete what [we] promised God [we'd] do,
> and [we'll] do it together with [all God's] people.
> (We repeat, so determined are we to do this.)
> [We] are ready to offer the thanksgiving sacrifice
> and pray in the name of God.
> [We'll] complete what [we] promised God [we'd] do,
> and [we'll] do it in company with [all God's] people,
> In the place of worship, in God's house,
> in Jerusalem, God's city.
> Hallelujah![31]

Song: "Halle, halle, hallelujah"[32]
Offering
Sharing

---

31. *The Message.*
32. Bell, "Halle, halle," In Nafziger, et al, ed., *Sing*, #17.

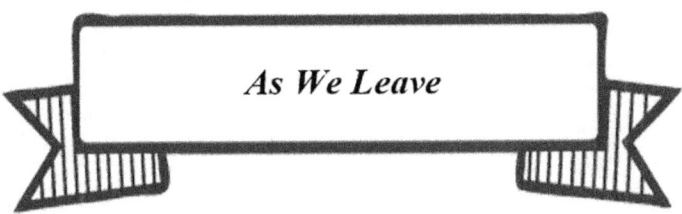

As We Leave

Sending Song: "God, we love you" (vs. 7):

> Hallelujah! Thank you, Lord, Amen! Amen!
> We are truly blessed, 'cause you are our best friend.
> We can sing and praise and shout here without end
> And we know you're with us where you do us send.
> God, we thank you for a world that's yours.
> We do thank you for the life that's ours.
> We shall leave here, knowing you go too.
> God, we know you're with us.
> This is true for sure.

Benediction

As with all the other material in this book, the above are samples meant to spark your imagination and creativity. By the power of the Spirit, engage God's gift of imagination and who knows what may come of it. Partner with God in the Creation that still has lots of room for creation!

Thank you, God, for that and thank you, God, for imagination and creativity.

APPENDIX A
For Further Reading

THE LIST BELOW MAKES no claims to being exhaustive. Many of you who read this book may well have read all of these and more in your pursuit of excellence and creativity in preaching. So, like the rest of this book, the intention is to point you in a direction. I have not included any commentaries. I have restricted myself to three themes. One is, obviously, "Preaching." The second is "Bible—What It is and How We Might Read It." And the third is a couple of books on "Faith and the Movies." A more complete bibliography that lists all the books referenced in this work follows after Appendix B.

PREACHING

Banting, Blayne A. *With Wit and Wonder: The Preacher's Use of Humor and Imagination.* Eugene, OR: Resource Publications, 2013.
Brueggemann, Walter. *Cadences of Home: Preaching among Exiles.* Louisville: Westminster John Knox, 1997.
———. *The Word Militant: Preaching a Decentering Word.* Minneapolis: Fortress, 2010.
———. *The Practice of the Prophetic Imagination: Preaching an Emancipating Word.* Minneapolis: Fortress, 2012.
Craddock, Fred B. *Preaching.* Nashville: Abingdon, 1985.
Johnson, Patrick W. *The Mission of Preaching: Equipping the Community for Faithful Witness.* Downers Grove: IVP Academic, 2015.
Keller, Timothy. *Preaching: Communicating Faith in an Age of Skepticism.* New York: Viking, 2015.
Lose, David. *Preaching at the Crossroads: How the World—and Our Preaching—is Changing.* Minneapolis: Fortress, 2013.
Meyers, Robin R. *With Ears to Hear: Preaching as Self-Persuasion.* Cleveland: The Pilgrim, 1993.
Plantinga Jr., Cornelius. *Reading for Preaching: The Preacher in Conversation with Storytellers, Biographers, Poets, and Journalists.* Grand Rapids: Eerdmans, 2013.

SERMON COLLECTIONS

Brueggemann, Walter. *The Collected Sermons of Walter Brueggemann.* Louisville: Westminster John Knox, 2011.

Buechner, Frederick. *Secrets in the Dark: A Life in Sermons.* San Francisco: HarperSanFrancisco, 2006.

BIBLE

Bell, Rob. *What is the Bible?: How an Ancient Library of Poems, Letters, and Stories Can Transform the Way You Think and Feel About Everything.* San Francisco: HarperOne, 2017.

Boyd, Gregory A. *Benefit of the Doubt: Breaking the Idol of Certainty.* Grand Rapids: Baker, 2013.

Charles, Howard H. *Opening the Bible.* Edited by J. Robert Charles. Elkhart: Institute of Mennonite Studies, 2005.

Enns, Peter. *Inspiration and Incarnation: Evangelicals and the Problem of the Old Testament.* 2nd ed. Grand Rapids: Baker Academic, 2015.

———. *The Bible Tells Me So: Why Defending Scripture Has Made Us Unable to Read It.* San Francisco: HarperOne, 2014.

Evans, Rachel Held. *Inspired: Slaying Giants, Walking on Water, and Loving the Bible Again.* Nashville: Nelson, 2018.

McKnight, Scot. *The Blue Parakeet: Rethinking How You Read the Bible.* 2nd ed. Grand Rapids: Zondervan, 2018.

McLaren Brian D. *A New Kind of Christianity: Ten Questions That Are Transforming the Faith.* San Francisco: HarperOne, 2010, 33–97.

Wangerin, Jr., Walter. *The Book of God: The Bible as a Novel.* Grand Rapids: Zondervan Publishing House, 1996.

Wright, N. T. *Surprised by Scripture: Engaging Contemporary Issues.* San Francisco: HarperOne, 2014.

FAITH & MOVIES

Detweiler, Craig. *Into the Dark: Seeking the Sacred in the Top Films of the 21st Century.* Grand Rapids: Baker Academic, 2008.

McNulty, Edward N. *Faith & Film: A Guidebook for Leaders.* Louisville: Westminster John Knox, 2007.

Pungente SJ, John & Monty Williams SJ. *Finding God in the Dark II: Taking the Spiritual Exercises of St. Ignatius to the Movies.* Toronto: Novalis, 2011.

Appendix B
The Bible and the Word of God

WHAT DO WE MEAN when we say, "The Bible is the Word of God?" As is evident in the bibliography, this is a topic much bigger than what can be held in one appendix. For a thorough discussion of this question, I invite you to read all the books under the topic "Bible" in Appendix A, and any others like it that are out there and you can get your hands on. What you will find here is a brief discussion that reflects where I am at and what has shaped my use of the Bible as I have written the sermons in this collection. I think it is also a view of the Bible that sets us free to use our imaginations as we read the Bible, as we chart pathways and build bridges to the twenty-first century, and as we get creative with our sermon writing and preaching.

To address that initial question, I suggest we need to address a few others. One of those other questions is: "When did the Bible become the Word of God?" Let's look at this in two parts. At what point did what we call the Old Testament become the Word of God? When the stories were originally told and the poetry was originally spoken or sung? When the material was first written down? When editors assembled the Ancient Writings in their current form? When the Jews, probably after the Exile, began to assemble a canon, a canon that was a canon but an open canon? When Jesus and then the apostles used the materials in their preaching?

And the New Testament? When Paul first wrote his letters? When these letters were read, circulated and read again as part of early church worship? When the Synoptic Gospel Storytellers gathered their stories and edited them into the form that would say what they wanted to say? When Pastor John wrote his extended discussion of "Who is Jesus?" using stories from Jesus's life and preaching? When the bishops created the

Christian canon in the fourth century at the insistence of a pagan emperor? When Luther grudgingly accepted that even James and Revelation could be part of the canon? And what about the Apocrypha, is it also "Word of God?" And if not, why not?

Or did the entire canon become "Word of God" when my denomination printed its *Confession of Faith in a Mennonite Perspective* and called it such?[1] Perchance was it when I, by faith, decided that's what it is? Maybe it only finally becomes "Word of God" when we preach this Word to our congregations.

I recall a story told by Richard Middleton and Brian Walsh in their book, *Truth is Stranger Than It Used to Be*. They use it to discuss the nature of truth. It may be equally applicable to our discussion about the "Word of God." In the story, three umpires are having a beer after a game and are discussing the nature of their work:

> One says, "There's balls and there's strikes and I call 'em the way they are." Another responds, "There's balls and there's strikes and I call 'em the way I see 'em." The third says, "There's balls and there's strikes and they ain't *nothin'* until I call 'em."[2]

Is there objective truth? Is there only our perspective on truth? Or is truth entirely our own decision? Is there that which can be declared to be objectively the Word of God? Or is it the Word of God, but only Word of God for me if I accept it as that? Or, perchance is it only a collection of Ancient Writings until I, by faith, declare it to be the Word of God?

When teaching classes on this question, I have sometimes suggested that there are three ways we can talk about the Bible and the Word of God. One, the Bible *is* the Word of God. Two, the Bible *includes* the Word of God. Three, the Bible *proclaims* the Word of God. To declare the first strikes me as an act of idolatry. It has held us in its truth-destroying grip for too long and resulted in useless, even harmful, fights and quarrels fought with all the passion and energy of a life and death struggle. People are quickly labeled as faithful or unfaithful, speakers of truth or promoters of heresy, Christian or not Christian. More on this below.

The second seems to me to be too wishy-washy. If the Bible simply includes the Word of God, that is, the Word of God is mixed in with a whole bunch of other stuff, who will determine which text is Word and which is simply words? Where are the criteria we will use to make that

---

1. Mennonite Church USA. "Article 4: Scripture."
2. Anderson, *Reality*, 75. As told in Middleton and Walsh, *Truth is Stranger*, 31.

decision? Do we each simply pick and choose and hope we get it right? Or, do we more self-righteously and arrogantly argue that we are right and all others are wrong?

I have hitched my wagon to the third horse—the Bible *proclaims* the Word of God. Sometimes I flesh that out a little bit more and refer to the Bible as a collection of Ancient Writings that the church has decided speaks the Word of God to us. It is not so much God's book as it is the church's book. It is not something that was delivered on a set of tablets (golden no less) as was the book of Mormon, nor was it dictated by the Angel Gabriel on behalf of God as was Qur'an. It was written by human beings who were, they believed and we have since affirmed, inspired and directed by God's Spirit. But is it any more so than I believe my sermon each week has been inspired by the Spirit and written at the direction of that same Spirit? No, I am not claiming my sermons are equal with Genesis, Isaiah, or Paul. However, I believe the only real difference is that with Genesis, Isaiah, and Paul, along with the other writings collected in what we call "The Bible," unlike my sermons, the church has declared that they speak God's Word to us.

In the books listed in the bibliography, I believe both Bell and Enns arrive at this conclusion. Enns is on the way in *Inspiration and Incarnation*. However, he arrives there fully in *The Bible Tells Me So*. Boyd and McKnight both head in this direction, but then at some point grow faint of heart, and hold on to a view of the Bible that is inconsistent with their strongest arguments.

What does viewing the Bible this way do for us and the Bible? I think it sets the Bible free to actually be God's Word in all its creative and transformative power. No longer do we have to worry about words like "inerrant" and "infallible," two words and ideas that are not generated by the Ancient Writings, but rather have been imposed on same by people caught in the grip of the Enlightenment. No longer do the Ancient Writings have to square with twenty-first century science nor conform to twenty-first century historical methods. They can be what they always were and God intended them to be: Ancient Writings that *first of all* had meaning for ancient folk. To insist, for example, that Genesis 1 must be accurate within the context of Enlightenment science is to suggest God's favorite people were people of the Enlightenment and that the Bible was really only meant for them. That's an arrogance that outstrips any arrogance ever seen. God not only did not write just for us Enlightenment and post-Enlightenment folk, but is as offended by our Enlightenment idolatry as God was by Old Testament worship of Baal and Asherah.

Once we can let the Bible be what it is and what God intended it to be—the collection the church decided speaks God Word to us—we no longer have to insist on theological uniformity and agreement within its sixty-six books whose writings were produced and collected over a period of one thousand three hundred years or so. Given the incarnational nature[3] of the collection and the time period it covers, a time period that included the dramatic and almost inconceivable reshaping of philosophy, history, worldview, and faith that came with the arrival of Jesus, we shouldn't expect theological agreement and uniformity. In fact, because of the very dialogue and argument that goes on in these writings, the collection does a better job of speaking God's Word, a Word that could never, ever be contained in one theological perspective. Insisting on theological uniformity is an insult to the greatness of God's Word. No one person nor any one way of thinking can include all that is God and God's truth. It is when there is agreement that we should begin to suspect that we have lost touch with the truth.

In one class in a former congregation, I suggested an exercise. We looked at various stories in the Ancient Collection and then asked the question, "Is this a short story or a news article?" And, a follow-up question: "Does it matter?" Do the messages of Job and Jonah change if they are short stories instead of news articles?

In his study of Israel's ancient King David, *David's Truth in Israel's Imagination & Memory*, Walter Brueggemann addresses this matter, even more strongly than I do with my questions. Brueggemann asserts: "[W]e are not here interested in the 'historical David.' As though we could isolate and identify the real thing. . . . [The historical David] would not be nearly so interesting or compelling as the 'constructed' David that the tradition has given us."[4]

Brueggemann continues, "I intend to focus on the question of truth. That means I do not inquire about facticity, not what happened, but what is claimed, what is asserted here about reality."[5] And again: ". . . the truth

---

3. See Enns, *Inspiration and Incarnation*, on this topic.
4. Brueggemann, *David's Truth*, 13–4.
5. Brueggemann, *David's Truth*, 14.

of David here yields no certitude, certainly not any facticity, but nonetheless glimpses of reality."[6]

Letting go of "facticity" and "certainty" in these texts opens them up to be Story, without regard for whether they are a short story or a news article. Then they can become stories that we can jump into and find our place in. Suddenly, then, they are stories not about a man and a series of events that happened three thousand years ago, but rather stories about us and our reality. They can then speak to us and through us to the people in our congregations in ways and with a power never before possible. The stories are neither conservative history nor liberal myth. They are powerful carriers and proclaimers of the Word of God.[7]

Is it okay for Revelation to be a fantasy novel in the spirit of twenty-first century fantasy stories and science fiction? Is its message any different if we decide John of Patmos was given a certain message by God and then John chose the vehicle—highly imaginative fantasy literature—to deliver the message? Is Revelation, perhaps, a fine first-century example of creative preaching? Can the stories in Genesis 1–11 be myth and, as such, be even more powerful voices for God's Truth, the Word of God?

Having said all this, I confess that when I get to the first three Gospels, I am more inclined toward news article than short story. Without the historicity of the resurrection of Jesus, I don't thing Christianity has much, if anything, to offer our world. Yet even there, the Good News Storytellers had their own agendas and included, arranged, and told stories in a way that best suited their theological agendas. Putting together an accurate account of what actually happened the first Easter Sunday is next to impossible. Such is the nature of both eyewitness accounts and the writing of history. Nevertheless, as N. T. Wright argues in various places, including in *The Resurrection of Jesus, The Meaning of Jesus,* and *The Resurrection of the Son of God*, there is ample credible evidence for the historical resurrection of Jesus. Does that mean I am inconsistent in my reading of the Ancient Writings? I don't think so. Rather, I want to read the Bible as it was given to us and was meant to be read.

---

6. Brueggemann, *David's Truth*, 17.

7. Brueggemann argues that Pontius Pilate, in asking Jesus, "What is truth?" wanted the kind of truth that governments and law courts like. He goes on to say that "such posturing for truth is the destructive tendency of much of the right wing. But it is equally the case among self-styled 'liberals' who squeeze the scars of truth into universal myths and Old Testament flattening schemes. Against that, *only the narrative has its liberating say.*" (Brueggemann, *David's Truth*, 17. Emphasis mine.)

And then there is the matter of idolatry. I used to have little understanding of, and therefore little appreciation for, Evangelicals fascination with John's Good News Story Collection. Then, in 2002, I preached my first series on the book, and gained an appreciation and even love for the collection. That appreciation and love has only grown with the series I preached in 2010 and 2018. In fact, with the writing of my sermons for Palm Sunday, Good Friday, and Easter this past spring—calling each sermon "A Twist in the Tale—I am tempted to write a book on John's collection and calling it "A Twist in the Tale." I have come to see John's book as an extended theological and narrative argument for "Who is Jesus?" In John's argument on the question and for the purposes of our conversation about the Bible and the Word of God, there is no more important text than John 1:1–18. For our purposes, the three verses that matter most are verses 1, 2, and 14:

> In the beginning the Word already existed.
> The Word was with God,
> and the Word was God.
> He existed in the beginning with God . . .
> So the Word became human and made his home among us.
> He was full of unfailing love and faithfulness. And we have seen his glory, the glory of the Father's one and only Son.[8]

I believe this text is part of the confession of faith of all Christian preachers. We believe that Jesus, as a human being, was the embodiment—the *incarnation*—of the Word of God. Jesus was the Word of God and in and through Jesus, and everything about Jesus, we see and hear and experience the Word of God. How is it then, that some of us want to make a collection of "dried ink marks on the page" into the Word of God? Absolutely, the Ancient Collection, especially the New Testament, points to Jesus and the entire collection proclaims God's Word. However, I believe to call it God's Word is to create an idol.

When the escaping Hebrew slaves were gathered around Mt. Sinai, God was clear about a few things. One of those was: "You shall not make for yourself an idol, whether in the form of anything that is in heaven above, or that is on the earth beneath, or that is in the water under the earth."[9] God must have had a premonition of how tempting it would be for those Hebrews to carve or chisel or build something tangible that

---

8. NLT.
9. Exod 20:4. NRSV.

they could point to and say, "[T]hese are the gods who brought [us] out of the land of Egypt!"[10] It's so much more believable and tangible than a god with a weird name that wasn't really a name even and a god that took no shape or form whatsoever, a burning bush one day, a pillar of cloud another, and a whopping thunderstorm a third. It was also a lot easier to argue with, and fight against, the nations who had gods they could see and worship in temples and carry into battle with them if they, Yahweh's people, could do the same. How the heck did you make any claims for your god whatsoever and convince belief in him (or her) if you had nothing to show for it?

That temptation has not lessened over the centuries and millennia since the gold rings were melted and the golden calf cast at the foot of a sacred mountain. Particularly as Evangelicals but others as well, we like the certainty and solidity that comes with having a collection of "dried ink marks on the page" collected into one volume bound in leather. To be able to hold a Bible aloft and say this is the Word of God (usually meaning "and how I read it is how God reads it") creates a sense of drama and power and surety that is hard to resist. When we can preface any statement with "The Bible says," we feel we have truth and authority that must be listened to and abided by. That is idolatry.

The effects of creating a printed idol of the Word of God and having it replace the true Word of God, the Word becoming human, can be seen in a variety of ways throughout history. The most obvious earliest example is probably the Constantinian takeover of Christianity. There was safety and security in having Christianity be the religion of the Empire, protected by the Emperor. It meant the Emperor decided it was time to close the canon. It meant Christianity moved from being voluntary to being enforced. But it meant safety and security and certainty. Who could argue with that? Had Jesus remained the Word of God, it would have been obvious that the concessions the church was making were moving it further and further from who God was and how God had been revealed in Jesus. But if "dried ink marks on the page" are the Word of God, there was ample foundation in the now-written word of God for making the accommodations they were making.

The most recent obvious example, at least with how I see things, is what often seems like, from this side of the border, the apparently unqualified support American white Evangelicals, people in the pews

---

10. Exod 32:4. NLT.

as well as leaders, are giving a president whose public persona seems as far removed from who Jesus is as it is possible to be. If Jesus was seen by these Evangelicals as the Word of God, there would surely have to be some congruence between what they see in Jesus and what they see in their president. Such congruence will never be, and has never been, perfect nor complete, but it has probably never been as absent as it is in 2018. However, with "dried ink marks on the page" as the Word of God, for American white Evangelicals, it is as easy to make accommodations for the sake of political power as it was for the bishops in the fourth-century-Roman Empire.[11]

Just like God's form was not to be cast in wood, bronze, or gold and God's name was not to be clear and unambiguous, so God's Word is not to be enshrined in words printed in a book. "[T]he word of God is living and active,"[12] the author of Hebrews tells us. "Living and active" can simply not be imprisoned in "dried ink marks on the page." This living and active Word comes to us in a person and is carried for us in story, poetry, and dialogue, even argument, certainly disagreement. Story and poetry are open enough, fluid enough, begging for imagination enough to be able to carry something as big as the Word of God.

But remember, story and poetry carry the Word of God, they *are not* the Word of God. Disagreement, dialogue, and argument are needed to hold something as big, high, deep, and wide as the "wisdom and knowledge of God! How unsearchable are [God's] judgments and how inscrutable [the Lord's] ways!"[13] No one voice or perspective can carry all that. Such a one voice only barely scratches the surface, no matter how inspired and "God-breathed" that perspective might be. To think such a Word can be locked into one book is surely idolatry. Oh, it feels safe and secure if we can lock it in and know for sure, but that is what idolatry is about, safety and certainty.[14] Idolatry is not about "living and active." It

---

11. For a more complete discussion of the incongruence between the Gospel and white Evangelicalism's apparent unqualified support for a president and an American empire, see Zahnd, *Postcards*.

12. Heb 4:12. NRSV.

13. Rom 11:33. NRSV.

14. Two important books dealing with certainty and doubt and open-endedness are Boyd, *Benefit of the Doubt* and Enns, *The Sin of Certainty*. My sense is that Boyd still struggles with letting go completely of idolatry when it comes to the Bible. He has trouble accepting the logical conclusion of his own well-articulated arguments. As I said elsewhere, Enns in *The Bible Tells Me So*, along with *The Sin of Certainty* and Bell in *What is the Bible?*, takes us where we need to go.

is about locked in and safe and secure and being able to control. There is, however, no controlling the Word of God and that is why you need person and story and poetry and disagreement.

It is into such a container, lake, or ocean that we as preachers invite our people to jump and find out what's there, imaginations fully engaged. As Paul of Tarsus tells us, translated by Eugene Peterson: "We are servants of Christ, not his masters. We are guides into God's most sublime secrets, not security guards posted to protect them."[15] To lock that Word into printed words is to attempt to be its master and therefore Christ's master. To allow God's Word to be carried in whatever way it may be carried, is to free it up. In all humility, acknowledging that we will always find far less and show our people far less than is to be found, we shepherd our folk into this wonderful world of God to see what might be there for us in our situation.

So preach the word, giving creativity and imagination free reign. Never try to lock in what God has left open. Never try to control or limit that which God has made "living and active." Never insist that you know and others don't. Allow all of it together, ancient and modern, to speak to us a Word that will never be fully spoken.

Go with God, to love and serve the Word, the World, and the People.

---

15. 1 Cor 4:1. *The Message*.

Bibliography

Achtemeier, Elizabeth Rice. *Nahum–Malachi*. Interpretation. Atlanta: John Knox, 1986.
African American traditional. "Over my head." In Nafziger et al, ed. *Sing the Journey*, #18.
Anderson, Walter Truitt. *Reality Isn't What It Used to Be*. San Francisco: Harper & Row, 1990, 75.
Batterson, Mark. *In a Pit with a Lion on a Snowy Day*. Colorado Springs: Multnomah, 2006.
———. *Wild Goose Chase: Reclaim the Adventure of Pursuing God*. Colorado Springs: Multnomah, 2008.
Baxter, Jr., Jessie R. "This World is not my Home." In Homer F. Morris, et al. *Favorite Songs and Hymns*. Dallas: Stamps-Baxter, 1939, #1.
Beery, Adaline H. "Lo, a gleam from yonder heaven." In Slough, ed. Hymnal: A Worship Book, #591.
Bell, John L., arr. "Halle, halle, hallelujah." In Nafziger et al, ed. *Sing the Journey*, #17.
Bell, Rob. *What is the Bible? How an Ancient Library of Poems, Letters, and Stories Can Transform the Way You Think and Feel About Everything*. San Francisco: HarperOne, 2017.
Bible Gateway. "BibleGateway.com: Search for a Bible Passage in 65 Languages and 208 Versions." https://www.biblegateway.com/passage/.
Boberg, Carl. "How great thou art." In Oyer et al., ed., *Mennonite Hymnal*, #535.
Bolz-Weber, Nadia. *Pastrix: The Cranky Beautiful Faith of a Sinner & Saint*. New York: Jericho, 2013.
Boyd, Gregory A. *Benefit of the Doubt: Breaking the Idol of Certainty*. Grand Rapids: Baker, 2013.
Brooks, Phillips. "O Little Town of Bethlehem." In Slough, ed., *Hymnal: A Worship Book*, #191
Brown, Brené. *Daring Greatly: How the Courage to Be Vulnerable Transforms the Way We Live, Love, Parent, and Lead*. New York: Gotham, 2012.
Brueggemann, Walter. *The Bible Makes Sense*. Revised edition. Cincinnati: St. Andrews Messenger, 2003.
———. *Cadences of Home: Preaching among Exiles*. Louisville: Westminster John Knox, 1997.
———. "The Creatures Know." In *The God of All Flesh and Other Essays*, 13–24. Eugene, OR: Cascade, 2015.
———. *David's Truth in Israel's Imagination & Memory*. Philadelphia: Fortress, 1985.

———. *Hopeful Imagination: Prophetic Voices in Exile*. Philadelphia: Fortress, 1986.

———. *The Message of the Psalms: A Theological Commentary*. Minneapolis: Augsburg, 1984.

———. *The Practice of the Prophetic Imagination: Preaching an Emancipating Word*. Minneapolis: Fortress, 2012.

———. *Praying the Psalms: Engaging Scripture and the Life of the Spirit*. Eugene, OR: Cascade, 2007.

———. *Spirituality of the Psalms*. Minneapolis: Fortress, 2002.

———. *Texts Under Negotiation: The Bible and Postmodern Imagination*. Minneapolis: Fortress, 1993.

———. *The Word Militant: Preaching a Decentering Word*. Minneapolis: Fortress, 2010.

Bryne, Rhonda. *The Secret*. New York: Atria, 2006.

Burge, Gary M. *John*. The NIV Application Commentary. Grand Rapids: Zondervan, 2000.

———. *Letters of John*. The NIV Application Commentary. Grand Rapids: Zondervan, 1996.

Canadian Mennonite. November 25, 2013. Vol. 17, #23.

Carpenter, Delores, and Nolan E. Williams. *African American Heritage Hymnal*. Chicago, IL: GIA Publications, 2001.

Carr, Patrick. *Cash: The Legend*. New York: Sony BMG Music Entertainment, 2005.

Cash, Johnny, vocalist. "The Beast In Me." By Nick Lowe. Released 1969. Track 3 on Johnny Cash, *Johnny Cash*. Columbia, LP.

———. vocalist. "Born To Lose." By Frankie Brown and Ted Daffan. Released 1964. Track 8 on Johnny Cash, *The Original Sun Sound of Johnny Cash*. Get Back Records GET 7511, LP.

———. vocalist. "Delia's Gone." By Karl Silbresdorf and Dick Toops. Released 1962. Track 7 on Johnny Cash, *The Sound of Johnny Cash*. Columbia, LP.

———. composer and vocalist. "Folsom Prison Blues." Released October 11, 1957. Track 11 on Johnny Cash, *With His Hot and Blue Guitar*. Sun Records, LP.

———. "Ghost Riders In The Sky." By Stan Jones. Released May 30, 1979. Track 5 on Johnny Cash, *Silver*. Columbia, LP.

———. vocalist. 1974. "If Not For Love." By Larry Michael Lee and Glenn Tubb. Released 1971. Track 4 on Johnny Cash, *A Man in Black*. Columbia, LP.

———. vocalist. "Keep Me From Blowing Away." By Linda Ronstadt. Released 2012. Track 33 on *Bootleg Vol. IV: The Soul of Truth*. Columbia Nashville Legacy, compact disc.

———. *Man in White*. San Francisco: Harper & Row, 1986.

———. composer and vocalist. "Redemption." Released 1994. Track 11 on Johnny Cash, *American Recordings*. American Recordings, compact disc.

———. vocalist. "A Thing Called Love." By Jerry Reed. Released 1972. Track 3 on Johnny Cash, *A Thing Called Love*. Columbia, LP.

Carion, Christian, dir. *Joyeux Noel*. Screen play by Christian Carion. Produced by Christophe Rossignon and Benjamin Hermann. Sony Pictures Classics, 2005.

Cassavetes, Nick, dir. *My Sister's Keeper*. Story by Jodi Picoult. Screenplay by Jeremy Leven & Nick Cassavetes. Produced by Mark Johnson et al. Alliance Atlantis, 2009.

Claudius, Matthias. "We plow the fields and scatter." Translated by Jane M. Campbell. In Slough, ed., *Hymnal: A Worship Book*, #96.

Cook, Jerry with Stanley C. Baldwin. *Love, Acceptance, & Forgiveness: Equipping the Church to be Truly Christian in a Non-Christian World*. Ventura, CA: Regal, 1979.

Connors, Stompin' Tom, composer and vocalist. "The Singer (The Voice of the People)." Released 1990. Track 20 on Stompin' Tom Connors, *A Proud Canadian*. Capitol, compact disc.

Croly, George. "Spirit of God, descend." In Slough, ed., *Hymnal: A Worship Book*, #502.

Darwish, Mahmoud. "a candle in the dark." https://semiclassicallimit.wordpress.com/2012/08/09/mahmoud-darwish-a-candle-in-the-dark/

Dickens, Charles. *A Christmas Carol*. The Original Manuscript Edition. New York: W. W. Norton & Company, 2017.

Dyer, Dr. Wayne. *Excuses Begone! How to Change Lifelong, Self-Defeating Thinking Habits*. Carlsbad, CA: Hay House, 2009.

———. *Inspiration: Your Ultimate Calling*. Carlsbad, CA: Hay House, 2006.

———. *The Power of Intention: Learning to Co-create Your World Your Way*. Carlsbad, CA: Hay House, 2004.

Dylan, Bob, composer and vocalist. "Blowin' in the Wind." Released May 27, 1963. Track 1 on Bob Dylan, *The Freewheelin' Bob Dylan*. Columbia Records, vinyl.

Elfstrom, Robert, dir. *Gospel Road: A Story of Jesus*. Screenplay by Johnny Cash & Larry Murray. Produced by Johnny Cash & June Carter Cash. 20th Century Fox, 1973.

Enns, Peter. *The Bible Tells Me So: Why Defending Scripture Has Made Us Unable to Read It*. San Francisco: HarperOne, 2014.

———. *Inspiration and Incarnation: Evangelicals and the Problem of the Old Testament*. 2nd ed. Grand Rapids: Baker Academic, 2015.

———. *The Sin of Certainty: Why God Desires Our Trust More Than Our "Correct" Beliefs*. San Francisco: HarperCollins, 2016.

Evans, Rachel Held. *Inspired: Slaying Giants, Walking on Water, and Loving the Bible Again*. Nashville: Nelson, 2018.

Excell, Edwin O. "Count Your Blessings." In Harry P. Armstrong, ed., *Spiritual Life Songs*. Nashville: Abingdon, 1983, #39.

Farjeion, Eleanor. "Morning has broken." In Slough, ed. *Hymnal: A Worship Book*, #648.

Friesen, Raymond Richard. "The Theology of the Martyrs: A Study of the *Martyrs Mirror* as a Source for Understanding Anabaptist Theology." MA thesis, University of Manitoba, 1988.

Halley, Henry H. *Halley's Bible Handbook: An Abbreviated Bible Commentary*. Grand Rapids: Zondervan, 1961.

Handel, George Frideric. "Hallelujah." In *Messiah*, 171.

———. *Messiah*. Choral ed. Watkins Shaw, ed. London: Novello & Company Limited, 1992.

Hanh, Thich Nhat. "Thich Nhat Hanh's Translation of the Metta Sutta." Teaching (mostly) Asian Religions. August 18, 2014. https://teachingasianreligions.com/2014/08/18/thich-nhat-hanhs-translation-of-the-metta-sutta/.

Hankey, Catherine. "I love to tell the story." In Oyer et al., ed., *The Mennonite Hymnal*, #593.

Harron, Don. *Olde Charlie Farquharson's Testament: From Jennysez to Jobe and After Words*. Markham, ON: Red Deer, 2010.

Hauerwas, Stanley. *Hannah's Child: A Theological Memoir*. Grand Rapids: Eerdmans, 2012.

Hay, Louise. *You Can Heal Your Life*. Carlsbad, CA: Hay House, 2004.

Haydn, Joseph, and Hoffmann v. Fallersleben, writers. "Deutschland, Deutschland über Alles.» Released 1995. Track 12 on *Deutschland, Deutschland Uber Alles*. FZ-Verlag, compact dist.

Hays, Edward. *A Lenten Hobo Honeymoon: Daily Reflections for the Journey of Lent* Leavenworth, KS: Forest of Peace, 1999.

Hewitt, Garth. "Ten Measures of Beauty (Pray for the Peace)." Track 1 on Garth Hewill, *Journeys with Garth Hewitt: The Holy Land*. Myrrh, 1996, compact disc.

Hughes, Albert and Allen Hughes, dir. *The Book of Eli*. Screenplay by Gary Whitta. Warner Brothers, 2010.

James, Mary Dagworthy. "In the rifted Rock I'm resting." In Slough, ed. *Hymnal: A Worship Book*, #526.

Jonasson, Jonas, *The 100-Year-Old Man Who Climbed out of the Window and Disappeared*. Translated from the original Swedish by Rod Bradbury. San Francisco: Harper Collins, 2012.

Key, Francis Scott, and John Stafford Smith, writers. "The Star-Spangled Banner." On *Star Spangled Banner*, compact disc.

King, Martin Luther. "Martin Luther King I Have a Dream Speech." August 28, 1963. American Rhetoric. https://americanrhetoric.com/speeches/mlkihaveadream.htm.

Kirkpatrick, William J. "Praise the Lord, sing hallelujah." In Slough, ed. *Hymnal: A Worship Book*, #50.

Kristofferson, Kris, composer and vocalist. "Sunday Morning Coming Down." Released 1970. Track 12 on Kris Kristofferson, *Kris Kristofferson*. Legacy/Monument, LP.

Lavallée, Calixa, Adolphe-Basile Routhier and Robert Stanley Weir, writers. "O Canada." Released 2004. On *O Canada!: The National Anthem: The Perfect Anthology and History of Our National Anthem = Lhymne National: Lhistoire Et Lanthologie Musicale De Lhymne National*. XXI, CD.

Lennon, John, composer and vocalist. "Give Peace a Chance." Released 1969. Track 1 on Plastic Ono Band, *Give Peace a Chance*. Apple 1809, 7".

Leslie, Elsie, vocalist and composer. "One Door, and Only One." In *Salvation Songs for Children Number One*. Child Evangelism Fellowship, 1939, 22.

Lewis, C. S. *The Lion, the Witch, and the Wardrobe*. The book is available in a variety of editions.

Longfellow, Henry Wadsworth. "I heard the bells on Christmas Day." 1864. Wikipedia. https://en.wikipedia.org/wiki/I_Heard_the_Bells_on_Christmas_Day.

Lowry, Robert. "Shall we gather at the river." In Slough, ed. *Hymnal: A Worship Book*, #615.

Mailer, Norman. *The Gospel According to the Son*. New York: Random House, 1997.

Mangold, James, dir. *Walk the Line*. Screenplay by James Mangold & Gill Denis. Fox 2000 Pictures, 2005.

Martino, Steve and Jimmy Hayward, dir. *Horton Hears a Who*. Screenplay by Cinco Paul & Ken Daurio. Blue Sky Studios, 2008. Based on the book by Dr. Seuss, *Horton Hears a Who*.

McCutcheon, John. "Christmas in the Trenches." *Winter Solstice*. Rounder, 1984.

McKnight, Scot. *The Blue Parakeet: Rethinking How You Read the Bible*. 2nd ed. Grand Rapids: Zondervan, 2018.

McLaren Brian D. *A New Kind of Christianity: Ten Questions That Are Transforming the Faith*. San Francisco: HarperOne, 2010.

———. *Why Did Jesus, Moses, the Buddha, and Mohammed Cross the Road?* New York: Jericho, 2013.
Mennonite Church USA. "Article 4. Scripture." Mennonite Church USA. http://mennoniteusa.org/confession-of-faith/scripture/.
Middleton, J. Richard & Brian Walsh. *Truth is Stranger Than It Used to Be: Biblical Faith in a Postmodern Age.* Downers Grove, IL: InterVarsity, 1995.
Miles, Sara. *Take This Bread: A Radical Conversion.* New York: Ballantine, 2008.
Miller, James C. and Jack and Elsie Osborn. "Where the Roses Never Fade." http://www.digitalsongsandhymns.com/songs/4216.
Mohr, Joseph. "Silent Night." Translated by John F. Young. In Slough, ed., *Hymnal: A Worship Book*, #193.
Montgomery, James. "Go to dark Gethsemane." In Slough, ed., *Hymnal: A Worship Book*, #240.
Morison, John. "To us a Child of hope is born." In Slough, ed., *Hymnal*, #189.
Mukungu, Lubunda. "God loves all his many people." Translated by Anna Juhnke. In Slough, ed., *Hymnal: A Worship Book*, #397.
Nafziger, Ken et al. ed. *Sing the Journey: Hymnal: A Worship Book—Supplement 1.* Scottdale, PA: Faith & Life, 2005.
Neale, John M., translator. "O come, O come, Immanuel." In Slough, ed., *Hymnal: A Worship Book*, #172.
Nouwen, Henri J. M. *Reaching Out: The Three Movements of the Spiritual Life.* Garden City, NY: Doubleday & Company, 1975.
Ollenberger, Ben C. "The Book of Zechariah: Introduction, Commentary, and Reflections." *The New Interpreter's Bible, Vol. VII.* Nashville: Abingdon, 1996.
Overholtzer, Ruth P., ed., Jesse Irvin Overholtzer, contributor, Herbert G. Tovery, foreword, and E.J. Pace, illustrator. *Salvation Songs for Children Number One.* Child Evangelism Fellowship, 1939.
Oyer, Mary, et al, ed. *The Mennonite Hymnal.* Scottdale, PA: Herald, 1969.
Pace, Adger M., and R. Fisher Boyce. "O Beautiful Star of Bethlehem." Hymnary.org. https://hymnary.org/text/o_beautiful_star_of_bethlehem#Theme_by.
Pasquin, John, dir. *The Santa Clause.* Written by Leo Benvenuti & Steve Rudnick. Produced by Rober Newmyer et al. Walt Disney, 1994.
Peterson, Eugene. *Answering God: The Psalms as Tools for Prayer.* San Francisco: HarperSanFrancisco, 1991.
———. *Christ Plays in Ten Thousand Places: A Conversation in Spiritual Theology.* Eerdmans, 2005.
———. *Eat This Book: A Conversation in the Art of Spiritual Reading.* Eerdmans, 2006.
———. *First & Second Samuel.* Westminster Bible Companion. Louisville: Westminster John Knox, 1999.
———. *Five Smooth Stones for Pastoral Work.* Grand Rapids, Eerdmans, 1980.
———. *The Jesus Way: A Conversation on the Ways That Jesus Is the Way.* Grand Rapids: Eerdmans, 2007.
———. *Leap Over a Wall: Earthy Spirituality for Everyday Christians.* San Francisco: HarperSanFrancisco, 1997.
———. *The Pastor: A Memoir.* San Francisco: HarperOne, 2011.
———. *Practice Resurrection: A Conversation on Growing Up in Christ.* Grand Rapids: Eerdmans, 2010.

———. *Tell It Slant: A Conversation on the Language of Jesus in His Stories and Prayers*. Grand Rapids: Eerdmans, 2008.

Picoult, Jodi. *My Sister's Keeper*. New York: Washington Square, 2005.

Radmacher, Mary Anne. *Lean Forward into your Life: Begin Each Day as if It Were On Purpose*: San Francisco: Conari, 2007.

Rice, Anne. *Christ the Lord: Out of Egypt*. New York: Knopf, 2005.

Rights, Douglas LeTell. "Veiled in darkness Judah lay." In Oyer et al., ed., *The Mennonite Hymnal*, #114.

Rohl, Carl and W. Warren Bentley. "When I'm lonely and defenseless." Translated by Jean Wiebe Janzen. In Nafziger et al, ed., *Sing the Journey*, #93.

Scheidner, Aaron, dir. *Get Low*. Screenplay by Chris Provenzano and C. Gaby Mitchell. Sony Pictures, 2009.

Schwartz, Ted. *Laughter is Sacred Space: The Not-So-Typical Journey of a Mennonite Actor*. Harrisonburg, VA: Herald, 2012.

Scrosese, Martin, dir. *The Last Temptation of Christ*. Screenplay by Paul Shrader. Based on the book by the same title by Nikos Kazantzakis. Produced by Barbara De Fina. Production company: Cineplex Odeon Films. Distributed by Universal Pictures and Cineplex Odeon Films. Release date: August 12, 1988.

Sears, Edmund H. "It came upon a midnight clear." In Slough, ed., *Hymnal: A Worship Book*, #195.

Seuss, Dr. *Horton Hatches the Egg*. New York: Random House, 1940.

———. *Horton Hears a Who*. New York: Random House, 1954.

Simons, Menno. "The Cross of the Saints." In John Christian Wenger, ed. *The Complete Writings of Menno Simons*, 579–622. Translated by Leonard Verduin. Scottdale, PA: Herald, 1974.

Sleeth, Natalie. "In the bulb there is a flower." In Slough, ed., *Hymnal: A Worship Book*, #614.

Slough, Rebecca, ed. *Hymnal: A Worship Book*. Elgin, IL: Brethren; Newton, KS: Faith and Life; Scottdale, PA: Mennonite Publishing House, 1992.

Tate, Nahum. "While shepherds watched." In Slough, ed., *Hymnal: A Worship Book*, #196.

Taylor, Barbara Brown. *An Altar in the World: A Geography of Faith*. San Francisco: HarperOne, 2010.

———. *Leaving Church: A Memoir of Faith*. San Francisco: HarperOne, 2006.

Thring, Godfrey. "From the Eastern Mountains." In Oyer et al, ed., *The Mennonite Hymnal*. #140.

Trapp, Justin. "How Long Should Your Sermon Be?" July 19, 2017. http://justintrapp.com/how-long-should-your-sermon-be/.

———. "The Average Sermon Length of These 10 Well Known Pastors." November 6, 2017. http://justintrapp.com/the-average-sermon-length-of-these-10-well-known-pastors/.

Von Schmid, Christian. "O Come, All Ye Children." In Oyer et al, ed., *The Mennonite Hymnal*, #470.

Wade, John F. "O come, all ye faithful." In Slough, ed., *Hymnal: A Worship Book*, #212.

Wangerin, Walter, Jr. *The Book of God: The Bible as a Novel*. Grand Rapieds: Zondervan, 1996.

Watts, Isaac. "Joy to the world." In Slough, ed., *Hymnal: A Worship Book*, #318.

Wilson, Michael J., creator. *Ice Age*. Directed by Mike Thurmeier, Carlos Saldanha, Chris Wedge, Steve Martino, Karen Disher, and Chris Renaud. 20th Century Fox, Blue Sky, Hit Entertainment, and 20th Century Fox Animation, 2002.

Wink, Walter. *The Bible in Human Transformation: Toward a New Paradigm for Biblical Study*. Minneapolis: Fortress, 2010.

Work Jr., John W. "Go Tell It on the Mountain." In *African American Heritage Hymnal*, #202.

Wright, N.T. "How Can the Bible Be Authoritative?" NTWrightPage. http://ntwrightpage.com/2016/07/12/how-can-the-bible-be-authoritative/.

———. *How God Became King: The Forgotten Story of the Gospels*. San Francisco: HarperOne, 2012.

———. "The Resurrection: Historical Event or Theological Explanation? A Dialogue: Opening Statement." In Robert B. Stewart, ed. *The Resurrection of Jesus*, 16–23. Minneapolis: Fortress, 2006.

———. *The Resurrection of the Son of God: Christian Origins and the Question of God Vol. 3*. Minneapolis: Fortress, 2003.

———. "The Transforming Reality of the Bodily Resurrection." In Marcus J. Borg & N. T. Wright, *The Meaning of Jesus: Two Visions*, 111–128. San Francisco: Harper Collins, 1999.

Wynette, Tammy, vocalist. "D-I-V-O-R-C-E." By Bobby Braddock and Curly Putman. Released 1968. Track 7 on *D-I-V-O-R-C-E*. Koch, compact disc.

Zahnd, Brian. *Postcards from Babylon: The Church in American Exile*. St. Joseph, MO: Spello, 2019.

———. *Sinners in the Hands of a Loving God: The Scandalous Truth of the very Good News*. New York: Waterbrook, 2017.

www.ingramcontent.com/pod-product-compliance
Lightning Source LLC
Chambersburg PA
CBHW062012220426
43662CB00010B/1299